The English Language series

Series Editors: David Britain and Rebecca Clift

The English Writing System

VIVIAN COOK

A member of the Hodder Headline Group
LONDON
Distributed in the United States of America by
Oxford University Press Inc., New York

First published in Great Britain in 2004 by
Arnold, a member of the Hodder Headline Group,
338 Euston Road, London NW1 3BH

http://www.arnoldpublishers.com

Distributed in the United States of America by
Oxford University Press Inc.
198 Madison Avenue, New York, NY10016

British Library Cataloguing in Publication Data
A catalogue record for this book is available from the British Library

Library of Congress Cataloging-in-Publication Data
A catalog record for this book is available from the Library of Congress

ISBN 0 340 80863 2 (hb)
ISBN 0 340 80864 0 (pb)

1 2 3 4 5 6 7 8 9 10

Typeset in 10 on 13pt Times by Phoenix Photosetting, Chatham, Kent
Printed and bound in Malta

Contents

Acknowledgements

This book arose out of teaching courses at BA and MA level on the English writing system. Its first debt is to the students who followed these courses, some of whose work is mentioned in its pages and whose comments and reactions have shaped many of them. Various people helped with different aspects, particularly languages other than English and specialist areas of English – Benedetta Bassetti, David Britain, Rebecca Clift, Scott Jarvis, Phil Scholfield and Yuki Tokumaru – and contributed samples of texts – Carol Jackson and the staff at Prettygate Infants School for child samples; Sue Shepherd, Nicky Andrews and Helen Taylor for texts of various types; and staff and students of The Eurocentre and the Bell School Cambridge for tests with adult learners of English. It would never have been finished without the constant background help of Brad Mehldau, Gilad Atzmon and Wayne Shorter.

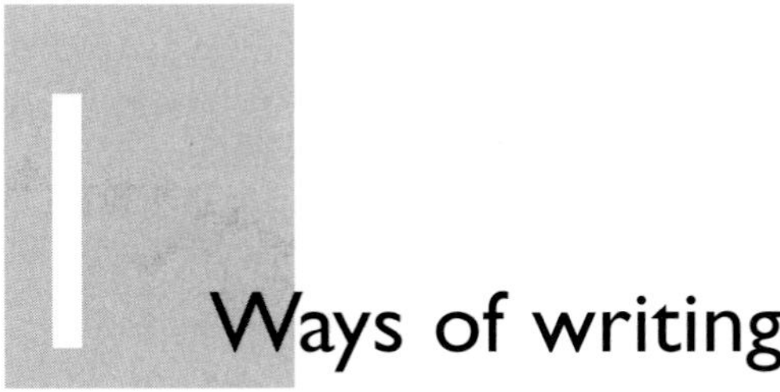

1 Ways of writing

INTRODUCTION

How does English writing actually work? The chapters of this book look at some answers to questions such as:

- How do people process words on the page? Reading English involves both linking letters to sounds and dealing with words as wholes.
- How does written English differ from spoken English? Written English is more than spoken English written down and has its own vocabulary, grammar and organization.
- What are the rules and regularities of English spelling? Far from being unsystematic, English spelling has complex rules relating sounds and letters, governing how letters can be combined and linking words to the vocabulary store in the mind.
- How is English punctuated and laid out on the page? Punctuation indicates grammatical and phonological structure; the way text is presented on the page conveys meaning.
- How do children and second language learners acquire the English writing system? Children progress through definite stages in the acquisition of written English, though some may get trapped at a particular stage. L2 learners bring to English the pronunciation and writing systems of their first languages.
- How has the English writing system changed over 1000 years? The historical development of the language and of writing technology has led to progressive changes in the writing system, even if it has not always kept pace with the spoken language.
- How has English writing system adapted to different circumstances? The American style of spelling shows some attempt at reforming spelling; e-mails and text messages have adapted traditional 'novel' spelling techniques to new media.

The aim of this book is then to show how the English writing system is connected to our lives in many ways, not something that is an ancillary to other aspects of language but vitally important to almost everything we do, from signing our wills to sending a text message.

The book covers an area that has seldom been treated as a whole within the study of English, bringing together approaches to English writing from linguistics, typography and psychology. It is designed to be used actively, each section having initial focusing questions, tasks to engage the reader in various aspects of English writing, final discussion questions and further reading; it makes liberal use of boxes to provide quotations, summaries and other information. After the broad discussion in this chapter, the later chapters are relatively self-contained so that readers can go straight to areas that interest them or can read them out of sequence.

Some conventions that will be needed should be mentioned. Words or sentences used as examples within the text are usually given in single quotation marks, say 'garden' or 'acknowledge'. Sometimes it is necessary to concentrate on the actual written form of the example – its letters, spaces, capitals, etc. In this case examples of English written forms are usually enclosed in angle brackets <>, <garden> and <acknowledge>. (This convention will not be used for characters in Japanese and Chinese in this chapter as it becomes cumbersome). Sometimes the actual pronunciation of the examples is important, mostly based on a British Received Pronunciation (RP) accent; this is given in phonetic transcript signalled by slants //, using the International Phonetic Alphabet (IPA) found in *Accents of English* (Wells 1982), /gɑːdən/ and /əknɒlɪdʒ/. A reference list of the symbols can be found on p. 215.

1.1 MEANING-BASED AND SOUND-BASED WRITING

Focusing questions

- Is English easier to read than Chinese? Why? (If you are not familiar with Chinese, look at Text 1 on page 4.)
- Is English spelling worse than Italian or Spanish? Why?

Key words

phoneme: the minimal sounds of a language that its speakers use to distinguish one word from another are its phonemes. In English the sounds /p/ and /b/ are different phonemes because they distinguish /piːk/ 'peak' from /biːk/ 'beak', 'tap' /tæp/ from 'tab' /tæb/ and so on.

morpheme: a morpheme is the smallest grammatical unit in the sentence, either a word in its own right such as 'cook' or part of a word such as the '-s' in 'cooks' and the '-er' in 'cooker'.

character: the name for a single symbol of a writing system such as Chinese, i.e. 人 ('person') is a character. The term is also used in computing for any distinct symbol such as the letter <a>, number <6> or other form <@>.

correspondence rules: the means of relating written symbols and sounds, say the letter <a> in 'rate' to the sound /eɪ/ or the sound /ŋ/ in 'long' to the letters <ng>, sometimes symbolized by ≡ ('corresponds to'), i.e. <a> ≡ /eɪ/ in 'page'.

orthographic depth: the scale for alphabetic languages going from 'shallow' writing systems with close links between letters and sounds, such as Finnish, to 'deep' writing systems with more complex links, such as English.

Some aspects of written language involve a relationship between written symbols and spoken sounds. So the letters in the written English word 'dollar' connect to the sounds in the spoken word /dɒlə/. Each element of the written word connects to a sound: the written letter <d> links to the spoken sound /d/, written <o> to spoken /ɒ/ and so on. When we read the word 'dollar', we discover that it means a certain kind of money only after we have worked out the sounds /dɒlə/.

Other aspects of writing involve a direct relationship between written symbols and meanings. The symbol <$> connects to the meaning 'dollar', without providing any clue to how it is said. Symbols such as <$> cannot be read aloud if they have not been encountered before – try <?> for example, incomprehensible without the explanation later in this chapter (*see* p. 21). They may have more than one spoken form. <#> for instance is called 'the pound sign' in the USA, 'hash' in England, even 'octothorpe' according to the Bell Lab researchers who introduced it into computing. The spoken form of <$> differs across the countries that use dollars, whether the USA, Zimbabwe, Singapore, Canada or many others. We can read and understand a symbol without knowing its spoken form.

Figure 1.1 presents these two relationships as a contrast between sound-based and meaning-based writing. Sound-based writing uses sounds as a bridge to connect letters and meaning; meaning-based writing goes directly from written symbols to meaning without involving sounds. This chapter explores the implications of these two relationships, which together form a substantial part of the English writing system. Part 1.1 of this chapter illustrates their characteristics from different languages, leading in to English itself. Part 1.2 looks at how an individual person uses both relationships to process written English.

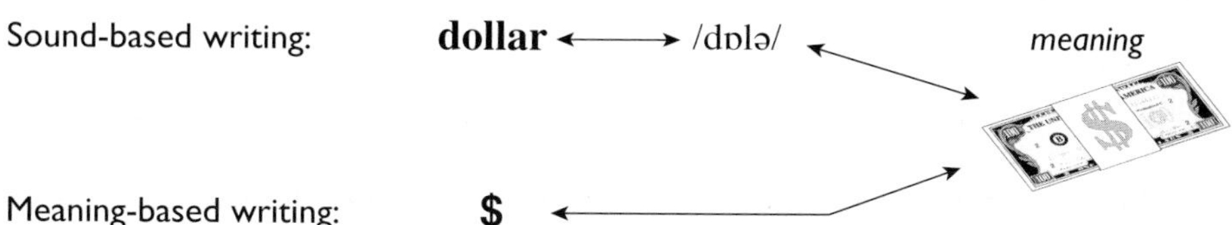

Fig. 1.1. Sound-based and meaning-based aspects of writing.

Meaning-based writing

No languages have writing systems that base themselves exclusively on either sounds or meanings. Some, such as English or Spanish, chiefly link letters and speech sounds; others, such as Chinese and Japanese, mostly link written symbols and meanings. Calling a writing system for a language sound-based or meaning-based refers to a preference for a particular way of writing rather than to an absolute distinction; probably the writing systems of all languages are a mixture of these two relationships.

Chinese is the chief example of a language with a writing system where written symbols connect directly to meaning. Text 1 below gives the Chinese version of article 1 of the United Nations *Universal Declaration of Human Rights*.

Text 1. An example of Chinese writing

人人生而自由,在尊严和权利上一律平等。他们赋有理性和良心,并应以兄弟关系的精神相对待。

(All human beings are born free and equal in dignity and rights. They are endowed with reason and conscience and should act towards each other in a spirit of brotherhood.)

Universal Declaration of Human Rights, article 1

Chinese writing consists of 'characters', each of which conveys a meaning rather than a particular spoken form. So the character 人 links to the meaning 'person', 上 to 'on', 生 to 'be born' and so on. Understanding 人 to mean 'person' does not require one to know that the Chinese word is actually 'ren'; knowing that 生 means 'be born' does not require one to be able to pronounce it as 'shang'. The character 人 is no more the Chinese word 'ren' than it is the English word 'person'. 人 conveys the meaning 'person' however it happens to be said.

The Chinese writing system has been called 'ideographic' (conveying ideas directly), a term seldom used nowadays, 'logographic' (showing meaningful units such as words) and 'morpho-syllabic' (based on both morphemes for meaning and syllables for sounds). The term 'meaning-based' is used here as being less tied to a particular theory.

Spoken Chinese has a non-regional form which is spoken everywhere called Putonghua, better known as Mandarin, and several regional 'dialects', such as Min, Cantonese and Hakka. These differ from each other as much as English differs from Greek. Speakers of one dialect of Chinese cannot necessarily understand speakers of another; in any other context they would be treated as distinct languages rather than dialects. Depending on the classification system, *The Languages of the World* (Katzner 1986) lists five main dialects, *Ethnologue: Languages of the World* (1996) lists 13.

Chinese, however, can be *read* by people who speak any of these dialects, since the characters have the same meaning regardless of the spoken forms they link to in Putonghua, Min or the other dialects. While the character 人 corresponds to different spoken forms in the various dialects, it means the same in all of them, just as <#> and <$> mean the same whatever they are called.

There are nevertheless some clues to the pronunciation of characters provided by components called phonetic radicals. The following characters all share the same radical, pronounced /tɕʻiŋ/ in Mandarin (but with different tones), namely 青 ('blue'), 情 ('feeling'), 清 ('clear') and 晴 ('fine'). Even if the clues about the character's spoken form conveyed in radicals may work for one dialect, they are unlikely to succeed across the board for other dialects.

The Chinese language is not then so much a single spoken language as a single writing system, having virtually the same characters with the same meaning everywhere it is used. Written Chinese is a unifying factor for people who would otherwise not understand each other, both in China and across the world. The exception is the differences that have evolved between the simplified characters of mainland China and the traditional characters of Taiwan. Apart from these, written Chinese is intelligible to the reader whichever variety or dialect of Chinese they speak.

Arabic numerals represent a global version of the same phenomenon. '0124' can be understood by anyone in the world who uses these number symbols, regardless of whether they call <1> 'un', 'ichi' or 'yksi'. Flight departure times on airport screens like '2015' make sense to the vast majority of passengers, whatever first language they speak. Most people in the world use the same numeral symbols with the same meaning, just as Chinese understand the same written texts whichever dialect they speak.

A meaning-based system relies on separate symbols for each meaning, <1>, <%>, 上, 人, not on symbols for each sound. The number of minimal distinctive sounds, that is, phonemes, in a language is quite small, ranging across the world between the 11 of Rotakas, an Indo-Pacific language, and the 141 of !Xu, spoken in southern Africa (Maddiesen 1984). English comes somewhere in the middle with around 44 phonemes in British RP, the precise number depending on the individual's accent. So in principle a writing system using phonemes needs a fairly small number of letters.

The number of words in a language is by comparison enormous and almost impossible to calculate. Nation (2001) reports 20,000 'word families' for English. The *Oxford English Dictionary* (*OED* 1994) contains 290,500 main entries and 616,500 distinct word forms. A meaning-based system therefore needs to call on a large number of separate symbols, at least a different one for each item in the dictionary. An educated Chinese speaker has to know approximately 5000 characters; a Chinese dictionary contains up to 40,000. A meaning-based system works efficiently with a language that has words with unvarying forms. Chinese 'words' always have the same form and have no inflections: 生 ('be born') for instance never changes to show present tense or plural number. No extra characters are needed for other forms of the word. But English words vary in form for past or present tense 'walk', 'walked', singular or plural 'walks', progressive tense 'walking', noun ending 'walker', 'walkers', etc., thus necessitating large numbers of new characters beyond the basic 20,000 if a meaning-based approach were adopted.

Sound-based writing

The main alternative to meaning-based writing is sound-based writing. Languages, however, vary in the type of sound unit that the written symbols connect to. One possibility is to link written symbols to syllables – the letter <U> corresponds to the syllable /ju:/ in 'UN'. Another is to link them to individual phonemes – the letter <g> corresponds to the phoneme /g/ in 'goal'. Such 'correspondence rules' go in both directions with letters corresponding to sounds – the *letter* <b> corresponds to the *phoneme* /b/ in 'bit' – and with sounds corresponding to letters – the *phoneme* /k/ corresponds to the *letter* <k> in 'kitten'.

Syllable-based writing

The Japanese writing system too uses characters called kanji which originally came from Chinese; the similarities between the two scripts can be appreciated by comparing Text 1 and Text 2. Japanese supplements these characters with two sound-based scripts called kana, that are used alongside the characters. One reason they were devised is that Japanese has different forms of the same word, unlike Chinese, and so some way of representing them in writing is needed without using wholly new characters.

Text 2. An example of Japanese writing

すべての人間は、生まれながらにして自由であり、かつ、尊厳と権利とについて平等である。人間は、理性と良心とを授けられており、互いに同胞の精神をもって行動しなければならない。

Universal Declaration of Human Rights, article 1

Text 2 gives the Japanese version of the same sentence, which combines kanji characters with kana symbols. The kana symbols correspond, not to phonemes, but to whole syllables of Japanese, usually consisting of a consonant and a vowel – technically called a mora as it differs in some ways from the English syllable. So the kana す corresponds to the syllable 'su', べ to 'he', て to 'te' and の to 'no', making up the word 'suheteno', meaning 'all', the first word in Text 2. The kana symbols reflect the full spoken forms of the Japanese word.

A syllable-based system, known as a syllabary, is also found in many Indian languages such as Tamil as well as in the native American language Cherokee. A syllabary works best with a language that has a limited number of spoken syllables, as in Japanese. English sometimes exploits the names of letters for a quasi-syllabic spelling, for example in the pub notice 'R U 18?', as we see in Chapter 7. The Japanese writing system is mixed in that it relies on both meaning-based characters and sound-based kana. In addition there are two kinds of kana, called hiragana and katakana, used for different types of word, and there is a Roman letter script called romaji. Reading a Japanese sentence in a newspaper may therefore involve using four different scripts.

Consonant-based writing

Most sound-based writing systems, however, use correspondence rules to relate symbols to phonemes rather than to syllables. This form of writing seems to have spread from Phoenicia in the Eastern Mediterranean some 3000 years ago. The written symbols do not necessarily correspond to every phoneme of speech. Text 3 gives the Arabic version of article 1, which is written from right to left.

Text 3. An example of Arabic writing

> يولد جميع الناس أحرارًا متساوين في الكرامة والحقوق. وقد وهبواعقلاً وضميرًا وعليهم أن يعامل بعضهم بعضًا بروح الإخاء.
>
> *Universal Declaration of Human Rights*, article 1

Arabic and Hebrew writing show the consonants of the spoken word but not the vowels (with some exceptions, such as, in Arabic, the use of four consonant symbols to double for vowels). Arabic has 28 symbols for the consonants; all but four letters vary in form depending on their position in the word. The Arabic word /ɭaʔiba/ لعب (he played) has three letters, going from right to left, ل for /l/, <ع> for /ʔ/, ب for /b/. The use of this type of writing system necessitates a language where the vowels are predictable from other features of the word, as is true of Arabic.

Would such a consonant-based system work for English? Task 1 reveals some of the problems. English vowels are far from predictable from the consonant spelling of the word. The vowel-less written word <n> could be 'on', 'an', 'in', 'no' or 'one', a rich source of confusion; <hv> could equally well be 'hive', 'hove', 'heave' or 'have'. A consonant-based system for English has nevertheless proved useful in text messaging, as will be seen in Chapter 7.

Task 1. English spelled with consonants

Read aloud the following short texts of English written only in consonant letters.

1 B, b, blck shp, hv y ny wl? Ys, sr, ys sr, thr bgs fll. N fr th mstr nd n fr th dm nd n fr th lttl by wh lvs dwn th ln. (nrsry rhym)

2 Hmn lf s vrywhr _ stt n whch mch s t b ndrd, nd lttle t b njyd. (Dr Jhnsn)

3 Lngstc thry s cncrnd prmrly wth n dl spkr-lstnr, n _ cmpltly hmgns spch cmmnty, wh knws ts lngg prfctly nd s nffctd by sch grmmtclly rrlvnt cndtns s . . . (Nm Chmsky)

4 D nt g gntl nt tht gd nght
Ld g shld brn nd rv t cls f dy
Rg rg gnst th dyng f th lght. (Dyln Thms)

Answers at the end of the chapter

Phoneme-based writing

In most sound-based writing systems, however, letters correspond in principle to all the phonemes of the language, including both vowels and consonants. The addition of vowels to the alphabet was the crucial change the Greeks made to the Phoenician system, as we see in Chapter 6.

Finnish, shown below in Text 4, has a writing system that relies heavily on the letter–phoneme link, using an alphabet of 21 letters, plus two more, <b> and <f>, in words borrowed from other languages. So the letter <k> corresponds to /k/, <a> to short or long /a/, <i> to short or long /i/ and so on. Each written vowel of Finnish corresponds to a distinct phoneme, <ai> to /a/ + /i:/ <aa> to long /a/. Each written consonant has to be pronounced: <kk> means one spoken /k/ followed by a second /k/.

Text 4. An example of Finnish writing

> Kaikki ihmiset syntyvät vapaina ja tasavertaisina arvoltaan ja oikeuksiltaan. Heille on annettu järki ja omatunto, ja heillä on toimittava toisiaan kohtaan veljeyden henki.
>
> *Universal Declaration of Human Rights*, article 1

Usually the term 'alphabetic' is reserved for languages that represent all the phonemes of the language, rather than for the consonant-based systems found in Semitic languages. The writing systems used in Europe are alphabetic, even if the actual alphabet varies from the Roman alphabets used in English and Spanish to the Cyrillic alphabets used in Russian and Bulgarian to the Greek alphabet. Coulmas (1996) defines an alphabet as 'a writing system characterized by a systematic mapping relationship between its symbols (graphemes) and the minimal units of speech (phonemes)'. In the terms used here, the 'alphabetic principle' links written symbols to the phonemes of the spoken language in sound-based writing based on phonemes rather than on syllables.

So, rather than the enormous list of separate items required in a meaning-based system, a sound-based system can use a relatively small set of symbols, say the 26 letters of the English alphabet (without counting capitals, etc.) or around 49 kana symbols. A sound-based system also requires rules to govern the correspondences between symbols and sounds – <m> links to /m/, て to 'te' and so on. The choice is between a large list of items and a small set of instructions, a difference that has many repercussions. Table 1.1 sums up the main differences between sound-based and meaning-based writing.

Table 1.1 Sound-based and meaning-based writing

Sound-based writing	Meaning-based writing
Symbols link to speech sounds	Symbols link to meanings
Needs:	Needs:
• some phonological properties, e.g. predictable vowels (Arabic)	• unvarying word forms, e.g. Chinese
• small number of symbols	• many thousands of characters
Syllabic: Japanese (kana), many Indian languages (Bengali, Tamil, Gujarati, etc.)	*Character-based*: Chinese, Japanese (kanji)
Consonantal: Arabic, Persian, Urdu, etc.	
Alphabetic: Spanish, Russian, Hindi, etc.	

English readers take it for granted that letters correspond to individual phonemes – the letter <p> in 'pat' links to the phoneme /p/, <a> to /æ/ and so on. Speakers of other languages find it just as obvious that written symbols relate to consonants, as in Arabic, or to syllables, as in Japanese. It may not be a coincidence that the analysis of speech into sequences of phonemes was invented by users of writing systems that rely on sequences of letters: 'every technical linguistics tradition that refers to segments arose in an alphabetic milieu or was influenced by such a tradition' (Faber 1992: 127). In various chapters we will come across the same chicken and egg problem: is writing represented as letters because we already know phonemes, or is language analysed as phonemes because we already know letters? Linguists such as Faber (1992) and Aronoff (1992) certainly believe that the study of phonology might have taken a different turn if it had been started by linguists who used L1 writing systems that were based on meaning or on syllables, etc., rather than on letter-to-sound correspondences. Indeed much phonological research of the past 30 years has gone beyond linear segments such as phonemes to distinctive features and syllables.

Figure 1.2 shows the approximate proportions of people who use the types of writing across the world. Although the languages with alphabet-based writing are most numerous, languages with character-based writing are not far behind, followed by syllable-based and consonant-based writing. These figures are necessarily rough approximations that include neither speakers of languages outside the top 50 nor users of more than one language. The Arabic consonantal writing system in particular is used by Muslims everywhere for religious reasons regardless of their first language;

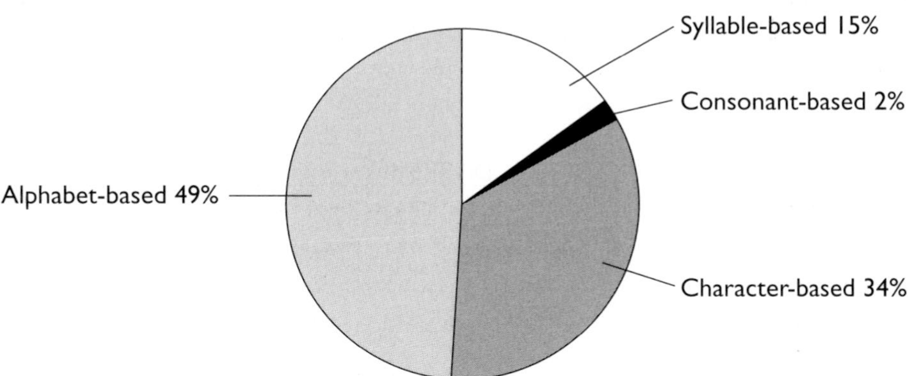

Fig. 1.2. Approximate proportion of types of writing system among the top 50 languages, by population. *Character-based*: at least 930 million users of Chinese (125 million Japanese). *Syllable-based*: at least 329 million users of Indian languages and Japanese. *Consonant-based*: at least 45 million users of Hebrew and Arabic. *Alphabet-based*: at least 1232 million users of English, Russian, Greek, etc. Figures for users are low estimates calculated from the 50 languages with most speakers (*Ethnologue: Languages of the World*), their grouping by system (Coulmas 1996) and the illiteracy rate in typical countries for each type (China, India, Egypt, Spain) (UNESCO).

Chinese characters are used wherever Chinese speakers are found, whether Singapore, Taiwan, Vancouver or London.

All of the writing systems seem to work perfectly well for their users, have been in use for many centuries if not thousands of years and are used by hundreds of millions of people every day. While the sheer number of symbols in character-based systems seems daunting to people brought up on sound-based writing systems, Japan has one of the highest literacy rates in the world, despite children having to learn 1945 characters in school. The practical difficulties of printing or typing large numbers of characters have now mostly been solved by modern computer technology.

Although the two types of writing have been presented here as alternatives, this is a matter of some controversy. It has been claimed that up to 97% of Chinese characters include phonetic radicals. DeFrancis (1984) asserts 'the universal phonological principle' that correspondence to sounds is the essential element in all writing systems. This is also argued in the context of individual processing of language (Perfetti *et al.* 1992), to be discussed in the next section.

If this universal phonological principle were true, Chinese too would have a sound-based core. The links between Japanese kanji and pronunciation may be more tenuous because of the differing periods at which kanji were borrowed from Chinese, whether they brought the Chinese word with them into Japanese or linked the character to a native Japanese word and so on. Japanese kanji may be a purer example of a meaning-based writing system than Chinese characters (Sproat 2000) because they are further separated from contemporary spoken words.

But, like the link between phonemes and linguists with sound-based backgrounds, there is a danger of researchers projecting their own first-acquired writing system onto the other languages of the world. An ancient Egyptian would doubtless see modern scripts as having a hieroglyphic base that has become corrupted over time. This phenomenon is called by DeFrancis (1996) 'The Law of the First Script': 'the first script learned is generally considered the most satisfactory, if not most perfect, of all possible systems.' Despite this warning, he goes on a few pages later to talk about 'the inefficiency of the Chinese system of writing' (DeFrancis 1996: 43).

Orthographic depth

It is more satisfactory to see writing systems as being on a continuum rather than as polar opposites. The scale of 'orthographic depth' from 'deep' to 'shallow' customarily ranges alphabetic languages according to the extent that their symbols correspond to spoken sounds, as we see in Figure 1.3 (Katz and Frost 1992). Finnish and Serbo-Croatian are near the shallow end because their letters correspond directly to phonemes; Arabic, Hebrew and English are towards the deep end since so much of their writing systems connect to sounds in ways that are far from straightforward.

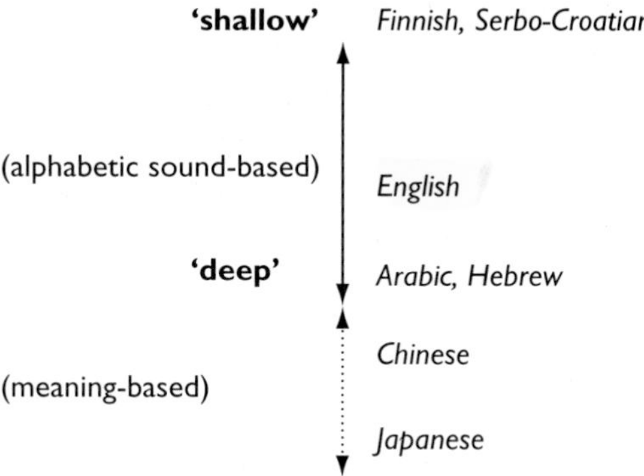

Fig. 1.3. Orthographic depth.

> An orthography in which the letters are isomorphic to phonemes in the spoken word (completely and consistently), is orthographically shallow. An orthography in which the letter–phoneme relation is substantially equivocal is said to be deep . . .
>
> (Katz and Frost 1992: 71)

If one accepts that all writing systems have some phonological element, the concept of orthographic depth can be extended to Chinese and Japanese, as in Figure 1.3. Chinese is deeper than English because its characters have even less connection to sounds than English letters. Japanese kanji go deeper as their links to spoken words are more remote (though of course actual reading in Japanese usually involves shallower kana as well).

A writing system rarely remains shallow for a long period of time. A writing system seldom keeps pace with the constant changes in spoken language, most notoriously in the increasing depth of English spelling since the Middle Ages when it was close to being a shallow system. The two shallowest languages, Serbo-Croatian and Finnish, only standardized their writing systems in the nineteenth century and doubtless will get deeper over the years. The only writing system that could achieve a perfect match would be a phonetic alphabet designed to transcribe the phonemes of speech fully, such as the International Phonetic Alphabet.

However close languages may come to being completely shallow or completely deep, they all draw to some extent on a mixture of sound-based and meaning-based writing, most notably Japanese where meaning-based kanji and sound-based kana are used in almost every written sentence. In 'deep' Chinese some radicals link to sounds; in 'shallow' Finnish some elements are not directly sound-based, such as the letter pair <ng> standing for a single phoneme /ŋ/ as it does in English 'sing', rather than to /n/ plus /g/.

The concept of orthographic depth in sound-based languages has led to considerable research. While in some ways orthographic depth is complementary to the scale between sound-based and meaning-based writing, there are two distinct factors: more-

or-less sound-based; more-or-less meaning-based. A greater reliance on sound-based elements does not necessarily mean less meaning; more meaning-based elements do not necessarily mean less sound. Sproat (2000) divides orthographic depth into two dimensions: type of phonography (consonantal, syllabic, etc.) and amount of logography (meaning-based units such as words or morphemes). English is classified as an alphabetic system with a small amount of logography, Chinese as a syllabic system with a fairly high amount of logography, Japanese as 'core syllabic' with a high amount of logography.

Principles of alphabetic systems

Going back to the conventional two-dimensional orthographic depth continuum, the overall depth of an alphabetic writing system depends on at least two other principles, the one-to-one principle and the linear order principle.

One-to-one principle

In Finnish one letter corresponds to a particular phoneme and, in reverse, a phoneme corresponds to a particular letter, with some minor exceptions. The letters match the sounds almost one-to-one, as they do in languages such as Italian and Spanish, popularly known as 'phonetic' languages. The principle of a one-to-one match between letters and sounds is sometimes seen as crucial to an alphabetic writing system; writing systems are regarded as defective if they depart from it. One of the driving forces behind the perennial movement to reform English spelling has been the belief that English breaks the one-to-one principle too often, as we see in Chapter 6.

Some ways in which English departs from the one-to-one principle are:

- *Multiple matches between letters and sounds*. Task 2 challenges the reader to find the 11 phonemes that correspond to the letter <a> and the 12 letter combinations that correspond to the sound /eɪ/. A single letter can correspond to many English sounds; <a> links to /eɪ/ in 'age', /æ/ 'bad', /ɑː/ 'bath', etc. The consonant <g> corresponds to /g/ in 'gate', to /dʒ/ in 'page', and apparently to nothing at all in 'though'. In reverse a single sound can correspond to many letters; the phoneme /eɪ/ links to <a> in 'lake', <au> in 'gauge', <et> in 'ballet', and so on. The phoneme /s/ can correspond to <s> in 'sit', to <c> in 'cell' or to <z> in 'waltz'. English does not have a consistent one-to-one correspondence between phonemes and letters in either direction but allows one-to-many mapping.
- *Pairs of letters and pairs of phonemes*. Many English letters go together in pairs, known as digraphs. The letter pair <sh> corresponds to the single phoneme /ʃ/ as in 'shirt', the pair <ng> to the single phoneme /ŋ/ in 'ring' and the pair <ea> to /iː/ in 'feat'. These break the one-to-one principle only if the writing unit is considered to be the single letter, not if the unit can be a digraph such as <sh> or <ng>. In reverse, at least two pairs of English phonemes correspond to single letters – the two phonemes /ks/ correspond to the single letter <x> in 'tax' and 'exit' and the two phonemes /juː/ correspond to a single letter <u> in 'student' in

British English. English writing cannot be converted into speech letter-by-letter. Nor, vice versa, can speech be converted into writing sound-by-sound. Some units are larger than the single letter or phoneme.

- *'Silent' letters.* Some letters do not correspond directly to sounds. So-called 'silent' letters such as the <g> in 'sign', the <b> in 'limb' or the <gh> in 'thought' are common in English. Again these break the one-to-one principle by not corresponding to a single sound in the spoken form and they will figure prominently in the spelling systems outlined in Chapter 3.

Task 2. Phoneme/letter correspondences

1 Find English words showing the 11 different phonemes that correspond to the letter <a>.

2 Find English words showing the 12 different letters that correspond to the sound /eɪ/ (as in the name for the letter <a>).

Answers at the end of the chapter

Linearity principle

A second principle of alphabetic writing systems is that the linear sequence of letters should be the same as the sequence of sounds. The order of the phonemes in 'mat' is the same as the order of letters – first /m/, then /æ/, then /t/. If the word 'mate' were approached in the same linear fashion, the order would be first /m/, then /æ/, then /t/, that is, the word 'mat'. The final <e> does not, therefore, signal an /iː/ at the end of the word, but that the *preceding* vowel <a> corresponds to /eɪ/ rather than /æ/. The final <e> is vital to the spoken correspondence of the preceding <a> but comes two letters after it. The information that 'silent' <e> provides is not linear since it is out of step with the letter sequence in the word. It nonetheless forms a vital part of English, reflected in the traditional advice to primary school children 'Fairy e waves its magic wand and makes the vowel before it say its name'. The rules for using silent <e> to mark preceding vowels are thus more abstract than the letter-to-sound rules seen so far and are dealt with in Chapter 3.

Another obvious area where English is non-linear is numbers. Currency symbols usually occur before the number so '£5' is read as 'five pounds', not 'pounds five' as the linear order suggests; a newspaper headline describes a '£1 m deal', combining a <£> out of sequence with an <m> for 'million', that is, 'one million pounds'. The number <1> corresponds to different words in <1> 'one', <10> 'ten', <100>, 'a hundred', <1000> 'a thousand', according to the number of '0's that come after it.

English thus breaks the linear order principle with its use of letters such as <e> that show what letters correspond to but are out of position in the word. Writing systems like the Devanagari script used in many Indian languages go further in putting some vowels before the consonants of a word; in Hindi a medial /i/ or /iː/ is written before the consonant it follows in speech. To read a word aloud, the reader has to reassemble the sequence of sounds; an English equivalent would be reading 'ibt' as /bɪt/ 'bit'.

Orthographic regularities

However, English also shows characteristics, called 'orthographic regularities' by Haynes and Carr (1990), that do not, strictly speaking, involve either sounds or meanings but are concerned with the actual combination of letters in words. Examples of orthographic regularities are:

- *Some combinations of letters are possible, others impossible:* <q> is only followed by <u> 'queen', 'equity', etc. There is no intrinsic reason why <q> could not occur by itself as it is pronounceable as /k/, as in the almost unique word 'Iraq'. (As we shall see in Chapter 3, many of the 'exceptions' to these regularities are words that were introduced fairly recently into English from other languages). Nor is there any reason why <th> is a possible digraph in, say, 'that' but <ht> is not in 'htat'. Initial <rh> is possible, as in 'rheumatism', but 'hr' now only exists in made-up names like C. S. Lewis' 'Hrossa'. Double <o> is frequent; double <a> is almost non-existent, apart from 'baa' and 'aardvark'.
- *Some letters and letter combinations typically occur in particular places in the written syllable:* <j>, <h> and <v> do not occur on their own at the ends of words, with rare exceptions such as 'Raj', 'Pooh' and 'spiv'. <k> occurs at the beginning of a word 'kill', but rarely on its own at the end – 'amok'. <ch> usually occurs at the beginning of the word as in 'chat' but <tch> at the end – 'match', although both correspond to /tʃ/. Double <l> can occur at the end of words as in 'dull' but not at the beginning 'llud', apart from the special rules for some proper names such as 'Lloyds' discussed in Chapter 3.

In other words, parts of the spelling of English and of other alphabetic languages do not divide simply into sound-based and meaning-based writing. A knowledge of the English writing system requires knowing not only how to link letters and phonemes and how to link whole words and meanings but also how to combine letters and locate them in the structure of words. Throughout this book issues about these orthographic regularities need to be raised, whether their place in the spelling system or their role in the child's development. They form a small but important part of the English writing system that cannot be reduced to either the phonology- or meaning-based relationships.

Other aspects of English writing

The English writing system has other conventions that are vital to its functioning but are not strictly related to either sound or meaning.

- *The direction of writing:* each line of written English goes from left to right rather than the right to left direction of Arabic, Hebrew and Urdu, or the top to bottom direction of some Chinese and Japanese (though most writing in these languages is now left to right). The only exceptions in English are short vertical texts such as shop-signs and, rarely, titles on the spines of books. This simple choice of direction can have many consequences for the shapes of letters, margins and other aspects of typography, as we see in Chapter 4, and may prove a stumbling block for those who have to switch direction for learning another language, say English people learning Arabic. English is also arranged in lines from top to bottom of the page, unlike older forms of Chinese and Japanese, which were arranged in columns from right to left. In English documents and books are read by turning pages from right to left, rather than from left to right.

- *The use of word spaces:* English uses spaces to show word divisions: <Everybody loves my baby> versus <Everybodylovesmybaby>, unlike for instance the native Canadian language Inuktitut, which has no spaces, or Chinese, which has even spaces between the characters. This deceptively simple aspect of writing nevertheless took many centuries to be invented and contributed to the development of silent reading, as we see in Chapter 6, now very much the norm in English.
- *The use of capital letters:* English uses capital letters *inter alia* to make grammatical differences such as proper name <Bill> versus common noun <bill>, and to indicate certain words <Monday>, <I>, etc., in ways that differ slightly from other European languages. The separation of lower-case from capital letters also took centuries to evolve and is not found in non-Roman sound-based scripts such as Devanagari.
- *The punctuation system:* English uses punctuation marks such as the full stop <.> and comma <,>, both to aid reading aloud and to show grammatical structure, as we see in Chapter 4. The marks themselves are more or less the same in European languages, but differ from, say, those in Chinese, as Text 1 demonstrates.

Definitions of 'shallow' and 'deep', such as those given in Figure 1.3, emphasize depth, not so much as a contrast between sound and meaning, but as a matter of consistency and clarity in linking letters to phonemes without reference to meaning. Hence increasing depth means breaching the one-to-one and linear principles, rather than relying more on meaning. Depth is seen as failure to correspond to sound rather than as success at conveying meaning; if anything, depth is a handicap in sound-based systems. While the depth continuum is clearly important, it does not cover the complex properties of the orthographic rules and conventions, which are neither meaning- nor sound-based but are unique properties of the actual written symbols of a language. Orthographic rules and other writing conventions form a third dimension to those of sound and meaning.

1.2 TWO WAYS OF PROCESSING WRITTEN LANGUAGE

Focusing questions

- Do you read English aloud letter by letter or word by word?
- When do people actually read something aloud in their everyday lives?

Key words:

mental lexicon: speakers of a language store all the words they know in a mental dictionary or 'lexicon' containing many thousands of items.

dual route model: a dual-route model of reading aloud has two processes or 'routes': the *phonological route*, which converts letters into sounds through rules, and the *lexical route*, which matches words as wholes in the mental lexicon.

Reading and writing are a natural and automatic part of most people's lives. We find it hard to conceive that other people use quite different writing systems from our own. In particular, users of sound-based systems tend to assume that theirs is the only sensible way of writing and that meaning-based languages such as Chinese and Japanese are inefficient alternatives, rather than being as unproblematic to their users as the ones they use themselves. For example, Diringer (1953: 76) claims 'Alphabetic writing is the last, the most highly developed, the most convenient, and the most easily adaptable system of writing'.

This section explores how both sound-based and meaning-based writing play a part in how an individual reads English. It draws mostly on ideas from the psychology literature. Even if English-speaking people chiefly rely on sound-based writing, they nevertheless make use of meaning-based writing at times. Just as there is a continuum of orthographic depth that applies to different languages, so there is a balance of phonological and lexical processes within the individual. Despite English being towards the shallow end of the orthographic depth continuum, both shallow and deep aspects are potentially available to the reader, as the two alternatives 'dollar' and '$' have already shown. Task 3 should demonstrate how this works out in English. The examples all come from publications ostensibly written in English and will be used to illustrate different ways of processing writing in the rest of this chapter.

Task 3. Read the following aloud

1 The child is father to the man.
2 25+59=84
3 Little Pig, Pillimore, Grimithistle, Pennywhistle, Great big Thumbo, father of them all.
4 Datta. Dayadhvam. Damyata, Shantih shantih shantih
5 A! Elbereth Gilthoniel! silivren penna míriel o menel aglar elenath, Gilthoniel, A! Elbereth!

Much research in psychology has used the 'dual route' model of reading aloud illustrated below in Figure 1.4, sometimes called the 'standard' model (Patterson and Morton 1985). The two ways of writing discussed earlier are paralleled by two alternative mental processes for reading words aloud, usually called the phonological and lexical 'routes'.

The phonological route changes a written word directly into sounds without connecting to its meaning, a sound-based process: a word like 'tip' is changed, letter by letter, from <tip> into the three phonemes /t/ /ɪ/ /p/, allowing us to read /tɪp/ out loud. This is an almost mechanical process of converting one form of representation into another, using correspondence rules in the mind to link <t> to /t/, <i> to /ɪ/ and so on. The number of rules depends on the orthographic depth of the language; to convert Finnish from letters to sounds presumably means consulting fewer rules in the mind than it does for English. The size of the unit may vary – English requires pairs of letters such as <th> for 'bath' or three letters such as <dge> for 'ledge'. But in principle following this route is a matter of turning an input made up of letters into an output made up of sounds.

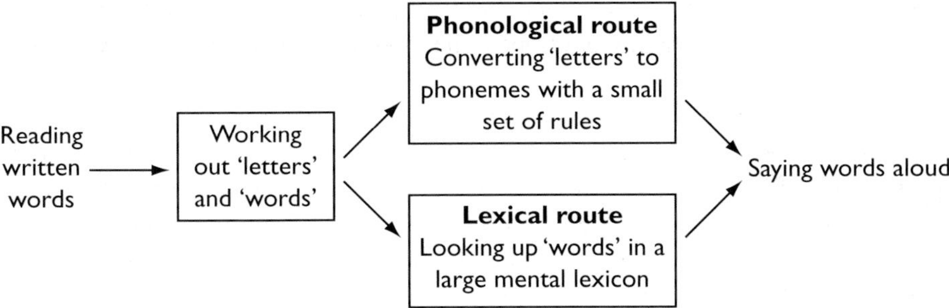

Fig. 1.4. The 'dual-route' model for reading.

The alternative lexical route changes a written symbol like <%> into the item 'per cent' with the pronunciation /pəsent/. Each symbol corresponds to a whole item with a meaning and a pronunciation, whether it is one letter or many letters long. The language user's mind contains a large mental dictionary complete with all the information about each lexical item that the person knows; someone who knows the word 'man' knows not only its basic meaning, say 'member of the human species', but also its pronunciation /mæn/, the way it behaves syntactically, 'a man' versus 'man' versus 'the man', its oddities of morphology 'man' versus 'men', its range of meanings, including 'piece in the game of draughts', and its spelling <man>.

Although this mental lexicon is probably very different in form from a printed dictionary, it must include much the same information and indeed go beyond it in terms of aspects such as collocation with other words 'my good man' and word association 'man'/'woman' that are not included in most printed dictionaries. Reading <%> forces the reader to consult this mental lexicon to retrieve its meaning, 'expressing a proportion out of a hundred', and its pronunciation, /pəsent/. Chapter 3 discusses some forms that this representation of the item takes in the mind. Once the individual letters of the word have been recognized, the lexical route ignores them and treats the word as a whole, looking it up as a complete item in the mental lexicon, along with its whole pronunciation.

The first task when reading aloud is to work out the letters and words. This is in itself far from unproblematic and varies according to the overall type of writing system being used. The process of reading aloud then divides into the two routes: the phonological route which uses correspondence rules to convert letters to sounds one by one, and the lexical route which matches words as wholes against a mental lexicon. Following the phonological route, the word 'free' is changed into /friː/ according to the correspondence rules of English. The reader has to know not only the phonemes of English but also the set of correspondence rules that connects letters and sounds. The meaning of 'free' is not relevant so long as there are rules for changing it into /friː/. Undoubtedly this is what most English people think they are doing when they read aloud – changing written letters into spoken sounds.

Following the lexical route, on the other hand, means matching the symbol against the items in the mental lexicon, each with its written form stored alongside other information – <%> 'per cent' /pəsent/, <£> 'pound' /paund/ and so on. <%> is matched against an item in the mental lexicon '%' that is pronounced /pəsent/, and so can be read aloud. The pronunciation is only one of the item's attributes; we do not need to know how <%> is pronounced to know what it means. Calling this the 'lexical' route does not necessarily commit oneself to a particular unit of meaning, whether morpheme, word or compound word – are <%> or <€> or <&> actually words? Chinese is often called a morphemic writing system because each character relates to a single morpheme, though some compound 'words' may use more than one character. The Chinese word is indeed hard to define, partly as it is not indicated by word spaces. Some aspects of English spelling are also based on morphemes rather than words. For instance the regular past tense morpheme is spelled as <ed> regardless of whether it corresponds to spoken /t/ 'looked', /d/ 'spooled' or /ɪd/ 'planted', as we see in subsequent chapters.

Users of a particular language favour a particular route. Chinese readers rely almost entirely on the lexical route: 人 has no clear connection to phonemes. Finnish readers rely almost totally on the phonological route: 'kaikki' can be processed entirely as individual letters and phonemes. However, both systems may be used even within a single language, most obviously so in Japanese where the characters and syllabic kana are mixed together in the same sentence.

Sentence 1 in Task 3 'The child is father to the man' can be processed almost entirely through the phonological route. Figure 1.5 shows the two routes applied to the reading of the last word 'man'. The phonological route turns the word into phonemes letter by letter, <m>, <a> and <n> into /m/ /æ/ /n/. If this routine were used for the other words in the sentence, however, the complexity of the correspondence rules in English would soon be revealed. Because of its breaches of the one-to-one principle through digraphs, the two letters <th> in 'father' correspond to a single phoneme /ð/, not to two phonemes, and the two letters in <ch> similarly correspond to a single phoneme /tʃ/. Because of the 'silent' letters in English, the letter <r> in 'father' has no spoken counterpart for readers in England, though it does for those in Canada, say.

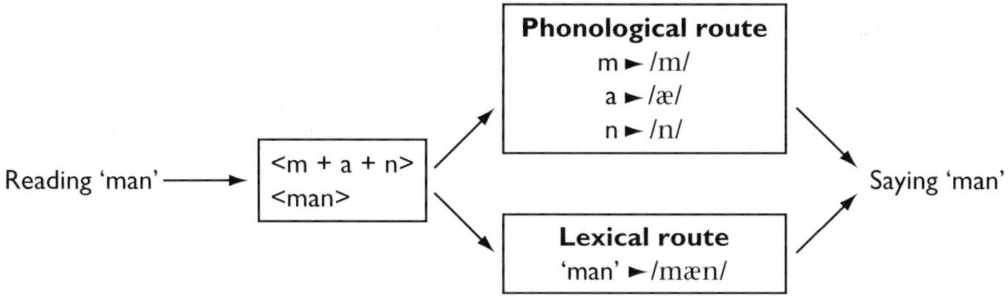

Fig. 1.5. Reading 'man' aloud.

The word 'man' may also be processed through the lexical route. <man> is checked as a whole against the items in the mental lexicon and is found to match an item with the pronunciation /mæn/. Both routes can yield the same result, whether the reader treats the word letter-by-letter or as a whole.

Sentence 2 '25+59=84' is not so much a sentence as a universal mathematical equation but can nevertheless be read aloud as English. Since English has no sound-based rule for linking <=> and <25> with phonemes, these symbols can be read aloud only through the lexical route. Each of them has to be checked against the pronunciation of a whole item in the mental lexicon – <25> to 'twenty-five' /twentɪfaɪv/ and so on. Indeed, most readers have to choose between two spoken forms for <+>, 'and' /ən(d)/ and 'plus' /plʌs/, and between three for <=>, 'are' /ɑː/, 'make' /meɪk/ and 'equal' /iːkwəl/. Figure 1.6 shows how the phonological route is blocked for the symbol <+> as it is not covered by any letter-to-sound correspondence rules.

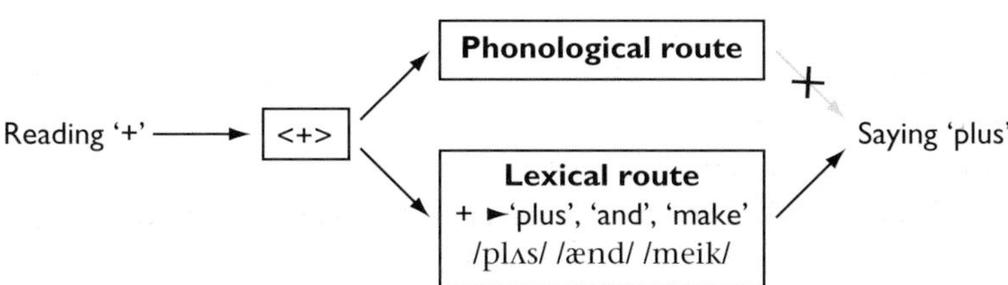

Fig. 1.6. Reading <+> aloud.

Unless familiar with nursery rhymes, readers will not have previously met the words in the finger-counting rhyme in Sentence 3 'Little Pig, Pillimore, Grimithistle, Pennywhistle, Great big Thumbo, father of them all.' Yet words like 'Pillimore', 'Grimithistle' and 'Thumbo' are unlikely to make them even stumble in reading aloud. Figure 1.7 shows how the phonological route converts 'Pillimore' letter by letter to /pɪlɪmɔː/, give or take a few additional rules for double <l> and final <ore>. The great advantage of the phonological route is that words that are completely unknown can still be read aloud.

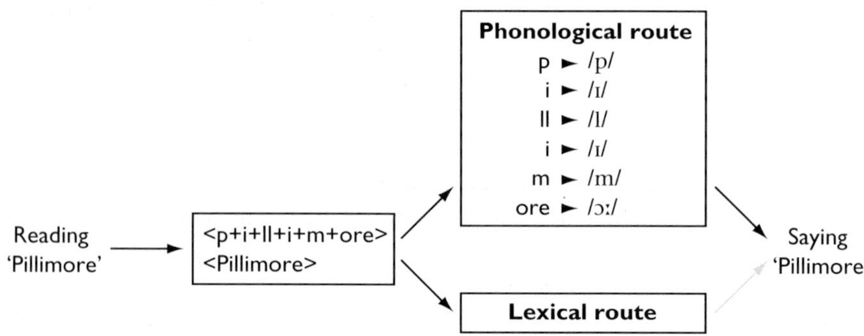

Fig. 1.7. Reading 'Pillimore' aloud.

Sentence 4 'Datta. Dayadhvam. Damyata. Shantih shantih shantih' shows how the ability to match sounds to letters extends to words that are not English. To most readers of *The Waste Land* these lines have little meaning without Eliot's footnote 'Shantih . . . "The Peace which passeth understanding".' Yet this does not prevent anybody from reading the word aloud using the phonological route and, ignoring non-English spelling such as the final <ih>, yielding something like 'shanty' /ʃæntɪ/. In principle any sequence of letters can be handled by the phonological route; it allows words to be read aloud without the reader understanding what they mean. So people can not only invent new words like 'Darth Vader' or 'Hogwarts' but also entire languages, such as Tolkien's Elven in Sentence 5 'A! Elbereth Gilthoniel! silivren penna míriel o menel aglar elenath, Gilthoniel, A! Elbereth!' Readers can be relied on to apply the letter-to-sound rules to any new sequence of letters they encounter – if they are forced to.

The main evidence for the existence of a phonological route is the ability to read unfamiliar and novel forms aloud. Literally any writing can be read aloud as English, whether 'Thumbo', 'Elbereth' or 'Gilthoniel'. The phonological route is capable of dealing with new and unknown words. Hence new names for businesses can be invented such as 'Accenture' or 'Consignia'; products can be put on the market called 'Nutrileum' or 'Olay'; pop groups can be called 'Sugababes' or 'Blackalicious'; aliens can be christened 'Klingons' or 'Mogwai', in the certain assurance that people will be able to pronounce their names, as we will see in Chapter 7. The ability to pronounce any sequence of letters as English stretches to foreign names. Though newsreaders may wince when they encounter foreign names, they can nevertheless read them aloud as English, whether the Russian writer Aleksandr Solzhenitsyn, the South African people's poet Mzwakhe Mbuli or the Zimbabwean singer Eska Mtungwezi, even if their pronunciation bears scant resemblance to that in the original languages.

The lexical route on the other hand cannot cope with novelty; it is unable to handle a new symbol that does not match anything in the mental lexicon. The novel symbol <‽> seen earlier in the chapter was uninterpretable if the reader did not know that the symbol is actually called an interrobang, combining an exclamation mark and a question mark, found in the computer font *Wingdings 2* if not in the *Oxford English Dictionary* (1994). Attempts to create new symbols without using letters often create problems for reading aloud, for example the symbol used by the Artist formerly known as Prince.

The lexical route is also called the visual route as it relies on the reader seeing a particular word before matching it against the words stored in the mind. It is the mental counterpart of meaning-based writing since it relies on a large mental store of visual items rather than on a set of rules. Hence it provides a short-cut to meaning not available through the phonological route. Indeed, in a sense it dispenses with the need to read aloud since the meaning of the word can be established independently of its pronunciation. The lexical route is also called 'addressed phonology', as the process involves looking up the phonology in a mental address like the address of a file in a computer, whereas the phonological route is called 'assembled phonology', meaning that the sounds of the word are put together bit by bit.

The size of the written unit varies in both routes. The units of the phonological route may be single letters such as <b> or two letters (the <gh> of 'laugh') or three (the <tch> of 'patch'). The units of the lexical route may also consist of single symbols such as <£> or several letters making up a high frequency whole word such as <and>. Neither route relies solely on individual letters in English.

The two overall types of writing system discussed in Part 1 are in a sense neutral between silent reading and reading aloud. The great leap forward in reading in Europe was taken about the eighth century AD when people realized that reading could be silent even when the writing system was sound-based. Until then libraries could be noisy places; libraries still insist on silence to this day. Reading aloud may be a side issue for most modern readers. Apart from reading aloud in the primary school and from reading bed-time stories to children, most adults seldom read aloud, except for professional newsreaders, ministers of religion and Members of Parliament. So, while we boasted above that any new combination of letters could be read aloud after a fashion, this existence is potential rather than actual. Most readers of Tolkien's Elven poems doubtless never read them aloud.

The dual model's final step of saying the word aloud is unnecessary in ordinary silent reading; the 'sounds' as well as the 'meanings' may just exist in our minds and not need physical expression. The lexical process means that people can read perfectly well in silence. Once they have decoded the words of the text and looked them up in their mental lexicon, they have understood all they need. The lexical route makes a direct connection between the text and the meaning. Even using the phonological route does not mean that texts have to be read aloud, since the discovery of silent reading: Finnish libraries are no noisier than Chinese libraries.

The lexical route in English

Just as orthographic depth claimed that languages do not use exclusively one type of writing or another, so an individual reading a language does not use only one route or the other. As we have seen, symbols such as <4>, <£> and <&> are treated as wholes by the lexical route since they do not fit letter-to-sound rules. Most English texts contain a few examples of this kind, particularly when numbers are involved, say prices <£5.99> or dates <11.05.03>. They may also have acronyms <WHO> or other systems based on the names of the letters <R U OK?>, again with no direct correspondences between letters and individual phonemes.

Task 4. Spelling high frequency words

Which of these high frequency words might be wrongly pronounced if the phonological route alone were followed in reading them aloud?

> was, it, would, is, new, that, have, years, of, some, do, said, his, like, two, people, just, the, then, and

Possible answers are at the end of the chapter

In a sense it has been cheating to illustrate the lexical route with symbols like <+> that are not strictly part of the English writing system. But the lexical route is also used for processing everyday words of English in every sentence. The lexical route must, for example, be available for the many English words that do not fit the correspondence rules. Take the infamous spelling of 'yacht'. Using the phonological route, <yacht> would be read aloud as /yætʃt/, to rhyme with 'matched'; instead it has to be remembered as a unique word /yɒt/, rhyming with 'hot', that is to be accessed via the lexical route to the mental lexicon.

Readers of English must therefore use the lexical route alongside the phonological route. Not only do many written words have virtually unique spoken correspondences, such as 'waltz' /wɒls/ and 'hiccough' /hɪkʌp/, but there are also many 'exceptions' to the usual phonological correspondence rules, such as 'great' /greɪt/ with the pronunciation of 'grate', not of the expected 'greet' /griːt/. One-off words like these cannot be handled easily by the phonological route but need to be checked against individual items in the mental lexicon. That is to say, the written forms of many English words are remembered as single items rather than generated by rules.

The main evidence for the lexical route comes from experiments using words with different frequencies of occurrence (Perfetti 1999). Take the words 'time' and 'bull'. If they were being read by the sound-based route, there should be no difference in processing time between them as they both have four letters and three sounds. If the processing times differ, this suggests that the lexical route is being used and that some words are accessed more rapidly as wholes than others. 'time' is in fact no. 68 in the *British National Corpus* (*BNC* 1995) frequency list, and 'bull' is no. 10,114. As we see from Task 4, many high frequency words would correspond to bizarre spoken forms if only the phonological route were employed.

One possibility is that there is not so much a continuum for frequency as a separate mental store for high frequency words. Seidenberg (1992) has claimed that high frequency English words such as 'new' and 'was' are accessed through the lexical route, that is, are stored as wholes. This has already been hinted at in the processing of <man> through the lexical route in Figure 1.5. A reader does not bother to change common words such as 'to', 'is' or 'this' into sequences of sounds, but matches them as wholes. To test this, readers can carry out Task 5 by crossing out the <e>s in a short English text. This task will be discussed further in Chapter 5.

Task 5. Deleting the <e>s

Cross out all the 'e's in this passage. Work straight through the passage, that is to say, do not have second thoughts or go back and check your answers. Answer the comprehension question at the end.

> The very famous water diviner Jane Rowe led a highly adventurous life. The Government asked her to divine for gold in an unsuccessful mine in the middle of the jungle. When she reached the mine, she became more and more uneasy as she perceived that the natives had cursed the place. At first the miners didn't believe her. Then the oldest miner was badly stung by a bee; the chief clerk broke five toes and was in great pain; the mine tunnel collapsed and they called it a day. Miss Rowe became seriously ill and the mine was soon closed.

Question: What was Jane Rowe's job?

Answers are at the end of the chapter

I compared native and non-native speakers of English on this task. To my surprise native readers failed to notice the <e> in 'the' on average 2.2 times; interestingly non-natives were much better, averaging only 1.1 omissions. Readers can now check their own performance by counting how many of the <e>s in the 12 examples of 'the' in the passage they missed. If 'the' were being processed through the phonological route, <th> would change into /ð/ and <e> into /ə/. For the <e> in 'the' to be invisible, readers must be treating 'the' as a whole, although as Perfetti *et al.* (1992: 228) remark, 'By age 20 even a college student who is a very infrequent reader will have encountered "the" over 50,000 times'. To the concept of the silent letter we can now add that of the invisible letter.

Much of the time English readers therefore recognize common words as wholes, probably at least the 100 most frequent English words, which add up to 45% of the words in most texts. Text 5 shows the same short text with the top 100 words in italics to demonstrate the proportion of written English they make up, here 47 words out of 100. Most are grammatical words, as one sees from the BNC top ten words in frequency: 'the', 'of', 'and', 'a', 'in', 'it', 'is', 'was', 'to', 'I'. Recognizing words as wholes through the lexical route is then vital for the skilled reader of English.

Text 5. High frequency words

> Words that belong to the most frequent 100 English words are given in italics (47/100).
>
> *The very* famous water diviner Jane Rowe led *a* highly adventurous life. *The Government* asked *her to* divine *for* gold *in an* unsuccessful mine *in the* middle *of the* jungle. *When she* reached *the* mine, *she* became *more and more* uneasy *as she* perceived *that the* natives *had* cursed *the* place. *At first the* miners didn't believe *her*. *Then the* oldest miner *was* badly stung *by a* bee; *the* chief clerk broke five toes *and was in* great pain; *the* mine tunnel collapsed *and they* called *it a* day. Miss Rowe became seriously ill *and the* mine *was* soon closed.

The two processing routes are thus closely intertwined rather than a matter of choosing one or the other. Both processes must be available from the initial phase of recognizing the word (Perfetti 1999). When readers encounter the word 'these', how do they know whether it is a high frequency word that they can look up as a whole in their mental lexicon or something they can treat letter by letter with correspondence rules? Or if they see 'thesis', at what point do they realize it cannot be read as a whole but must be dealt with by correspondence rules? With the pair 'these'/'thesis', this is crucially important since the clue to whether initial <th> corresponds to /ð/ as in /ðiːz/ 'these' or to /θ/ as in /θiːsɪs/ 'thesis' is only provided by the <is> at its end. The reader must in a sense explore both routes simultaneously until it is clear which one is going to succeed. The reader accepts 'thesis' because the phonological route produces an acceptable word of English first. Seidenberg (1992) claims that the difference between a fast and a slow reader of English is how many words they can recognize via the lexical route, that is, how big is the stock of words they recognize as wholes. The phonological route slows reading down.

Just how the two routes interact is controversial. Perfetti *et al.* (1992) claim that the phonological route is basic to all processing of writing, Kreiner (1992) that it is only used when the lexical route fails. Even deaf students have in a sense a phonological route, demonstrated by their difficulty in reading tongue-twisters despite not being able to hear them (Hanson *et al.* 1991).

The two routes (*see* Table 1.2) are also relevant to the acquisition of reading, as we see in Chapter 5; a phonics method for teaching reading favours the phonological route, a look-and-say method the lexical route. Dyslexia too is linked to the two routes: some dyslexic people cannot use the lexical route (Castles and Coltheart 1993). In aphasia, some people only lose one of the routes rather than both (Funnell 1983). Furthermore, the two routes make a crucial difference to the difficulty of learning a writing system in another language, as will be seen in Chapter 5: compare at one extreme the problems of an English-speaking person learning Italian with those of the same person learning Chinese.

Table 1.2 The two routes

	Phonological route	**Lexical route**
Converts written units	To phonemes	To meanings
Also known as	Assembled phonology	Addressed phonology
Needs	Mental rules	Mental lexicon of items
Works by	Correspondence rules	Matching
Can handle	Any novel combination	Only familiar symbols
Used with	Any words	High frequency words

Orthographic regularities in processing

The last section mentioned some orthographic regularities of English that are based neither on letter-to-sound correspondence rules nor on memory for whole items. For example double letters such as <ff> occur only at the end of words, 'cliff', not at the beginning 'fflick' (apart from some Welsh names like 'Ffion'); only a few vowels may occur without a following consonant, <a> and <i> are rare ending a word, exceptions being 'ska' and 'spaghetti'; <y> is preferred over <i> when there is no following consonant, 'cry', 'only'; <y> corresponds to /ɪ/ in word endings, 'city', but to /j/ in word beginnings, 'yawn' and 'yes'; <q> is always followed by <u>, 'queue', 'quit', and so on.

These regularities are not based on the phonological route since they are not straightforward letter-to-sound correspondence rules (although they could, at least in part, be covered by complex context-sensitive rules, as will be seen in Chapter 3). Nor is there any intrinsic reason why 'bbe' is any less pronounceable than 'ebb' or 'cri' than 'cry'. These patterns do not apply solely to individual words like 'yacht' or 'does' in the manner of the lexical route but to whole groups of words: initial <c> corresponding to /k/ applies to 'call', 'cough', 'cry' and a host of other words; final <ck> corresponding to /k/ to 'trick', 'lack', 'clock' and another host of words. Orthographic regularities often apply to the positions of letters within the word rather than to phonemes. So they are typical neither of the lexical route, which has no rules, nor of the phonological route, which does not use letter positions. Indeed, Besner and Chapnick Smith (1992) propose a third processing route in which visual forms of words are looked up in the lexicon but passed to a phonological process without accessing their meaning, that is, <$> could lead to the spoken form /dɒlə/ in the mind.

But do these orthographic regularities have as much reality for readers as the phonological and lexical routes? Based on experiments by Olson *et al.* (1985) and Treiman (1993), I tested native speakers of English with pairs of real and concocted words. They had to say which word was spelled correctly out of 'room'/'rume' for the lexical route (same pronunciation, one spelled right); which word sounded like an English word out of 'fense'/'felce' (one corresponds to a real English spoken word spelled in a different way, 'fence') for the phonological route; and which word looked like a real word out of 'truve'/'truv' for orthographic regularities (one has possible English spelling, one does not, though neither is a word of English). The shortest response time for choosing between the words (800 milliseconds) was for the lexical route but there was little difference between the phonological route (1504 milliseconds) and the orthographic regularities (1658 milliseconds). The lexical-based route had the most answers correct (99.3%) but orthographic regularities were about as easy as the sound-based route, with 88.8% and 88.5% correct, respectively.

In other words the lexical route relying on memory of individual words was easiest and fastest; the other routes that required 'rules' of some type were slower and more difficult. This small-scale experiment hints that orthographic regularities are processed as quickly and easily by English native speakers as sound-based rules, though it is of course difficult to claim that the tasks used for the three aspects make exactly the same demands on the subjects. Chapter 5 examines the extent to which this also applies to non-native speakers. Other chapters will show how orthographic regularities contribute in large measure to the complexity of the English writing system.

Various alternatives to the dual-route models have been proposed in recent years, particularly as part of the theory of connectionism. This claims that the mind does not have discrete processes and modules but consists of a single unified system of connections. Spelling, like everything else, is learnt by weighting connections following the properties of the input: the heavier the weighting the more a connection is activated. So an orthographic unit gets linked to a phonological unit by occurring with it time and again: the more often the reader sees <b> linked to /b/ the stronger the connection becomes. Seidenberg and McLelland (1989) trained a computer by feeding in 2884 monosyllabic English words and then tested what it had 'learnt'. Only 2.7% of its suggested pronunciations were mistakes, showing that some of the regular patterns of English can indeed be acquired from sheer input without postulating either rules or whole-item learning.

There are, however, problems with this approach. Though few in number, the mistakes appear highly unlikely for any human reader to make; 'lewd' came out as /lɪd/, 'feud' as /flʌd/ and 'zip' as /vɪp/. Many of the thorny problems of English spelling to be discussed in Chapter 3 were avoided by using only monosyllables. It has also proved difficult to get the computer to handle the very fact that motivated researchers to establish a phonological route in the first place, namely the ability to pronounce novel words that have not been previously encountered (Perfetti 1999): 'bang' and 'mang' have little difference in difficulty for a human reader but considerable difference for a computer. The proof of this model comes from computer simulations and their postulated analogies with human processing. At best one can say that in principle connectionism forms an alternative to dual or triple processing models but the evidence from actual human processing of written language is scant.

This chapter has looked at the English writing system in relationship to some general properties of writing with regard both to writing systems of particular languages and to the mental processing of written language. It has set the scene by describing something of the complexity involved in the study of a writing system and demonstrating the need for it to be treated as interacting elements and processes rather than as a unified whole. It has introduced a conceptual difference between rules and items, whether seen as sound-based rules versus meaning-based items, or as the phonological route versus the lexical route, that will echo throughout the remaining chapters.

Lastly, some background needs to be provided for the actual term 'writing system'. As displayed below (*see* box), Perfetti (1999) sees a hierarchy between the writing system that 'determines in a general way how written units connect with units of language' and the 'orthography – the system that actually implements the writing system'. In this sense the writing system of English is the overall relationships described in Part 1, that is, a sound-based alphabetic system; everything else is the orthography of English, which implements the writing system through its detailed spellings and correspondence rules. Other writers such as Sproat (2000) introduce the concept of 'script' as 'a set of distinct marks conventionally used to represent the written form of one or more languages' and regard the writing system as an implementation of the script: English uses a Roman script rather than an Arabic or a Cyrillic script. Script should not be confused with language – even Hebrew script is also used for Yiddish (Sampson 1985).

Coulmas (1996), on the other hand, gives two meanings to 'writing system': sense 1 'the basic types of graphic systems designed to represent language . . .', which is equivalent to Perfetti's use; and sense 2 'spelling, i.e. a system of rules underlying the use of the graphemes of the language', contrasting with 'orthography' 'Correct spelling and that part of grammar that deals with the rules of correct spelling'. This meaning of writing system includes Perfetti's 'orthography' and covers the correspondence rules of the language; it reduces orthography to a standard of 'correctness', based on conformity to an authority such as a dictionary, bringing in the social factor that so often occurs in discussion of English writing.

Keeping to a single definition of 'writing system' throughout this book would fail because of the diverse worlds of psychology, linguistics and typography that it draws on. Following Sproat (2000) and Sampson (1985), 'writing system' will be treated as an overall cover term for the way that a particular language and its users systematically employ writing.

Definitions of the term 'writing system' and similar terms

Consider first *the writing system*, which determines in a general way how written units connect with units of language. . . . the orthography – the system that actually implements the writing system (Perfetti 1999: 168)

A 'script' is just a set of distinct marks conventionally used to represent the written form of one or more languages . . . A 'writing system' however is a script used to represent a particular language. . . . We will use the terms 'orthography' and 'writing system' interchangeably' (Sproat 2000: 25)

writing system A set of visible or tactile signs used to represent units of language in a systematic way . . .: [sense 1] the basic types of graphic systems designed to represent language . . .; [sense 2] spelling, i.e. a system of rules underlying the use of the graphemes of the language. (Coulmas 1996: 560)

orthography Correct spelling and that part of grammar that deals with the rules of correct spelling (Coulmas 1996: 379)

In the main 'writing system', 'script' and 'orthography' will be used interchangeably, though I shall tend to use 'writing system' when a script is cited as exemplifying a particular *type* of writing, and 'orthography' in connection with alternative conventions for using a given set of written marks (Sampson 1985: 20)

DISCUSSION TOPICS

1 Could English use a character-based writing system like Chinese?
2 How 'shallow' do you think English really is?
3 What other examples are there of English breaking the one-to-one and linearity principles?
4 Is there any justification for believing, as some do, that alphabet-based writing is the most advanced form?
5 How could English spelling be improved if there are indeed two routes for processing it?
6 How useful is reading aloud for English adults? How important is it to teach reading aloud to children?
7 What other letters might be 'invisible' to English readers apart from the <e> of 'the'?
8 Why do you think English spelling has such a bad reputation?

ANSWERS TO TASKS

Task 1. English spelled with consonants

1 Baa, baa, black sheep, have you any wool? Yes, sir, yes sir, three bags full. One for the master and one for the dame and one for the little boy who lives down the lane. (nursery rhyme)

2 Human life is everywhere a state in which much is to be endured, and little to be enjoyed. (Dr Johnson)
3 Linguistic theory is concerned primarily with an ideal speaker-listener, in a completely homogeneous speech community, who knows its language perfectly and is unaffected by such grammatically irrelevant conditions as . . . (Noam Chomsky)
4 Do not go gentle into that good night
Old age should burn and rave at close of day
Rage rage against the dying of the light. (Dylan Thomas)

Task 2. Phoneme/letter correspondences

1 Different correspondences for <a>: /eɪ/ 'age', /æ/ 'bad', /ɑː/ 'bath', /ə/ 'about', /iː/ 'beat', /e/ 'many', /aɪ/ 'aisle', /əʊ/ 'coat', /ɔː/ 'ball', /uː/ 'beauty', /ɒ/ 'cauliflower'.
2. Different correspondences for /eɪ/: <a> 'lake', <au> 'gauge', <et> 'ballet', <ai> 'aid', <er> 'foyer', <ay> 'stay', <é> 'café', <ea> 'steak', <eigh> 'weigh', <ée> 'matinée', <ae> 'sundae', <ey> 'they'.

Task 4. Spelling high frequency words

Some are hard to judge but probably: 'was' /wæs/ not /wɒz/ (cf. 'gas'), 'have' /heɪv/ not /hæv/ (cf. 'cave'), 'of' /ɒf/ not /ɒv/, 'some' /səʊm/ not /sʌm/ (cf. 'tome'), 'said' /seɪd/ not /sed/ (cf. 'paid'), 'two' /twəʊ/ not /tuː/ (cf. 'twin').

Task 5. E-deletion

<e>s are underlined.

> The very famous water diviner Jane Rowe led a highly adventurous life. The Government asked her to divine for gold in an unsuccessful mine in the middle of the jungle. When she reached the mine, she became more and more uneasy as she perceived that the natives had cursed the place. At first the miners didn't believe her. Then the oldest miner was badly stung by a bee; the chief clerk broke five toes and was in great pain; the mine tunnel collapsed and they called it a day. Miss Rowe became seriously ill and the mine was soon closed.

Answer to question: Jane Rowe was a water diviner. (Note: this was present simply to make people read for meaning rather than just look at the letters).

FURTHER READING

Some useful general follow-up reading on the topics covered in this chapter includes:

- Sampson, G. (1985) *Writing Systems: A Linguistic Introduction*. London: Hutchinson. The best linguistic style introduction to writing systems in general.
- Sproat, R. (2000) *A Computational Theory of Writing Systems*. Cambridge: Cambridge University Press. This covers much about meaning-based and sound-based relationships within a modern framework.

- Coulmas, F. (1996) *The Blackwell Encyclopedia of Writing Systems*. Oxford: Blackwell. An invaluable reference source on everything to do with writing systems.
- Patterson, K.E. and Morton, J. (1985) From orthography to phonology: an attempt at an old interpretation. In K.E. Patterson, J.C. Marshall and M. Coltheart (eds), *Surface Dyslexia*. London: Erlbaum, 335–59. A basic psychological article on the two-routes processing model.

A useful website on writing systems with further examples of scripts using the *Universal Declaration of Human Rights* is *The Language Museum* (www.language-museum.com). The originals can be seen at (www.unhchr.ch/udhr/navigate/alpha.htm).

2 The multi-dimensions of spoken and written English

Views on the relationship between speech and writing

Writing is not language, but merely a way of recording language by means of visible marks (Bloomfield 1933: 21)

Language and writing are two distinct systems of signs; the second exists for the sole purpose of representing the first (de Saussure 1916, trans. Baskin 1960: 23)

. . . an identical spoken and written language would be practically intolerable; if we spoke as we write, we would find no one to listen; and if we wrote as we speak, we should find no one to read. The spoken and written language must not be too near together, as they must not be too far apart (T.S. Eliot, cited in Hughes 1996)

If it sounds like writing, I rewrite it (Elmore Leonard 1985)

INTRODUCTION

So far as most linguists are concerned, written language has no existence in its own right, but is a shadow cast by speech: 'the spoken language is primary and . . . writing is essentially a means of representing speech in another medium' (Lyons 1968: 38). Some typical views about speech and writing are seen in the box above; the two other linguists, Bloomfield and de Saussure, agree with Lyons; the two writers, T.S. Eliot and Elmore Leonard, have rather different views. Text 1 below gives three short authentic English texts. Two are written language, one a transcript of spoken language. If Lyons and the others were right in thinking that writing is speech written down, all the three texts should have essentially the same characteristics.

Text 1. Samples of written English

A. The car benefit cash equivalent is calculated on a percentage of its price, set according to the level of your business travel in the car during the tax year (with subsequent reductions for age, unavailability and private use payments).

B. [Lovely morning] Er well this is it. You know I I've been like a spring lamb for about the last week and a half. [Haha] I do. I keep boinging about because it's just it's just so nice. [Yes Yes].

C. Have just finished Perdido Street Station – odd book; I thought the prose style let it down till it got going and then it turned into a straight action story towards the end.

Yet it is instantly obvious that the first text is written language and the second is a transcript of spoken language; only the third text is at all problematic. Some of the differences lie in their grammatical structure: the complex noun expression in the first, 'The car benefit cash equivalent' is characteristic of written language; the pronouns in the second 'it . . . you . . . I . . . I . . . I . . . I . . . it . . . it . . .' are characteristic of spoken language as well as the hesitation 'er', the 'well' and the restart 'it's just it's just so nice'. The vocabulary is also different: 'unavailability' is as much written language as 'boinging' is spoken language. Despite the linguists' assertions, writing does more than represent speech.

This chapter then is concerned with the relationship between speech and writing, how the differences between them originate, and the effects that writing has on the lives of individuals and societies.

2.1 DIFFERENCES BETWEEN THE VISUAL AND ACOUSTIC MEDIA

Focusing questions

- Do you think writing depends on speech or is independent?
- What do you think are the essential differences between speech and writing?
- How would you say something to sound excited? How would you convey the same feeling in writing?

Key words

tone: a tone is a unit of pitch change for a given language, English having about seven tones, such as a high fall $^{Y}e_{s}$ or a high rise ye^{s}, used to convey the speaker's attitude, grammatical distinctions and other types of meaning.

tone-group: the stretch of speech in English organized around a single tone is called a 'tone-group'. Depending on the particular meaning the speaker wants to convey, 'Life is short' could in principle be organized as one tone-group /Life is short/, as two /Life/is short/ or /Life is/short/, though three is unlikely /Life/is/short/.

To state the obvious, speech is spoken sounds passing through the air; writing is visible signs on a surface. Producing a spoken sentence means co-ordinating complex movements of the muscles of the mouth and lungs; producing a written sentence means co-ordinating complex movements of the hand and fingers with a pen or keyboard. Understanding a spoken sentence starts by hearing sound waves with the ears, understanding a written sentence by seeing visual shapes with the eyes. These obvious physical differences between the acoustic and visual channels have many consequences for the relationship between speech and writing.

Task 1. Comparing speech and writing

1 Listen to someone speaking spontaneously for a minute, say by turning on the radio, then answer the questions on page 52.
2 Read the following text for a minute: then answer the questions on page 53.

Oxford High Street
The High Street in Oxford, otherwise known as 'The High', is one of the most famous streets in the world. It follows a slight curve rising from the River Cherwell to Carfax, the centre of town. Its finest buildings are mostly churches or colleges of the university. On the right going up the hill you first pass fifteenth century Magdalen College, pronounced locally to rhyme with 'maudlin'. Then after Longwall Street comes St Edmund's Hall, alias 'Teddy Hall', followed by All Saints, a college for graduates, and University College, shortened to 'Univ'. . . .

Writing is permanent, speech is fleeting

Written language has a solid existence outside of our minds. Sumerian clay tablets tell us how much barley was sold at a market in the Middle East some 5000 years ago; the *Voyager* spacecraft will fly on into space displaying its cryptic symbolic message for millions of years to come. Whether or not anybody understands the tablet, whether or not some alien race eventually deciphers the *Voyager* message does not matter: they are potentially there for someone to read until they are physically destroyed. Everyday writing is seldom so enduring: last week's shopping list vanishes; yesterday's newspaper goes out with the rubbish. But in principle writing is permanent, waiting to be activated in someone's mind. Graffiti on London walls still abuse two Romans called Publius and Titus 2000 years later, even if now in a museum. The instructions for filling out a tax return in Text 1A can be read or consulted whenever needed; although they have doubtless been superseded by the current year's tax form, this does not destroy the written sentence. The only exception to this is the world wide web, whose pages are in a constant state of flux, hence forcing references in academic texts to state the date when they were accessed rather than the date of publication.

Speech, however, is impermanent (setting aside for the moment devices such as tape-recorders). Second by second, minute by minute, spoken language is said and is gone. Speech is bound to the fleeting moment. The only reason that spoken Text 1B can be discussed at all is because it has been taken out of the time flow, first by the tape-recorder, then by the transcript; it is only permanent because it has been converted into written language. There are no records of what Sumerians actually said because there are no transcripts of their speech, let alone recordings; all that is directly known of their spoken language comes from the written record. What was said a week ago, or indeed a second ago, has vanished, unless it has been converted into some other form or deliberately tape-recorded.

The contribution of memory and other cognitive processes

This difference in permanency has immediate consequences for the processing of written and spoken language. Understanding speech depends not just on perceiving the actual sounds of speech, but on storing them in working memory while the sentence is processed. A person who hears a spoken sentence like Text 1B has to keep information in the mind as he or she processes the sentence – what 'it' refers to, what 'I do' refers to, who is 'boinging about' and so on. Speech has a moving window; for things before the window we rely on memory, for speech to come, on prediction: we can look neither backward nor forward. Speech is uttered linearly in time; we hear it sound by sound, even if it is converted to a non-linear form in our minds.

Writing, however, is all present at the same moment of time. Readers can look back at the beginning of the book if they get lost, look forward to the end if they get bored or set the book aside to read at a later time. So, if readers forget what a pronoun refers to or get lost in a grammatical construction, they can effectively press replay and try again. It is like the difference between watching a play and reading a book. The play is not under the spectators' control and proceeds remorselessly even when they have lost the hang of the plot. The book can be read at the readers' own pace for however long they want; any misunderstanding can be cleared up by going back a few pages.

One obvious consequence is speed. Though there is considerable variation from one person to another and it is difficult to measure speech and writing in the same way, estimates suggest that people speak and listen in the region of 150 words per minute, read on average 250–300 words and copy texts at about 22 words a minute (Bailey 2000). So far as literary composition is concerned, a fluent literary writer like Anthony Trollope used to set himself the task of writing 1800 words every morning; more fluent writers such as Edgar Wallace, who usually wrote a 70,000 word book in 72 hours, and Erle Stanley Gardner, known to write a book in an evening, 'cheated' by dictating to shorthand typists.

The individual necessarily uses different mental processes for speech and writing. Speech is intensive on working memory in a way that writing is not. Indeed, as seen later, people's memory systems are claimed to work differently in literate and non-literate societies.

Spontaneity versus editing

Speech is normally unrehearsed; people do not plan what they say except in special circumstances, which can indeed become close to written language read aloud, as in political speeches. Nearly all speech is necessarily an unedited first draft; it cannot be changed, improved or deleted after it has been said because the text is no longer available for editing. The woman who uttered Text 1B may wish that she had not repeated 'I I' or that she had tidied up the sentence 'because it's just it's just so nice' before she said it; she may even regret the odd verb 'boinging'. But there is nothing she can do about it now it has been said. However much speakers rephrase their mistakes, this does not erase the first botched attempt. Speech therefore comes out with the characteristic mistakes and distortions of a first draft that has not been checked or edited. Apart from a few gifted or trained public speakers, people do not plan in detail a polished version of what they are saying; there is no word-processing of spontaneous speech.

Most written language is, however, planned and edited. Apart from private registers like diaries, people monitor what they are writing as they go along. What the reader sees is therefore usually the last draft, possibly of many. The civil servant who composed Text 1A doubtless had to check the list of tax reductions 'for age, unavailability and private use payments' against previous drafts and had to have the whole sentence sanctioned by committee before it could be printed. Writing can be worked over time and again until it conveys just what the writer wants; Joseph Grand in Camus' *La Peste* spends much of his life reworking the first sentence of his novel: 'One fine morning in the month of May an elegant young horsewoman might have been seen riding a handsome sorrel mare along the flowery avenues of the Bois de Boulogne'. Readers can check the written sentence to make certain that they have understood; on the tax return it may be vital to ensure that they know how to calculate the cash equivalent. Children indeed have to be taught that a piece of writing can evolve through different drafts (Perera 1984). Only when they are taught to cross out do they come to see that writing can be revised as many times as they like.

Oddly enough modern technology has blurred this first-draft nature of written language by introducing new types of first-draft writing, for example e-mail, as seen in Text 1C, and text messaging. E-mail messages resemble spoken language rather than written in some respects, for example in having sentences without subject pronouns as in Text 1C 'Have just finished Perdido Street Station' and verb-less expressions 'odd book'. Many users treat e-mail writing as first-draft and hardly bother to tidy it up before sending; indeed the first e-mail program I used in the 1980s would not let me edit the spelling once typed.

Relationship to situation

Writing also involves a different relationship between language and situation from speech. In speech pronouns may refer to people who are present without further explanation: 'He's an idiot!' describing the driver who is overtaking on the inside lane; 'They're all mine' pointing to a pile of books; 'It's a boy!' announcing a birth. Out of context it is impossible to tell to whom the pronouns refer. Written language has to supply the details that are quite obvious in the spoken situation; 'I thought the driver who was passing in the inside lane was an idiot'. As Vygotsky 1962: 99) says, 'In written speech we are obliged to create the situation, to represent it to ourselves'.

In the case of spoken language the listener and speaker are usually physically present in the same speech situation, apart from broadcasting and the telephone; they can see each other and they are aware of what is going on. So there is no need to specify who they are, where they are speaking, the date and time of day, and their respective roles. Listeners to Text 1B could link 'last week' to an actual date and would have found it obvious that the participants were talking about a heat wave, now almost opaque to us. So the ways in which language relates to the situation (deixis) have to vary between speech and writing. Because of the shared physical situation, the speaker does not have to spell out all the deictic links. The meaning of pronouns in speech is usually obvious – 'I', 'it', etc., – as are the specifications of place – 'here', 'there' – and time – 'last week', 'now', 'tomorrow'. The self-evident details about the situation do not have to be supplied.

There is no need, however, for reader and writer ever to meet. A book or a tablet can still be read centuries or millennia after the writer has died; e-mails can be exchanged between people who have no idea where the other person is located. So, in writing, the pronouns 'I' and 'you' need either to be identified or to be avoided. Time is indefinite in writing unless specified: to pinpoint 'tomorrow' you need to know 'today'. A written document can be read anywhere by anyone, not just by those actually present in the speech situation. A written text either has to spell the situation out or to be so neutral that it can apply to any situation. Again Text 1C is problematic as it assumes a shared context in which it is obvious that 'Perdido Street Station' refers to a book.

Social roles

The social roles of speaker and listener in spoken language often differ from those of writer and reader in written language. Speakers tell you overtly about their states of mind, 'I think', 'I believe', called private verbs as they refer to unobservable states of the speaker's mind: writers do so rarely. Speech often requires the listener to do something, whether obey a command ('Stand up!'), answer a question ('What's the time?') or respond to a 'tag' ('Seaman is playing well, isn't he?'). Such calls for action by the recipient are far less possible in writing; Text 1A has no commands, questions or tags at all. Speech is seldom separated from the speaker.

In a sense, speaking is two-way in that interaction between speaker and listener is immediate; writing is one-way with, at best, slow consecutive interaction between writer and reader, for instance readers' letters to the editor. The participants in speech affect each other; it takes two to have a conversation. Text 1B uses the broadcasting device of an on-air dialogue with another person to convey the interaction of speech, since the whole of the actual audience is not accessible; this is often built-in to radio broadcasts through phone-ins, as here, or through two presenters who chat cheerfully to each other on air. Even in the monologue of a lecture, the behaviour of the audience has an impact on the speaker: no English academic forgets the disconcerting experience of lecturing for the first time in a culture where agreement with the speaker means head-shaking rather than head-nodding. Speech normally involves a visible social interaction between the participants, whether the carefully marked-out roles of a job interview or the informal roles of casual conversation.

In written English the role of reader seldom involves immediate interaction with the writer. The reader's enjoyment or lack of comprehension cannot feed back to the writer from one moment to the next. The problem for writers is how to communicate in the absence of a social relationship. This relates to the greater neutrality of writing; there is no need to know even the name of the civil servant who drafted the income tax form Text 1A; their individuality, personality or identity is irrelevant to the purpose of writing. In many circumstances a writer is not identified. Nor is the reader addressed directly. It is a shock when Sterne's *Tristram Shandy* challenges his reader 'How could you, Madam, be so inattentive in reading the last chapter?'

Unique features of visual and written media

Last come the sheer physical differences between the two media, which can be exploited in speech and writing. The pitch of the voice goes up and down in speech, enabling spoken language to use intonation for signalling grammatical structure or emotional attitudes, such as the English rise $\mathrm{y^{e^{s}}}$, fall $\mathrm{^{y}e_{s}}$, and combined fall–rise $\mathrm{^{y}e^{s}}$. To some extent the punctuation system of written English signals similar meanings to the tones of speech through 'Yes?', 'Yes!' or plain 'Yes.' and marks out the tone-groups with commas and full stops. But, as can readily be seen, the meanings of the three spoken tones given here do not correspond exactly to those of the three punctuation marks; a rising tone is not necessarily a question; the doubting fall–rise tone has no written equivalent. Punctuation also has other purposes that are not signalled in speech at all, such as the use of capital letters to signal proper names and sentence beginnings, as seen in Chapter 4.

Speakers also have to stress words and syllables. Sometimes this is to maintain an overall rhythm in speech 'The <u>rain</u> in <u>Spain</u> stays <u>mainly</u> in the <u>plain</u>', sometimes to distinguish one word from another '<u>per</u>fect' (adjective) versus 'per<u>fect</u>' (verb), sometimes to emphasize a particular word or element 'Hoagy <u>Carmichael</u> wrote Stardust' (not George Gershwin), 'Hoagy Carmichael wrote <u>Star</u>dust' (not Moondust), 'Hoagy Carmichael <u>wrote</u> Stardust' (rather than just performing it), and so on. Although written English provides the possibility of underlining or italicizing emphasized words, as just demonstrated, in most texts this is used sparingly, particularly as many printers detest underlining. Other languages may use different written means for distinguishing stress: French and Italian use the grave accent for instance to show the stressed syllables in 'voilà' and 'città'. Spanish and Greek show stress with the acute accent in 'mágico' or 'άνδρας' ('man').

Nor do the spaces of written language correspond to pauses of spoken language. Speech comes out in a fairly continuous stream with pauses used for reasons such as hesitating, breathing, planning, etc. Spoken words are rarely marked out by pauses, even if this division is potentially available for some kind of emphasis: 'Read.my.lips. This.is.my.final.answer.' Modern English writing, however, puts spaces between words so that the word divisions are immediately obvious: 'Read my lips. This is my final answer.' Writing is neatly pre-packaged into word chunks, speech is not. A radio phone-in went astray when the caller was talking about 'Ali G', the television satirist, the presenter about 'allergy', a misunderstanding prevented in writing by the word space (and the capital letters).

These distinctive aspects of written English are discussed at greater length in later chapters. Although some of the systems of speech and writing run parallel in expressing similar features of meaning through different means, many are quite dissimilar. Written language can conveniently show different words by varying the spelling, 'inn' versus 'in', or 'whole' versus 'hole' (Chapter 3). Many of the devices of written language have no spoken equivalent (Table 2.1). The way capital letters distinguish proper nouns 'Art' from ordinary nouns 'art' cannot be duplicated in speech (Chapter 4). How for instance do you 'say' the e-mail 'emoticons' popular in the 1990s such as <:-(and {;-)? However trivial such symbols may be, they are not available in the spoken language.

Table 2.1 Spoken sounds versus written symbols

Speech is spoken sounds	Writing is written symbols
Speech is fleeting	Writing is permanent
Speech is linear in time	Writing can be consulted, regardless of time
Speech is processed 'on-line'	Writing is stored 'off-line'
Speech can be produced and comprehended at around 150 words per minute	Writing can be read at up to 350 words per minutes
Speech is spontaneous first-draft	Writing is carefully worked, final-draft
Speech is linked to a definite shared context	Writing has an indefinite non-shared context
Speech attributes definite roles to the listener	Writing attributes indefinite roles to the reader
Speech can use sound features such as intonation	Writing can use written features such as punctuation

2.2 SPECIAL FEATURES OF WRITTEN ENGLISH

Focusing questions

- What aspects do you think are distinctive about written English?
- How do you think literacy has affected your ways of thinking in general?

Key words

content words versus function words: content words such as 'table' or 'truth' or 'see' are best explained in the dictionary (lexicon); function words (also known as 'grammatical' or 'structure' words), such as prepositions 'by' or 'for' or determiners 'a' or 'an', express the grammatical relationships in the sentence.

lexical density: the proportion of features such as content words to function words in a text.

register: a variety of a language defined by its situational use rather than its speakers, for example academic prose or gossip.

involved production: 'high informational density and exact informational content' (Biber 1988: 107).

informational production: 'affective, interactional and generalised content' (Biber 1988: 107).

text-sentence: a unit 'of written text customarily presented as bracketed by a capital letter and a period' (Nunberg 1990) is a *text-sentence*, as opposed to a lexical sentence, which is a grammatically or conceptually complete unit.

This section looks at some of the distinctive characteristics of written language. To illustrate the argument, Text 2 (below) gives some English road signs and a brief newspaper story.

Text 2. Short written texts

1 Some road signs in England

A&E not 24 hrs ACCIDENT AHEAD No loading at any time
GIVE WAY WEAK BRIDGE Reduce speed now
Humps for ½ mile SLOW WET TAR
Low bridge 2 miles ahead Keep Clear
Give way to oncoming vehicles Soft verges for 2 miles
Sorry for any delay Queues likely No footway for 400 yds
STOP when lights show Delays possible until Sept 2003

The Highway Code (1999)

2 A newspaper article

Riot fears allayed

Fears of disturbances during the annual May Day anti-capitalism protests appeared largely unfounded yesterday as police described the thousands-strong demonstrations in London as 'peaceful and good-humoured'. Up to 6000 people gathered in Trafalgar Square in a peaceful joint protest – including trade unionists and anti-globalisation groups – and listened to speeches from a variety of activists.

But trouble brewed in Piccadilly, central London, as a crowd marched down Coventry Street where there were angry skirmishes. A hard core of about 100 demonstrators charged the police line, throwing cans and bottles and shouting 'police scum'.

Scotland Yard said there had been eight arrests.

Local newspaper

Vocabulary

Some words exist primarily in the written form and are rare in speech. For instance 'footway', 'oncoming vehicles', 'unfounded' or 'allayed' are more likely in written than spoken texts. Written notices often preserve older forms of English; the road sign uses 'footway' rather than British 'pavement' or American 'sidewalk'; a notice in my home town, Colchester, in England, still orders 'No parking on the greensward', a word usually associated with Robin Hood; a notice by an Essex university footpath says 'Cyclists must dismount', summoning up a Victorian image of gentlemen getting off horses. It is not so much that particular words are totally excluded from speech or writing as that they occur more commonly in one medium or the other. Most people would not say 'allayed', 'unfounded' or 'thousands-strong' when talking about the May Day demonstration, nor would they write such words as 'boinging' in Text 1B earlier, or 'thingy' or 'loo', common in my own speech.

Grammar

The grammar of written English also has distinctive characteristics. It may be inevitable that the only verbs in the road signs are commands, 'GIVE WAY', 'Reduce speed' and that the verb 'be' is omitted '[There are] Humps for ½ mile', 'Queues [are] likely'. It is not, however, so obvious that *all* written English is weighted towards noun expressions rather than verb expressions. Typical examples from one day's *Guardian* newspaper include 'the petulant and ultimately discredited performance of the prosecutor's star witness, a 14 year old girl known as Bromley'; 'the direct local effects of a hydrogen explosion in the most probable target areas' and 'the NHS system of funding – comprehensive and inclusive insurance with treatment free at the point of delivery'. In each case an expression with a noun feels more natural in writing than one with a verb. The headlines on the same day provide more examples: '£66 crackdown on bad behaviour by pupils', 'Hard boys drifting into a life of crime', 'Stormy scenes at AstraZeneca AGM'. A noun-based notice that must have baffled travellers at Gatwick Airport near London is:

> NCP long-term off-airport car park courtesy coach pick-up point

Not that the notice at Narita Airport in Tokyo is any easier to fathom:

> Passenger service facilities charge tickets.

The same tendency to minimize verbs is seen in the way written language uses noun expressions derived from verbs, that is to say, participles ending in 'ed' and 'ing'. 'Hard boys drifting into a life of crime'; 'using oil as a bargaining ploy', '. . . led to oil prices quadrupling, motorists waiting . . . and the global economy beginning a slide . . .', 'being tough on the causes of crime'. Verbs also tend to be in the 'full' form in writing rather than contracted: 'shall not' rather than 'shan't', 'will not' rather than 'won't', etc. Writing uses the passive voice where the 'actor' is not identified to preserve the writer's neutrality; 'the latest grim find was made in the cellar' claims my local paper, rather than 'PC Jones made a grim find in the cellar.'

Many examples from the same newspaper illustrate the prevalence in written language of phrases linked by prepositions; 'the direct local effects of a hydrogen explosion <u>in</u> the most probable target areas', 'insurance <u>with</u> treatment free <u>at</u> point <u>of</u> delivery', 'Crackdown <u>on</u> bad behaviour <u>by</u> pupils'. Much of the apparent complexity of written language comes from stringing together phrases with prepositions or particles in this fashion, as seen in later texts.

Figure 2.1 displays some of the frequency characteristics of written and spoken English. This graph is based on Leech *et al.* (2001), who analysed the 100 million words of the *British National Corpus* (*BNC*) into those categories that showed the greatest difference in frequency between spoken and written English. Setting aside interjections and undecidable words, the figure gives the 10 categories that have the biggest difference per million words, usually about double. Thus written English has proportionately far more common nouns (singular and plural, 'book'/'books'), general adjectives, articles 'the', singular proper nouns 'London' and the preposition 'of'. Spoken English on the other hand has a far higher incidence of 'I', 'it', 'you', and base verbs such as 'give'.

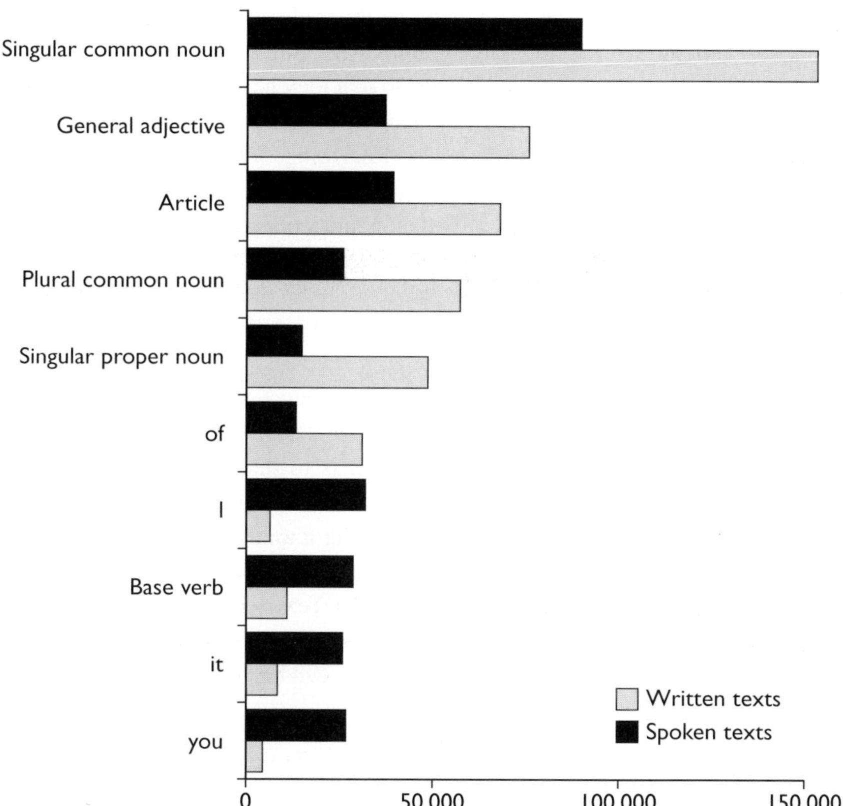

Fig. 2.1. Frequency of the top 10 most differentiated categories per million words in the *British National Corpus* for spoken and written English. (Data source: Leech *et al.* 2001.)

One issue that needs to be introduced here is the contrasting ways that particular grammatical categories are treated in the analysis of written and spoken English. For example, in speech a word is defined in terms of its grammatical characteristics, since there are no clear spoken divisions between words: a spoken word is 'a minimum free form' (Bloomfield 1933: 178). The spoken phrase 'The two cats' has three words since 'the', 'two', 'cats' can all potentially be said in isolation and have separate entries in dictionaries; the form 's' and the cluster 'tw' never occur as utterances on their own and so do not count as words. In writing, however, an 'orthographic word' is defined in terms of its form: whatever comes between two spaces is a word. While these two definitions are rarely in opposition, they are nevertheless different ways of conceiving of words. Indeed, some linguists argue that words are artefacts imposed on speech by linguists who learnt to read in languages where word spaces form part of the script rather than being 'really' there (Faber 1992).

More serious perhaps is the difference between the definition of sentence in the analysis of speech and writing. Again, the analysis of spoken language uses a structural definition, typically based on an idea of completeness: a sentence is grammatically complete and can stand by itself, echoing the traditional definition of a sentence as a complete thought but moving it to a grammatical rather than semantic plane. Most linguists use the term sentence descriptively so that they have to recognize both major sentences which have a subject and a predicate in English, say 'The dog swims', and minor sentences consisting of phrases, 'Good morning, John', answers to questions 'On Thursday', or single words 'John' (Bloomfield 1933).

The analysis of written language, however, again uses a definition that is based on form: a sentence is anything that starts with a capital letter and ends with a full stop. So 'Come in.' is a written sentence, as is 'Green.' or 'In the morning.'. A single written sentence may include several elements that would pass as separate sentences in the spoken language, partly corresponding to separate clauses. One of the prime functions of punctuation is indeed to bind elements together into a single sentence with commas, dashes and semi-colons as will be seen in Chapter 4.

The solution put forward by Nunberg (1990) is to distinguish lexical sentences from text-sentences. Lexical sentences are defined in the conventional way by completeness in grammatical or semantic terms, having a main verb, etc. Text-sentences are 'units of written text customarily presented as bracketed by a capital letter and a period', called by some 'orthographic sentences'. Text-sentences may thus contain more than one lexical sentence. Consider some examples taken more or less randomly from an Angela Carter novel *Nights at the Circus* (1984):

> On that European tour of hers, Parisians shot themselves in droves for her sake; not just Lautrec but all the post-impressionists vied to paint her; Willy gave her supper and she gave Colette some good advice.

At least two lexical sentences are combined by the semi-colons and arguably two more pairs are combined by 'but' and 'and'.

> But the bones of birds are filled with air and mine are filled with solid matter and if the remarkable development of my thorax forms the same kind of windbreak as does that of a pigeon, the resemblance stops there and problems of balance and of elementary negotiation with the wind – who is a fickle lover – absorbed me for a long time.

Again the 'and's serve a crucial role in producing a single text-sentence, as do the dashes. The text-sentence combining several lexical sentences becomes important to writing as soon as written English rises above a certain level of sophistication.

Many text-sentences do not meet the classic 'completeness' definition of a single lexical sentence, to take three from *Nights at the Circus* at random:

> Extraordinary raucous and metallic voice; clanging of contralto or even baritone dustbins.
>
> About to join her hands in prayer.
>
> Which pithy quibble wouldn't sound badly set to music, either.

Many of the written sentences people encounter each day consist of short verbless sentences, called by Biber *et al.* (1999) 'non-clausal units' and sometime known as 'block' language, seen for example in part of a small ad from a local newspaper:

> Exciting telecoms business opportunities
>   not to be missed!
> No stock. Up-front bonuses
> Full or Part Time
> Ongoing commission
> Full support

Journal editors have tried over the years to eliminate the occasional 'incomplete' sentence from my own writing – one reviewer assumed this showed I was a non-native speaker of English – rather than accepting them as a necessary component of a varied prose style. A written sentence begins with a capital. Ends with a full stop. So there.

Much written language consists of short sentences that do not form part of a longer discourse, whether the written language on a train ticket, the names on a road sign, the entries on a destination board, the labels on pill bottles, the items on a restaurant menu, the notes on a phone-pad, the file names on a computer, or many other everyday pieces of written language, even, as Biber *et al.* (1999) confirm, some academic prose. Spoken language usually demands greater coherence; short verbless sentences are spoken in response to a question – 'What's the advantage?' 'No stock' – that is, implicitly linked to a larger grammatical structure. Spoken language tends to be analysed as part of larger units such as conversations and exchanges; much written language does not necessarily relate to units of language higher than the text-sentence but stands on its own. It is then important to make clear whether one is discussing lexical or text-sentences.

The lexical density of writing

Put together, these vocabulary and grammar differences add up to the overall factor called 'lexical density'. This relies chiefly on the division between content words and function words, to be dealt with more fully in Chapter 3. Content words are nouns such as 'accident', verbs 'reduce', adjectives 'wet' and so on; they have meanings that can be looked up in dictionaries. Function words are prepositions such as 'at', conjunctions 'as', articles 'the' and the like; they signal the structure of the sentence and make sense in terms of grammatical rules rather than entries in the dictionary.

The difference in density can be shown by underlining the content words in written Text 1A and spoken Text 1B, both shown earlier.

1 The <u>car benefit cash equivalent</u> is <u>calculated</u> on a <u>percentage</u> of its <u>price</u>, <u>set</u> according to the <u>level</u> of your <u>business travel</u> in the <u>car</u> during the <u>tax year</u> (with <u>subsequent reductions</u> for <u>age</u>, <u>unavailability</u> and <u>private use payments</u>). [21 content words out of 39]

2 Er well this is it. You <u>know</u> I I've been like a <u>spring lamb</u> for about the <u>last week</u> and a <u>half</u>. I do. I <u>keep boinging</u> about because it's just it's just so <u>nice</u>. [9 content words out of 36]

At a glance one can see that, though the texts are about the same length, there are far more content words in the written text than in the spoken. The proportion of content words to function words is thus higher in the written text, as it is in virtually all written texts, particularly the short verbless text-sentences discussed above like 'Total monthly charge'. Written language has different characteristics in terms of the grammatical categories of the words it uses.

Task 2. Novelists' prose and lexical density

Test the characteristics of written language on these two examples of novelists' prose by: (i) calculating roughly the proportion of content to function words in each; (ii) seeing how much they depend on nouns and noun expressions derived from verbs.

1 Soon we are in the Veneto: walls of terracotta and ochre, a red-roofed town in the shadow of a hulking mountain; elderberries along the track; gardens of irises and pink roses; the junkyards and sidings of Mestre.

As we move swiftly along the causeway across the grey-green water of the lagoon, the beautiful city draws itself into our eyes: towers, domes, façades. If a few years late, we are here at last. The two of us stand in the corridor with the luggage and look out over the water. I speak her name softly to myself, and she, somehow sensing it – or is it chance? – speaks mine. (117 words)

Vikram Seth (1999) *An Unequal Music*. London: Phoenix, 326–7.

2 I'd hold my arms out straight till they ached and I'd spin. I could feel the air against my arms, trying to stop them from going so fast, like dragging them through water. I kept going. Eyes open, little steps in a circle; my heels cut into the grass, made it juicy; really fast – the house, the kitchen, the hedge, the back, the other hedge, the apple tree, the house, the kitchen, the hedge, the back – waiting to stop my feet. I never warned myself. It just happened – the other hedge, the apple tree, the house, the kitchen – stop – onto the ground, on my back, sweating, gasping, everything still spinning. (115 words)

Roddy Doyle (1993) *Paddy Clarke Ha Ha Ha*. London: Minerva, 173.

Lexical density is then a measure of the proportion of content words to function words in a text: the more content words, the greater the density. Written language has a higher overall density than spoken texts. Halliday (1985) calculated the proportion in written language to be about one function word to 1.2 content words, in spoken language about one to 0.6. The increase in numbers of noun expressions, the need to spell out the situation more fully, the greater use of prepositional phrases and participles, and other grammatical factors, all conspire to make writing denser. Such denseness would lead to information overload in speech, as everyone who has heard a conference speaker read a written paper aloud can vouch. The feeling of density in written language is not simply a matter of spoken sentences being shorter or simpler than written but of a greater concentration of content words. This shows up in the *BNC* frequencies cited in Figure 2.1 above. Common nouns occur 209,687 times per million words in written English, 127,224 in spoken, that is, nearly twice as often in written English; pronouns ('you', 'it', 'I') occur 19,665 times in written English, 83,809 in spoken, that is about a quarter as often.

Functions of writing

The intrinsic differences between speech and writing inevitably lead to writing being used for different purposes. Its permanency means writing is used for records that can be preserved for the future, whether minutes, examinations, contracts or the tablets of Moses. Constitutions of countries and organizations are written down; even the so-called unwritten English constitution leads to a mass of written decisions and judgements. Hence, for most societies, writing is an authority that can be trusted in a way that speech cannot.

Much of the status of the written language derives from its permanent nature. In modern societies 'serious' literature is written down as novels, not improvised as oral epics; poetry is largely found in books, not folk songs; music is mostly played from written scores rather than improvised. In many societies, holy writings capture the very words of God. Most people regard writing as more important than speech, with perhaps the only exception being linguists; 'One could nearly say that in a "literate culture" speech is the spelling of writing' (Kress 2000: 18).

It is also important to remember the sheer range of ways in which written language is used. The image of a typical piece of spoken language is a conversation like the radio chat in Text 1B earlier; the image of the typical piece of written text is a continuous text like the extracts from novels in Task 2. Text 2 already displayed some short traffic signs; Chapter 4 has examples of newspaper headlines, café placards and street notices. Perhaps the majority of the writing people encounter does not consist of the elaborate sentences of a novel or a continuous text. Looking around from my keyboard, I see 'Kodak CD-RW' on a packet of disks, 'SIGN THE PLEDGE OF RESISTANCE' on a postcard, '*Tempo plus*' on a packet of paper handkerchiefs, 'MS.PACMAN' on a CD-ROM, 'Making sense of school' on the heading of a newspaper article pinned up on the wall. People take for granted the pervasiveness of written language in our everyday life, whether the train ticket, the text message, the public notice, the credit-card slip, the price tag or the hundred and one other everyday uses. Many of these are short fragments of language, not the conventional stereotype of writing as polished prose, even if these uses have seldom found their way into corpora of English or into English grammars.

Some languages indeed have a complete, or almost complete, separation between spoken and written language. This is particularly so in situations of diglossia where there are two versions of a language with very different uses, a High form for official occasions and a Low form for everyday life. In several countries the spoken language differs extremely from the written, for example the difference between High German and Swiss German in Switzerland. Some versions of the language may in effect not have a written form, like Ulster Scots in Northern Ireland. In many areas the written form of one language has been suppressed by another as happened to written English during the years of Norman rule, to be discussed in Chapter 6. Written Arabic is an interesting example where there is a gulf between the 'classic' form used internationally for religion and other purposes and the very different spoken Arabics of the countries of the Middle East and North Africa.

The claim is often heard that the function of language is communication. Malinowski (1923) showed early in the twentieth century that language is used not just for conveying information but also for creating and maintaining social relationships without communicating specific ideas, which he called 'phatic communion'. Halliday (1975) developed this approach into the three adult functions for language: the ideational (communicating 'ideas'), the interpersonal (having social relationships) and the textual (connecting language to itself). Written language should not be considered only as a way of communicating information from one person to another but also as a way of cementing social relationships. For example, the language of the internet chat room conveys little real information but serves phatic communion, as we shall find in Chapter 7.

To go from social functions to psychological, Chomsky has often insisted that the main function of language is to serve the internal needs of the human mind and that communication is an 'epiphenomenon' added on to this (Chomsky 2002). To make a computer analogy, the rationale for Windows was to make an operating system that each personal computer (PC) could use, and secondarily to have a way of communicating between PCs. Language is how the human mind copes with the world. Written language improved the results of mental processes by freeing the mind from its own limitations, by equipping it with an external storage device. This enabled the final product to be made permanent, to be consulted whenever the person wants. But also it provided a way of working out things on paper, of carrying out intricate operations that could not have been done in the mind – compare the limitations of mental arithmetic with the open potential of calculations on pen and paper.

Registers

As we have seen, the complex differences between speech and writing are often a matter of degree, of having more or less of some property rather than not having it at all. Mostly they are signs of more general patterns of variation between different 'registers' of language – 'varieties defined by their situational characteristics' (Biber *et al.* 1999: 135). Biber (1988) conceptualized registers in terms of five dimensions of variation, 'defined by distinct groupings of linguistic features that co-occur frequently in texts' (Biber 1995: 19). The dimension that links most closely to spoken and written English is 'involved production' to 'informational production', shown in Figure 2.2.

At the 'involved production' end come registers of language in which the participants interact with each other to the greatest extent. The linguistic features characteristic of involved production in English are mostly familiar from the discussion above. Here is a selection of the 34 touchstones for this dimension, with examples from Text 1; many also figure on the list of most differentiated categories in Figure 2.1.

Some features that score positively towards a register being at the involved production end of the scale are the proportions of:

- private verbs: 'doubt', 'believe', 'know': 'I <u>thought</u> the prose style let it down'
- 'that' deletion: 'I thought (<u>that</u>) the prose style let it down'
- contractions ''s', ''ve': 'I'<u>ve</u> been like a spring lamb'
- second person pronouns 'you': '<u>You</u> know . . .'
- first person pronouns: 'I', 'we': '<u>I I</u>'ve been like a spring lamb'
- pronoun 'it': 'till <u>it</u> got going'.

Features that score negatively and place registers at the informational end of the scale include the proportions of:

- nouns: 'car', 'cash'
- longer words: 'unavailability', 'subsequent'
- prepositions: 'on', 'to', 'of': '<u>with</u> subsequent reductions <u>for</u> age'
- attributive adjectives: '<u>odd</u> book'
- passives: 'The car benefit cash equivalent <u>is calculated</u> on a percentage of its price'
- place adverbials: 'towards the end'.

Adding together the scores for the 34 features that count towards this dimension yields an overall score for a particular register, locating it on the continuum shown in

Involved production

telephone conversations
face-to-face conversations

personal letters
spontaneous speeches
interviews

romantic fiction
prepared speeches
mystery and adventure fiction
general fiction
professional letters
broadcasts
science fiction
religion
humour
popular lore; editorials; hobbies
biographies
press reviews
academic prose; press reportage
official documents

Informational production

Fig. 2.2. Biber's dimensions of involved versus informational production (spoken registers in italic type). (Adapted from Biber 1988: 128.)

Figure 2.2. The registers that score most highly for involved production are telephone conversations and face-to-face conversations, both spoken language (shown in italics in Figure 2.2). Registers with high scores for informational production are academic prose and official documents, which are written language. In between these extremes come a range of registers: personal letters, though written, are fairly close to the involved production end, but so are spoken interviews. Science fiction and biographies (written) are toward the informational end. Romantic fiction (written) is closer to involved production than other types of novel. Broadcasts (spoken) and general fiction (written) are closer to the informational end. And so on for many other registers of language. Chapter 7 looks at the position of e-mails such as Text 1C on this continuum.

Broadly speaking, written language registers tend to be towards the informational end, spoken registers towards the involved production end, but there is considerable overlap. For example, personal letters are more involved than many spoken registers and broadcasts are more informational than many written registers. Task 3 tests the use of this continuum with some short pieces of English.

Task 3. Types of spoken and written English

Here are some fragments of English texts. Try to decide where each one fits into Biber's continuum from Involved production to Informational production by scoring the proportion of nouns, private verbs, contractions, first- and second-person pronouns, prepositions, etc., and then see whether this separates them into spoken versus written. The sources for the texts are given on page 53.

1 Gains arising on disposals of assets on or after 29 November 1994 may be deferred where shares are acquired under the Enterprise Investment Scheme (EIS) within specified time limits.
2 So much a part of him did his theories of unsuccessful action and unsatisfied love become that in 1895 and 1896, when a beautiful married woman fell in love with him, he spent the first year in idealised chastity, meeting her only in museums and railway carriages.
3 thanks I opened the photo oK – yes not bad glazed eyes somewhat.see you soon
4 And the thing is that the journalists I mean I've met some of these people – they know nothing about the country at all. They go to the Ledra Palace Hotel for example and they sit at the bar and they absorb you know one or two facts from a few people.
5 The principle of Greed (last resort) overrides convergence; Procrastinate selects among convergent derivations. In addition we have several conclusions about expletive constructions, theta theory, economy and convergence.
6 How are you doing? I'm here at work waiting for my appointment to get here, it's Friday. Thank goodness, but I still have tomorrow, but this week has flown by, I guess because I've been staying busy, getting ready for Christmas and stuff.
7 Beautiful? She frowned a little, examining her reflection. She did seem to have a little more colour in her face from being outside so much; but other than that, she looked just as bland as she always had.
8 Well he's always er or at least for a long time had that view er I gather he expressed it first around May erm he's an admirable minister he's he's done extremely well and I'm very sad he should go.

Some differences between speech and writing are inescapable; some are a matter of convention about the suitability of particular grammatical forms or vocabulary for one or the other medium. Many differences between spoken and written language are in fact signs of other factors. This brings us back to Text 1C, the e-mail message 'Have just finished Perdido Street Station – odd book. . . .' The 1990s saw an active academic debate over whether e-mails are more like spoken or written English, which will be discussed in Chapter 7. Features like the missing subject 'Have just finished' and verb-less clause 'odd book' for instance seem to resemble spoken language.

Literacy and cognition

A remaining issue of controversy is the effects of literacy on the people who acquire it; according to Ong (1982) 'Writing is a technology that changes thought'. Largely because of the properties of writing outlined earlier, such as permanency, societies that use writing inevitably differ from those that do not. This difference extends to the members of these societies. Studies of non-literates in Russia suggest that their thought processes are different from those of literates. The Soviet psychologist Luria (1976) set non-literates the problem:

> In the far North, where there is snow, all bears are white. Novaya Zemlya is in the North and there is always snow there. What colour are the bears there?

The typical answer would be:

> I don't know . . . There are different sorts of bears.

The non-literates base their answers on their concrete experience; their reasoning is less abstract than that of literates. However, this difference might not be the result of writing itself so much as the other factors that go with formal education, in particular the use of imaginary contexts rather than real contexts; school education forces children to ascend a ladder of abstraction from the concrete situation (Donaldson 1978).

It is also claimed that people who can read store information in their minds differently from those who cannot read. Goody (2000) for instance shows how a sacred oral text in a Ghanaian tribe varies from one elder's account to another; even the same elder may tell it differently on different occasions. Oral epic poems such as the Old English *Beowulf* (circa 1000 AD or earlier) were delivered spontaneously, a feat made possible by the use of rhythmic formulas, as in contemporary rap. Without a written language, a society does not insist on a single correct version of the truth. Compare the multifarious versions of oral stories in circulation such as jokes or local myths, for example the giant black cat sighted in so many areas of eastern England, with the 'authentic' report of a car accident in the newspaper. One has a changing nebulous form, the other a clear-cut outline. Cultures with written language may organize their memories and their view of reality differently from those with spoken language.

Indeed, some research has shown that literacy has an effect on the way that the brain is organized. Petersen *et al.* (2000) showed that the brains of literate people process words and pseudo-words in the same way but the brains of illiterate individuals process them differently. Moreover, the very fact that someone can read and write affects how they conceive of language. Adults' perceptions of spoken language are influenced by their knowledge of writing. As Olson (1996: 100) puts it, 'Writing systems create the categories in terms of which we become conscious of speech'. Literate English speakers for example believe there are more sounds in 'ridge' /rɪdʒ/ than there are in 'rage' /reɪdʒ/ (Derwing 1992) because of the extra letter <d> in the written form, as seen in Chapter 5. In part this debate concerns how acquisition of a different form of language affects the individual's other language knowledge; partly it is part of the debate on linguistic relativity about whether language influences thinking itself, which has been revived in recent years (Levinson 1996).

As seen in Chapter 6, one of the crucial developments in the writing of sound-based systems was the discovery of silent reading, made possible by the invention of the word space around the eighth century AD. This meant reading could be a private activity – no one else knew necessarily what you were reading – and led to a more individualistic voice free from the public nature of speech or spoken reading.

An influential movement in current psychology treats the crucial element in language acquisition as the child's recognition that other people have minds of their own (Tomasello 2000). The basis of language is a 'theory of mind' in the speakers' own minds, in the sense that human beings recognize that other people also think, except for cases of extreme autism. Hence 'theory theory' is the general theory based on the concept of theory of mind. Speech and reading aloud still provide an external fact that people can relate to; with silent reading the other's mind has moved into our own; their inner voice echoes in our mind without any external signs. Novels can make readers feel that they are experiencing the lives of the characters or the author from within: we have felt what Anna Karenina feels, seen what Leopold Bloom has seen, or understood how Jane Austen perceived the world. Silent reading at least feels as if it gives us insight into how other minds work.

The problem with interpreting the effects of literacy on human societies and the human mind is disentangling written language from the rest of cultural behaviour. The structures of society could be shaped in part by writing; or it could be the nature of society that necessitates recourse to certain functions of written language (Table 2.2). The Sumerian inventories of barley must have arisen out of a particular trading situation; it was not that people who had invented records on tablets looked around for things to record with them but that they needed a system for what they were already doing. Scribner and Cole (1981) countered the overall position that literacy *per se* affects people by researching the Vai script used in Liberia; this differs from most written scripts in being used for informal purposes rather than as a record of great events, etc. Users of Vai showed none of the cognitive changes that literacy was believed to bring. Later research by Bennett and Berry (1991) looked at the Cree syllabary used in northern Ontario, which has wider functions than Vai among its users, yet there were no effects on cognitive functioning apart from the ability to manipulate certain visual shapes.

Table 2.2 Spoken English versus written English

Written English:

- uses a slightly different range of vocabulary to spoken English, say 'dismount' and 'greensward'
- uses more noun expressions such as 'the NCP long-term off-airport car park courtesy coach pick-up point', more verb-derived noun expressions 'using oil as a bargaining ploy' and more prepositional phrases 'crackdown on bad behaviour by pupils'
- is lexically denser, that is to say, it has a higher proportion of content words to function words
- has higher status, both in 'official' attitudes to written documents such as contracts and laws, and in the 'unofficial' attitudes of everyday people
- is typically closer to informational production than involved production, though there is considerable variation across registers

The overall danger in comparing two objects such as speech and writing as done in this chapter is that it prevents us seeing their own unique features. Comparing George Bush with George W. Bush will yield a list of similarities and dissimilarities in terms of height, intelligence, foreign policy and so on; but it will never tell us the peculiar qualities of either. Comparing an apple and a pear takes us some way towards knowing about apples but still cannot define their unique flavour. The study of written language has to move on beyond the continual comparison with spoken language to consider its unique qualities.

DISCUSSION TOPICS

1 To what extent are linguists right in claiming spoken language is primary?
2 In what ways are spoken and written English necessarily different?
3 How does it matter if people employ written language forms in spoken English, spoken language forms in written English?
4 Can the writer of English really convey the emotions that are shown by intonation in speech through written devices?
5 Why *should* written English be lexically denser than spoken English?
6 How has your own thinking been changed by the ability to write, if at all?
7 Are you convinced by the argument that differences of register are more important than differences between spoken and written language?
8 Has written English become more like spoken English in recent years or are there simply changes in both?

ANSWERS TO TASKS

Task 1. Comparing speech and writing

Question 1

1 What was the first sentence you heard?

2 Did the speaker make any grammatical mistakes, hesitations, repetitions, etc?
3 Would you understand what the speaker was talking about in a week's time? In a year's time?

Question 2

1 Try to remember the first sentence you read.
2 Did the writer make any grammatical mistakes, hesitations, repetitions?
3 Would you understand what the writer was writing about in a week's time? In a year's time?

Task 3. Types of spoken and written English

Sources for texts:

1 Official document (Inland Revenue, *Filling in your 1995 Tax Return*).
2 Biography (Ellman, R. (1979) *Yeats, the Man and the Masks*. London: Norton.).
3 Personal e-mail.
4 Face-to-face conversation (Crystal D. and Davy D. (1975) *Advanced Conversational English*. London: Longman.).
5 Academic prose (Chomsky, N. Bare phrase structure. In G. Webelhuth (ed.), *Government and Binding Theory and the Minimalist Programme*. Oxford: Blackwell, 383–440.).
6 Personal letter (Biber, D. (1988) *Variation across Speech and Writing*. Cambridge: Cambridge University Press.).
7 Romantic fiction (Cross, M. (1991) *Heartsong*. London: Mills & Boon.).
8 Radio interview (BBC Radio 4).

FURTHER READING

- Halliday, M.A.K. (1985) *Spoken and Written Language*. Oxford: Oxford University Press. Highly readable, brief introduction.
- Biber, D. (1988) *Variation across Speech and Writing*. Cambridge: Cambridge University Press. The basic source for statistical comparison of speech and writing.
- Tannen, D. (ed.) (1982) *Spoken and Written Language: Exploring Orality and Literacy*. New Jersey: Ablex. This contains several of the core papers referred to in the chapter.

Approaches to English spelling

3

INTRODUCTION

If you ask English-speaking people about rules of spelling, they typically start reciting 'i before e except after c' – the rule of thumb that 'explains' the <ie> of 'field' as opposed to the <ei> of 'receive', explored in Task 1 below. Ask them for more rules and at best they offer vague memories from primary school about silent <e> or about words ending in <y>. Yet they can spell the vast majority of words they need. True there are problem words such as 'accommodate', 'ecstasy' or 'desiccate', true some individuals have persistent spelling problems, but by and large most people can spell with a high degree of proficiency.

Task 1. The I before E rule
'i before e except after c'
Which of these words fit the rule and which don't?
weight, deceive, sleigh, ceiling, either, leisure, species, caffeine
In what ways could the rule be improved by specifying it more precisely?
Suggestions are at the end of the chapter

The 'i before e' rule is the tip of a large iceberg of spelling patterns and rules that people know with little conscious awareness. In a truly 'shallow' alphabetic system that observed the one-to-one and linearity principles seen in Chapter 1, the only rules necessary would be the correspondences between letters and phonemes – <p> links to /p/, <a> to /æ/ and so on; in reverse /p/ links to <p>, /æ/ to <a> and so on. Straightforward correspondences like this work satisfactorily for a few parts of English – written <b> corresponds to spoken /b/ 99% of the time and, in reverse, spoken /b/ corresponds to written <b> 98% (figures from Carney (1994)). But this simple relationship does not work for most letters and sounds, if only because there are more sounds than individual letters – approximately 44 phonemes in RP (listed on page 215) to 26 letters of the alphabet (excluding capitals, etc.).

Opinions on the importance of spelling

. . . orthography, in the true sense of the word, is so absolutely necessary for a man of letters, or a gentleman, that one false spelling may fix a ridicule upon him for the rest of his life. (Lord Chesterfield: *Letters to His Son*, 1775)

Take care that you never spell a word wrong. Always before you write a word, consider how it is spelled, and, if you do not remember, turn to a dictionary. It produces great praise to a lady to spell well. (Thomas Jefferson to his daughter Martha, 1783)

Good spelling, like good grammar, is a distinct mark of culture. (*The Common Sense Spelling Book*, 1913)

Part 3.1 starts this chapter by looking at some rules for English spelling that can be stated quite readily, at least as rough approximations. They illustrate general properties of English that mostly go unnoticed and demonstrate how English spelling depends on particular aspects of English phonology and grammar as well as on correspondence rules. Then Part 3.2 outlines three systematic approaches that linguists have applied to English spelling, namely those originated by Richard Venezky, Ken Albrow, and Noam and Carol Chomsky. This chapter also draws throughout on the invaluable *A Survey of English Spelling* by Carney (1994). Though these approaches handle more or less the same facts, they are far from compatible.

3.1 BASIC RULES FOR ENGLISH

Focusing questions

- What rules of thumb do you consciously use for English spelling?
- How useful would it be to teach children large numbers of rules for spelling English?

Key words

content words: nouns, verbs and adjectives, such as 'brick', 'see' or 'blue', that have meanings that are best explained in the dictionary and are numbered in thousands; new ones can readily be coined.

function words: articles, prepositions and the like, such as 'the' and 'to'; they are considered part of the grammatical structure of the sentence and are numbered in hundreds; new ones cannot be created.

two 'th' sounds: in terms of phonetics, there are two 'th' phonemes in English – the voiced consonant /ð/ heard at the beginning of 'this' and the unvoiced consonant /θ/ heard in 'thistle', though both typically correspond to the spelling <th>.

This section outlines four basic rules of English. These are not intended as laws like the law of gravity but as informal generalizations that explain a reasonable amount of the facts, on a par with 'most ginger cats are toms'. Some of them are developed further in the linguistic approaches described later. Some derive from the school teaching tradition, some have never been taught in school.

The three-letter rule

Why are two words with identical spoken forms spelled differently, say 'in' and 'inn' or 'be' and 'bee'? English spelling distinguishes some of these pairs in terms of function words versus content words, as mentioned briefly in Chapter 2. This distinction has been utilized in several traditions of language teaching and linguistics in one way or another.

Content words are nouns, verbs, adjectives and so on, like 'glass', 'pay' or 'red'. Their meanings can be looked up in a dictionary; there are many thousands of them in English, and they can be added to at any time – an open set.

Function words are prepositions, articles, conjunctions and so on, such as 'of', 'the' or 'but'. They relate chiefly to the grammatical structures of the language rather than to the dictionary; there are perhaps a couple of hundred of them in English, and no new ones can be added – a closed set. An incidental identification cue comes indeed from the writing system itself: one convention for book titles in English is to give initial capital letters to the content words but not to the function words: 'The Taming of the Shrew', say, or 'Murder on the Orient Express'.

Task 2. Function words

Here are two lists of function words and content words. What peculiar characteristics can you see about the spelling of function words?

- Function words: the, by, in, so, I, there, of, this, as, a, to, an, up, be, or, us
- Content words: official, theory, ass, inn, theft, eye, buy, theme, add, two, awe, etymology, ill, bee

Answers in text and at the end of the chapter

For our purposes, the crucial point is the differences in spelling between function and content words (*see* Task 2 above). All the one- or two-letter words of English are function words – 'by', 'to', 'an', etc. Content words on the other hand have three letters or more. So a content word that happens to have the same pronunciation as a two-letter function word has an extra letter to make it longer – 'bye', 'two', 'Ann'. The overall rule is seen in Rule Box 1: 'Content words must have more than two letters' predicts the spelling for word pairs such as 'we'/'wee', 'I'/'eye', etc. This does not mean that all function words are necessarily short, as can be seen from 'toward' or 'nevertheless', only that all words under three letters are function words.

Rule Box 1. The three-letter rule
Content words must have more than two letters.

Examples:

in/inn, oh/owe, he/heehee, no/know, by/bye/buy, so/sew, to/two, we/wee, or/ore/oar, be/bee, an/Ann, I/eye/aye

Exceptions:

- *Common*: go, ox, ax (US), pi, re
- *Exotic*: aa, ai, ba, bo, bu, etc.

There are of course exceptions to the three-letter rule. An obvious two-letter *content* word is 'go', which appears to be a normal verb, apart from its grammatical use in the 'going to' future in English – 'It's going to rain tomorrow'. Interestingly enough, as Albrow (1972) points out, 'go' has not only been spelled 'goe' in the past but also has a present tense third-person form 'goes' with an <e> instead of 'gos'. A few, fairly uncommon, nouns also have two letters, for example <ox> and the American spelling <ax>. The names of musical notes used to have a two-letter spelling (actually derived from the first two letters of the opening word of each line of a Latin hymn, a familiar technique in creating alphabets) 'do re mi fa so la si'; a nineteenth century convention converted these into names for scales by adapting some spellings to the three-letter rule with an extra <h> or <y>, 'doh ray fah soh lah', as well as changing <si> to <te>. And there are highly unusual two-letter words known only to Scrabble players, such as 'bu' and 'od'.

The three-letter rule captures a simple yet powerful property of English spelling. Yet it is certainly not one of the rules children encounter in school. People who are told about it are often surprised that they were previously unaware of something so obvious. The rule depends, not on the sounds of English, but on the overall grammatical distinction between content and function words, like other rules to be seen later.

The 'th' rule

The division between content words and function words also comes into play in the correspondence rule for the <th> digraph at the beginning of words. English pronunciation reserves the voiced fricative phoneme /ð/ for the opening <th> of function words such as 'the', 'they' and 'this'. The voiceless phoneme /θ/ corresponds initially to <th> in content words such as 'therapy', 'thrash' or 'thistle'.

Since the <th> spelling corresponds to both phonemes, the correspondence rule means linking initial <th> to /ð/ in function words but to /θ/ in content words. The correspondences for <th> at the end or in the middle of the word are more flexible, either /ð/ as in 'rather' and 'father' or /θ/ as in 'bath' and 'ether'. The rule is 'Initial <th> corresponds to a voiceless /θ/ in content words and to a voiced /ð/ in function words', as given in Rule Box 2. Inevitably there are exceptional words in which <th> corresponds to /t/ as in 'Thames' and 'Anthony', or to zero as in 'asthma'.

Rule Box 2. The 'th' rule

Initial <th> corresponds to a voiceless /θ/ in content words, to a voiced /ð/ in function words.

- Initial **<th>**

/ð/	/θ/
the	therapy
they	Theydon Bois
there	theory
their	theft
them	thimble
this	thistle
that	thatch

- **medial or final <th>**
  /ð/ rather, father, whether, . . .
  /θ/ bath, ether, . . .

Again, readers have to know a particular aspect of English grammar before they can decide whether <th> corresponds to /ð/ or to /θ/. Give them a nonsense word like 'thark' and they will immediately read the <th> as /θ/. Show them 'they' and they will say /ðeɪ/; reveal to them that it is part of a longer word 'Theydon Bois' (a town in Essex) and they change it to /θeɪ/. But they also have to know that the rule only applies to the beginnings of words; using the 'th' rule means knowing the structure of words; which phoneme <th> corresponds to depends upon context as well as grammar.

Rules for surnames

English often distinguishes surnames from other nouns or adjectives by variation in spelling, as well as by capital letters, as shown in Rule Box 3. One possibility is to double the final consonant; 'hog'/'Hogg', 'kid'/'Kidd', 'star'/'Starr'. Another is to add a final <e>: 'lock'/'Locke', 'brown'/'Browne', 'boil'/'Boyle'. Or indeed consonant doubling and an extra final <e> are found together: 'lily'/'Lilley', 'crab'/'Crabbe', 'leg'/'Legge'. Or <i> may change to <y>, sometimes with an extra final <e> as in 'pie'/'Pye', 'smith'/'Smythe', and 'wild'/'Wylde'. Colour names as surnames seem less susceptible to change, though 'Whyte' and 'Greene' do occur.

Rule Box 3. Rules for surnames

Surnames are often distinguished from other nouns:

- By having a final <e>: brown/Browne, trollop/Trollope, clerk/Clarke
- By doubling the final consonant: bun/Bunn, kid/Kidd, web/Webb
- By having <y> rather than <i>: smith/Smythe, wild/Wylde

This does not take into account those surnames that have particularly idiosyncratic spellings in British English, perhaps to their owners' pride, such as 'Beauchamp'

/biːtʃəm/, 'Cholmondeley' /tʃʌmlɪ/, 'Featherstonehaugh' /fænʃɔː/ 'Marjoribanks' /maːtʃbæŋks/ and 'St John' /sɪndʒən/. These often form the basis of jokes and puns; a TV sitcom has Mrs Bucket insisting her name is pronounced as 'bouquet' /buːkeɪ/; the swindler Horatio Bottomley when informed that a Mr Cholmondeley was present insisted his own name was /bʌmlɪ/; P.G. Wodehouse has a character called 'Psmith' ('the p is silent'), Terry Pratchett one called 'Teatime' ('pronounced Teh-ah-tim-eh'). There are two groups of London dancers, one called the Cholmondeleys (all female), the other the Featherstonehaughs (all male).

The rules for surnames assist the reader by providing an additional clue that a word is a surname. Spelling distinguishes not just parts of speech but also subcategories of nouns. Though it is doubtful whether English people are at all consciously aware of these regularities in surnames, they nevertheless apply the rules all the time. It is impossible for me to provide my surname 'Cook' in a shop without being asked 'with or without an "e"?', even if a quick count in my local phone book yields a ratio of 5.7 'Cook's to every 'Cooke'.

The unusual feature about surnames, as Carney (1994) points out, is that variation in spelling is tolerated rather than forbidden, as it is for other types of word, even if it is now felt strange if an individual spells their name in different ways on different occasions. The name Shakespeare was spelled in at least 12 ways by his contemporaries ranging from 'Shakes-speare' to 'Shakspere' (http://shakespeareauthorship.com/name1.html#2). The possessor of a particular surname is effectively allowed to spell it any way they like. The same licence seems to be true of the wide variation in spellings of place names, whether 'Leominster' /lemstə/, 'Bicester' /bɪstə/ or 'Marylebone' /mærɪlebəʊn/.

Doubling consonants

One of the most frequent mistakes with English spelling is to double consonants when they are not needed, 'carefull', and to use single consonants, when two are required, 'refered'. Task 3 tests some common mistakes made by native speakers of English.

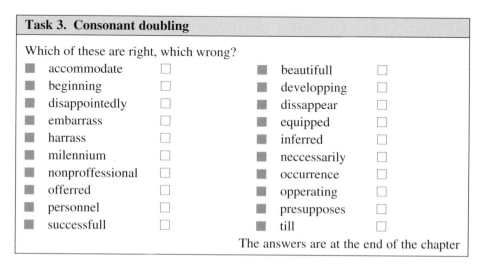

Task 3. Consonant doubling

Which of these are right, which wrong?

accommodate	☐	beautifull	☐
beginning	☐	developping	☐
disappointedly	☐	dissappear	☐
embarrass	☐	equipped	☐
harrass	☐	inferred	☐
milennium	☐	neccessarily	☐
nonproffessional	☐	occurrence	☐
offerred	☐	opperating	☐
personnel	☐	presupposes	☐
successfull	☐	till	☐

The answers are at the end of the chapter

The problem is that a doubled written consonant does not mean that the spoken consonant is double the length or is said twice, even if this is so in Finnish and once was so in English. Instead, consonant doubling is used to convey different aspects about the word, such as the fact it is a proper name as shown in the last section.

Rule Box 4 gives the main rule for consonant doubling in English spelling. Many vowel correspondences in English fall into two groups, sometimes called, 'short' and 'long' vowels, more often known to spelling researchers as 'checked' and 'free'.

Rule Box 4. Consonant doubling

Doubled consonants are chiefly used to show that the vowel that precedes them is 'checked' rather than 'free'.

- <a> /æ/ 'navvy' versus /eɪ/ 'navy'
- <e> /e/ 'better' versus /iː/ 'Pete'
- <i> /ɪ/ 'dinner' versus /aɪ/ 'diner'
- <o> /ɒ/ 'lobby' versus /əʊ/ 'lobe'
- <u> /ʌ/ 'running' versus /uː/ 'rune'

When they are 'free', the written vowels <a e i o u> correspond to /eɪ iː aɪ əʊ juː/, when they are 'checked' to /æ e ɪ ɒ ʌ/. So one of the issues in reading English is knowing which of the free and checked alternates a particular letter corresponds to: should <a> link to /æ/ or to /eɪ/ in a given word? One clue is provided by the consonant or consonants that follow the vowel: if the consonant is doubled then the vowel is checked; if single, the vowel is free. So 'dinner' corresponds to checked /ɪ/ because it has double <n>; 'diner' corresponds to free /aɪ/ because there is only one <n>. Task 3 above gives some further examples. The consonant doubling rule is complementary to the use of <e> to show that the preceding vowel is 'free', that is, 'mat' versus 'mate'. Both these rules will be discussed further later in this chapter.

Some consonants do not double, say <hh, jj, qq, ww, xx, yy>; others double rarely, such as <vv> 'skivvy' or <kk> 'trekked'. What counts as a doubled consonant is not always two occurrences of the same consonant: other forms may stand in for it. Some digraphs effectively function as the doubled form of a single letter when doubling is required to show the preceding vowel is checked, a kind of substitute doubling. <ck> 'backing' occurs rather than <kk>, <tch> 'match' rather than <chch> and <dge> 'ridge' rather than <jj>. Final silent <e> also provides another substitute for the rare double <v> as in 'love' or 'give'.

The consonant doubling rule for free and checked vowels is only one reason why consonants are double or single in English, and ignores for instance the problems with Latin-derived prefixes such as 'communication', 'address' and 'illegal'. Nevertheless it represents a handy generalization about English, which would for example get people out of trouble in such words as 'beginning' and 'beautiful' in Task 3 above.

So, to use English spelling, you need to know English. In other words, it is impossible to deal with English spelling as a system for connecting letters to sounds or vice versa, without taking into account not only the system of English phonology, for instance the distribution of the voiced /ð/ phoneme, but also the system of English grammar, for example the uses of function words and the types of nouns. English spelling is in a sense designed for someone who already knows English phonology and grammar: hence the problems it poses for young children or for adult learners of English as a second language, neither of which know English in the same way as an adult native speaker, as will be seen in Chapter 5.

The rules of thumb presented in this section appear to work adequately for particular areas, whether function words or surnames. It would be possible to go on adding more such rules, all of which work plausibly within a small area of English once one abandons the attempt to make the whole of English strictly observe the alphabetic principles outlined in Chapter 1.

The remainder of this chapter, however, reports some of the overall analyses that have been proposed for English spelling over the past few decades. These combine some of the ideas about English spelling captured by these rules with the general points made in Chapter 1. Since each of these analyses is a complex system in its own right, the fragments given here inevitably simplify them: readers need to consult the originals for a full account. In particular each approach has to cover much of the same ground as the others. Although particular topics are treated here within one approach, this does not mean the others do not account for them in their own way; for example the spelling of past tense 'ed' is here treated under Albrow's approach but it is also necessarily accommodated within the approaches of Venezky and Chomsky.

3.2 VENEZKY: CORRESPONDENCE RULES AND MARKERS

Focusing questions

- How many spoken correspondences can you find for written <c>?
- Do you think the 'silent' <e> in 'bite' has any use?

Key words

relational units: correspond to phonemes and may be one or more letters long, <t> 'tin', <th> 'thin', <tch> 'watch'.

markers: do not correspond to any one phoneme but affect the correspondence of other letters, for example <e> in 'rate' versus 'rat'.

graphemes: a grapheme refers to 'the basic symbol of a writing system' (Sproat 2000: 28) but the term is avoided by some because of its potentially misleading parallel to 'phoneme'.

syllable: in spoken English the structure of the syllable is seen as having an optional onset, a compulsory vowel nucleus and an optional coda: thus 'trip' has onset /tr/, nucleus /ɪ/ and coda /p/. In written English a crucial question is whether the syllable is open, that is, has no coda as in 'know', or is closed by a coda as in 'knot'.

free vowels: may occur in open spoken syllables, for instance /uː/ in 'to'.

checked vowels: may not occur in open spoken syllables, for example /æ/ in 'bat'.

simple consonant: a consonant is 'simple' if it functions as a single relational unit, regardless of whether this has a single letter such as <d> or more than one letter <sh>.

An important contribution to spelling analysis was made by Venezky's (1970) book *The Structure of English Orthography*, updated in some respects in his 1999 version *The American Way of Spelling*. This was originally based on the spellings of the 20,000 most frequent words in the Thorndike-Century *Senior Dictionary* (1941). Its aim was 'to show the patterning which exists in the present orthography' (Venezky 1970: 11); it only covers correspondences from writing to sounds.

General principles of English orthography (Venezky 1999)

1 Variation is tolerated.
2 Letter distribution is capriciously limited.
3 Letters represent sounds and mark graphemic, phonological and morphemic features.
4 Etymology is honoured.
5 Regularity is based on more than phonology.
6 Visual identity of meaningful word parts takes precedence over letter–sound simplicity.
7 English orthography facilitates word recognition for the initiated speaker of the language, rather than being a phonetic alphabet for the non-speaker.

The 'seven principles of English orthography' described in Venezky (1999) are displayed in the box above. These general insights have already been used here implicitly to some extent. The principle of tolerance of variation (1) allows English words to have alternate spellings, whether across dialects – American style 'honor' versus British style 'honour' – or within a single community – 'judgment' and 'judgement' both exist in England. The principle of capricious limitation on letter distribution (2) prevents English from using some of the combinations of letter that are actually possible. For example, there are no logical reasons why doubling is prohibited for the letters <a, i, h, v, z>, with a few exceptions like 'skivvy', 'flivver' and 'navvy', or why double <l> should not occur at the beginning of words, with odd exceptions such as 'llama'. The principle of regularity (5) extends spelling outside phonology and has already been seen in Part 3.1, which utilized aspects of grammar such as the content/function distinction: English spelling depends *inter alia* on knowing the distinctions between different types of nouns and between content and function words.

The principle that English spelling requires an initiated speaker (7) has already been mentioned and comes to the fore in Part 3.4 below: spelling depends on the user knowing many aspects of English other than phonology. Venezky's principle 3, on the multi-functions of letters, and principle 6, on the precedence of visual identity, are developed below. Principle 4, that spelling should respect the history of the word, is tackled in Chapter 6.

Venezky's starting point is deciding on the actual written units that form the basis of English spelling. Some writers have made spelling parallel phonology: just as the phoneme is the minimum distinctive unit in speaking, so the grapheme is the minimum distinctive unit in writing. That is to say, English has 26 graphemes equivalent to letters of the alphabet (setting aside upper- and lower-case, capitals, etc.).

But, as seen in Chapter 1, English spelling sometimes depends on pairs of letters, as in the <th> in 'this' discussed earlier, sometimes on triples, such as <tch> in 'match'. A spelling unit is therefore needed that spans more than one letter. English spelling also often depends on 'silent' letters, which are handled in very different ways in the three approaches described in this chapter. Venezky's solution to the problem of the units of spelling (*see* box below) is 'functional units', which fall into two types: relational units and markers.

Functional units

1 Relational units 'map directly into sounds' (Venezky 1999: 7)

2 'a marker is an instance of a letter that has no pronunciation of its own; instead, it marks the pronunciation of another letter, indicates the morphemic status of a word or preserves a graphemic pattern' (Venezky 1999: 7)

Relational units

'Relational units' correspond to individual sounds. So the relational units <a, b, c, . . .> correspond to individual phonemes: <a> links to /æ/ in 'fat', <b> to /b/ in 'bat', <c> to /k/ in 'cat' and so on. Relational units made up of pairs of letters also correspond to one phoneme: <gh> to /g/ in 'ghost', <ck> to /k/ in 'back', and so on. So do the relational units made up of three letters: <tch> corresponds to /tʃ/ in 'match' and the rare <rrh> to /r/ in 'diarrhoea'. The same letter may form part of different relational units, say <h> in <th, ch, sh, rh, gh, ph, wh>.

Some relational units are restricted to certain positions in the word or syllable. <wh> corresponds to /w/ only in initial position in the syllable (known as the 'onset') as in 'what' or 'nowhere', and is not found in final position. <ng> corresponds to /ŋ/ only at the end of the syllable (known as the 'coda') as in 'sing' or indeed 'singing'; <pph> corresponds to /f/ only in the middle of words (and probably in only one word 'sapphire').

The kind of correspondence rule that Venezky describes therefore links a relational unit in a particular structural place to a phoneme; it involves a knowledge of word and syllable structure as well as of phonemes. Let us illustrate by going through his rules for the relational unit <c>, given in Rule Box 5. In these and later statements of spelling rules the symbol '≡' stands for 'corresponds to' and 'Ø' for zero sound.

Rule Box 5. Venezky (1970): rules for <c> correspondences

1 <c> ≡ /tʃ/, 'cello'
2 <c> ≡ /ø/, 'czar'
3 <c> ≡ /s/ before <i/y/e>,'cell'
4 <c> ≡ /k/ otherwise, 'come'

Rule 1 gives the correspondence of <c> with /tʃ/ that occurs in a small number of words that are clearly Italian in origin – 'cello', 'concerto', 'ciao'. Rule 2 specifies that <c> corresponds to nothing /ø/, that is, is a silent letter, in a few words like 'victual', 'czar' and 'Connecticut' (non-US readers may need to be told that it is the second <c> that is silent). Rule 3 describes how the <c> correspondence with /s/ depends on the following vowel, namely <i, y, e> in 'city', 'cygnet' and 'centre'. Rule 4 is the standard correspondence of <c> with /k/ for all other <c>s, including <c> in front of other vowels as in 'cart' and 'cull'. This distinction is sometimes called 'soft' and 'hard' <c> in teaching books such as Shemesh and Waller (2000).

Establishing the correspondence for <c> in a particular word means starting with rule 1 and seeing if it belongs to this small group of /tʃ/ words, exploring rule 2 to see if it is on the list of 'silent' <c>s; checking whether the following vowel is <i, y, e> to apply rule 3; and then, if nothing has worked, <c> corresponds to /k/ in rule 4. The rules have to be applied in order. Rule 4 applies only after the first three have been exhausted; it is a default to catch anything not covered in the earlier rules. The rules in Venezky (1970), in a sense, state the exceptions before the rule itself; only after the reader has checked whether the <c> in 'cat' is 'silent' and whether it is followed by <e>, do they get to link it to a /k/ phoneme.

Markers

Graphemes that have functions other than direct correspondence with phonemes are called 'markers' by Venezky. For example <e> is widely used:

- as a marker for surnames, 'Cooke'
- to indicate the vowel correspondences before a preceding consonant, 'rip'/'ripe', dealt with below
- to prevent single consonants that rarely occur finally in English, <s> 'hous(e)', <v> 'jiv(e)'.

The following discussion deals with <e> only as a marker of vowels. The area of vowel correspondences is perhaps the most complex area of English spelling and will be limited in this section to some main topics. The next section will look at an alternative analysis of vowels and 'silent' <e> by Albrow.

The ideas that were touched on in the consonant doubling rule given above can now be developed. English spelling partly takes account of the syllable structure within which phonemes function. The spoken English syllable has to have a nucleus vowel (V), which may or may not have an initial onset and a final coda, consisting of one or more consonants (C); this is given in the formula (C)V(C), which shows that a compulsory V is preceded and followed by optional C, say 'I' /aɪ/ (V) versus 'buy' /baɪ/ (CV) versus 'aisle' /aɪl/ (VC) versus 'bile' /baɪl/ (CVC). In fact there may be more than one initial or final C in English, as one can see for example in the /tr/ of 'try' /traɪ/ or the /mp/ of 'lamp' /læmp/ or the /str/ and /ŋkθs/ of 'strengths' /streŋkθs/ with three initial Cs and four final Cs. Some vowels can only occur in a syllable with a final consonant: /æ/ and /e/ occur in CVC 'bad' and 'ten', but no English words end in these sounds. This is the motivation for calling these non-final vowels 'checked'.

Other vowels may occur at the end of a syllable without a coda, that is, in a CV syllable; for instance, final /iː/ in 'sea' and final /uː/ in 'too'; these vowels are called 'free'. Many of the correspondence rules of English spelling amount to ingenious ways of indicating whether the written single vowel corresponds to a free or a checked spoken vowel.

The free correspondences for the five vowel graphemes are the same as the names of the letters, <a>, <e>, <i>, <o> and <u>, and are given in Rule Box 6 below. Three of these are diphthongs, <a> /eɪ/, <i> /aɪ/ and <o> /əʊ/, rather than pure vowels; two are long vowels <e> /iː/ and <u> /(j)uː/. Hence the group is often referred to popularly in spelling books as 'long' vowels, for instance by Shamesh and Waller (2000). These free vowels may occur anywhere in the syllable, at the beginning 'eat' /iːt/, in the middle /biːt/ 'beat' and at the end 'knee' /niː/.

Rule Box 6. Free and checked vowels

	Free	Checked
<a>	/eɪ/ 'fate'	/æ/ 'fat'
<e>	/iː/ 'fever'	/e/ 'fed'
<i/y>	/aɪ/ 'ripe'	/ɪ/ 'rip'
<o>	/əʊ/ 'cone'	/ɒ/ 'con'
<u>	/(j)uː/ 'student'	/ʌ/ 'study'

The checked vowel correspondences for the five vowel letters can also be seen in Rule Box 6. The relational unit <a> corresponds to /æ/ 'fat' because the syllable ends in a single consonant <t>, the <e> in 'fed' to /e/ because of the following <d>, just as the <i> in 'rip' corresponds to /ɪ/, the <o> in 'con' to /ɒ/ and the <u> in 'study' to /ʌ/, compared to 'ripe', 'cone' and 'student'.

A written syllable ending in a vowel plus a consonant, <VC>, implies a checked vowel: the vowel of 'dim' is checked /ɪ/ because <i> is followed by a consonant <m> <VC>; the vowel of 'dime' is free /aɪ/ because <i> is followed by more than one consonant <VCC>. One exception where a checked vowel occurs at the end of a word may be /ɪ/ in British RP, which occurs in unstressed endings, for example 'city' /sɪtɪ/, though my own accent has a southern English short /i/ rather than /ɪ/ in such words. Checked vowels are often called short vowels, with rather more reason since the spoken vowels are indeed short. But there are of course more than five short vowels in English, such as /ə/ 'about' and /ʊ/ 'good'.

Conversely a syllable ending in a vowel and consonant plus a following silent <e>, <VCe>, suggests that the vowel is free, as in 'fate' /eɪ/, 'bide' /aɪ/ and so on. In Venezky's account the silent <e> marks the preceding vowel as free, that is, /eɪ/, rather than /æ/, /aɪ/ rather than /ɪ/, etc. *Without* a final <e>, the preceding vowel corresponds to the checked vowel, say /æ/ in 'fat' or /ɪ/ in 'bid'; *with* an <e> it corresponds to the free vowel, say /eɪ/ in 'fate' or /aɪ/ 'bide'. The final <e> effectively forces the reader into the free vowel correspondence for the preceding vowel. Hence the advice encountered in the first chapter – 'Fairy "e" waves its wand over the preceding vowel and makes it say its name' – is a quite reasonable account of the use of <e> as a marker, even if we don't believe in fairies. This is not to say that many frequent words of English do not break the e-marking rule by having a checked vowel, for example 'have' /hæv/, 'some' /sʌm/ and 'active' /æktɪv/, some of which are presumably handled by the lexical route.

The role of silent <e> is only one aspect of free/checked vowel correspondences. The type of consonant also plays a part. Venezky claims that 'functionally compound consonants' prevent e-marking. So 'hedge' has the checked vowel /e/ because the following consonant is the compound <dg>, rather than the simple consonant, <d> 'hide'. The consonant doubling rule seen earlier in Part 3.1 is another way of forcing a preceding checked vowel with a functionally compound consonant, as in 'supper' /ʌ/ versus 'super' /uː/ or 'rabbit' /æ/ versus 'rabid' /eɪ/. Task 4 checks the accuracy of this rule on the most frequent words with double consonant spellings in the BNC.

Task 4. Checked vowels and consonant doubling

Here are some of the most frequent words with doubled consonants in the *British National Corpus*. How many of these have checked vowels /æ e ɪ ɒ ʌ/ that go against the usual free vowel predictions?

across according to account all approach appropriate better
business committee community current difficult effect 'll
getting happy less little matter off office opportunity possible
process programme sorry staff still success suddenly support
will well

Glossing over these other factors slightly, Venezky's rule (1999: 173) for free/checked vowel correspondences is given in Rule Box 7. Part 1 of the rule then generalizes the effects of silent <e> by claiming that the first V in syllables with the structure V1 + simple C + V2 must be free. Thus the <a> in 'canine' corresponds to 'free' /eɪ/ because it is followed by a simple consonant <n> plus another vowel <i>, that is, <VCV>, just like the <a> in 'cane'. The <i> in 'silly', however, corresponds to checked /ɪ/ because the following consonant <ll> is doubled, that is, *not* a simple unit but <VCCV>: doubling means a checked vowel. The silent <e> marker is a dummy vowel that triggers the more general correspondence rule.

Rule Box 7. Venezky's rule for free/checked vowel correspondences
A stressed primary spelling unit corresponds to its free alternate when it is followed by: (1) a functionally simple consonant unit that in turn is followed by another vowel unit (including final <e>); or (2) a functionally simple consonant unit followed by <l> or <r>, and then by another vowel unit (including final <e>).

Part 2 of the same rule claims that the structures <VCl> or <VCr> force the vowel to be free, taking care of 'ladle' with a free /eɪ/ (simple consonant <d> + <le>) versus 'little' (complex consonant <tt> + <le>) with a checked /ɪ/, and of 'litre' (simple consonant <t> + <re>) so free /iː/ versus 'litter' (complex consonant <tt> + <er>) so checked /ɪ/.

According to Venezky, <e> plays 12 other roles as a marker, some of which are given in Rule Box 8, such as preventing a final <s> showing plural, as in the <e> in 'please' versus plural 'pleas'.

Rule Box 8. Some markers

final <e>	**marks 'free' vowel** 'mate'
	marks voiced consonant 'bathe'
	marks not plural 'goose'/'goos'
	marks homophones 'bell'/'belle'
<u>	**marks 'hard' pronunciation** 'guest'/'gesture'
<k>	**marks <c> ≡ /k/** 'picnicking'
<ë>	**marks non-silent final <e>** 'Brontë'

There is also far more to free and checked vowel correspondences than the presence of a following <e>. Here 'silent' <e> has been used chiefly as a marker that has no direct spoken correspondence itself but affects the vowel correspondence in another place in the word, that is, breaks the linearity principle described in Chapter 1.

Some other markers mentioned by Venezky are mentioned in Rule Box 8:

- <u> may mark a preceding <g> as corresponding to /g/, 'guess', 'guide', rather than to /dʒ/ 'gesture', 'gem'
- <k> before a suffix such as 'ing' marks <c> as corresponding to /k/: 'picnic'/'picnicking', 'panic'/'panicky'
- final <h> after a vowel may be a marker, as in 'hurrah' and 'pariah', though Venezky has not been able to determine its function.

To sum up, Venezky's system (Table 3.1) supports his principle (3) that 'letters represent sounds and mark graphemic, phonological and morpheme features'. English spelling is a complex system of interlocking features where the reader needs, on the

Table 3.1 Richard Venezky's approach

Aim: 'to show the patterning which exists in the present orthography' (Venezky 1970: 11)

Units: relational unit (sound-linked) <t, th, tch . . .>; functional units (markers) 'silent' <e, h, . . .>

System:

- correspondence rules <c> ≡ /tʃ/ in 'cello', to /s/ in 'cell', etc.
- silent <e> *inter alia* marks preceding 'free' vowel: 'mate'/'mat', etc.

(Main sources: Venezky (1970); Venezky (1999))

one hand, a complex knowledge of English to interpret the letters on the page, on the other, gains much more from them than their spoken correspondences.

Venezky provides an overall account that unites diverse aspects of English spelling; his approach is far more extensive than can be conveyed here. It should not be thought that the aspects of spelling dealt with at length in the next two sections are missing from his approach.

3.3 ALBROW: THREE SYSTEMS OF ENGLISH SPELLING

Focusing questions

- Is the unit of English spelling the letter, the word, combinations of letters or something else?
- Is more than one system involved in English spelling?

Key words

orthographic symbol: this unit of spelling consists of simple letters <c> 'come', complex symbols <ck> 'track', or discontinuous symbols <a_e> 'sale'.

A second major approach to English spelling is represented by Ken Albrow, whose book *The English Writing System* (1972) was part of the project Linguistics and English Teaching in the early 1970s. Albrow's aim is to provide a description of the English writing system for teachers based on the British functional tradition in linguistics now associated chiefly with Halliday. His analysis is neutral about direction: correspondences go both from speech to writing and vice versa, though for convenience they are usually stated as writing to speech. As with Venezky, the account here highlights only some of the aspects of English spelling he deals with. All approaches have to tackle many of the same issues, such as multiple correspondences and 'silent' letters.

Orthographic symbols

Albrow's unit of writing is the 'orthographic symbol', which may consist of simple symbols – the usual 26 letters – or of complex symbols made up of more than one letter, such as <ch> 'chop', <dge> 'badge' or <igh> 'light'. The same letter combination can form part of more than one symbol: the <th> that corresponds to /ð/ in 'this' is a different orthographic symbol from the <th> that corresponds to /θ/ in 'thistle'.

Orthographic symbols may also be discontinuous, that is to say, consist of letters separated by other elements. The word 'hive' for example contains the symbol <i_e> corresponding to the vowel /aɪ/. Where Venezky sees final <e> as a silent marker that the preceding vowel is free, Albrow treats it as part of the discontinuous complex symbols <a_e>, <i_e>, etc., with the space occupied by assorted simple consonants, 'ate', 'ice' and so on; the <e> is as much part of the <a_e> symbol as the <s> is part of the <sh> in 'shirt'. So <a_e> corresponds to /eɪ/ in 'mate' and 'bane', <o_e> to /əʊ/ in 'rope' and 'mole', despite the consonants that intervene.

Letters with no direct sound correspondence form part of larger discontinuous units that *do* have an effect on sound. The <g> of 'sign' is part of the complex orthographic symbol <ig>; the <h> of 'ghost' part of the symbol <gh>; the <e> of 'rune' part of the symbol <u_e> and so on. All the letters in the written word are either orthographic symbols in their own right or form part of larger orthographic symbols. Nothing is left over that can be called a 'silent' letter. Albrow's approach abolishes silent letters by making them part of orthographic symbols having more than one letter. It reflects the general recognition in functional linguistics that some units do not occur in a linear sequence, like phonemes or letters, but are discontinuous and extend over several segments, such as intonation patterns.

There are a few recalcitrant examples where a letter appears to have no direct correspondence and yet forms no part of a complex symbol. For example the <b> in 'debt' and 'doubt' does not seem important enough to suggest a complex symbol <bt> that corresponds to /t/ nor does the <th> in 'asthma' warrant a complex <sth> corresponding to /s/ in a few other words – 'isthmus'? It may be easier to admit a few 'dummy' letters to the system than to have orthographic units of very limited occurrence.

Three systems

A tenet of functional linguistics is that a language consists of many interacting systems rather than a single overriding system, in J.R. Firth's words – the doyen of British functional linguistics – 'a system of systems' (Firth 1951). A Venezky-style analysis states the correspondences for a relational unit as a single ordered list of many rules. In the Albrow approach the correspondence rules are shared out among three interacting systems.

Let us first look at the correspondences of the consonant <g>, seen in the rules given in Rule Box 9.

Rule Box 9. Correspondences for <g>

- System 1 **<g>** ≡ /g/ 'get'
  <gg> ≡ **short vowel**+/g/ **three-letter rule** 'egg', 'ebb'
- System 2 **<g>** ≡ /dʒ/ 'gem'
- System 3 **<g>** ≡ /ʒ/ 'genre'

Albrow's System 1 covers the correspondence of <g> with /g/ as in 'gold' and 'big', which accounts for 92% of the correspondences of <g> from speech to writing and 95% of the correspondences of /g/ from writing to speech (figures from Carney (1994)). System 1 also incorporates two general rules that affect <g> among other consonants. One is the familiar rule that doubled consonants indicate a preceding checked vowel: the <i> of 'bigger' corresponds to /ɪ/ not /aɪ/, the <a> of 'haggle' to /æ/ not /eɪ/. The other rule derives from the three-letter rule earlier in Part 3.1. A spoken content word that would logically correspond to two letters is padded out with an extra consonant to avoid confusion with two-letter function words. So the correspondence of <gg> with /g/ in 'egg' conforms to the same pattern as 'add', 'ebb', 'inn', 'odd' and 'err'.

System 2 covers the correspondence between initial <g> and /dʒ/ before <e/i/y>, as in 'gem', 'gin' and 'Egyptian'. Lastly, System 3 brings in the correspondence between <g> and /ʒ/ before <e> in words such as 'genre' and 'gendarme'.

Let us now see how vowels are covered in the three systems, given in Rule Box 10 and Rule Box 11.

Rule Box 10. Correspondences for <a>

- System 1 **<a>** ≡ /æ/ **'cat'**
  <a> ≡ /ɑː/ **before <ss>** 'pass' **and <lm>** 'psalm'
- System 2 **<a>** ≡ /ɑː/ 'grant'
  <a> ≡ /æ/ **before <ss>** 'lass'
- System 3 **final <a>** ≡ /ə/ 'data'

Rule Box 11. Simple vowel correspondences in systems 1 and 2

	System 1	System 2
<a>	/æ/ 'ant'	/ɑː/ 'grant'
<a>		/æ/ 'lass' **(before <ss> and <ff>) and** 'alp', 'gas', **etc.**
<e>	/e/ 'bed'	
<E>		/ɪ/ 'English', 'England' **(with capital <E>)**
<i>	/ɪ/ 'bid'	
<o>	/ɒ/ 'body'	/uː/ 'tomb'
<u>	/ʌ/ 'bud'	/ʌ/ 'bus', 'pus' **(words with single <s>)**
<y>	/aɪ/ 'my'	/ɪ/ 'cyst'

While vowel correspondences are distributed across the systems, Albrow's brief account does not itself provide examples for each vowel in all three systems. Sample correspondences for the simple vowel <a> are seen in Rule Box 10, first setting aside the links for <a_e>, <ea>, etc., which concern different orthographic symbols. In System 1 <a> typically corresponds to /æ/ 'cat' (91% according to Carney (1994) after allowing for reduction to schwa /ə/ in unstressed syllables, for example 'rival'). There are also correspondences between <a> and /ɑː/ as in 'grass', particularly before <ss>, 'pass', etc. and in some <lm> words 'almonds' and 'napalm'.

System 2 in a sense reverses the correspondences of System 1 so that <a> typically corresponds to /ɑː/ 'grant', but to /æ/ before <ss> 'lass' and 'mass'.

Albrow provides no examples of <a> in System 3. One possibility might be the /ə/ correspondence in 'data'.

British readers will have noticed that the correspondences for <a> and <u> in systems 1 and 2 are affected by regional accent. 'Pass' rhymes with 'lass' north of a line across England from roughly mid-Wales to the Wash. That is to say, <a> correspondences are System 1 <a> ≡ /æ/ in northern English accents without need for the complications about double <ss>. American English may need a different set of correspondences. Venezky gives a list of exceptional correspondences in American English between <a> and /a/ in 'father', 'spa' and so on, but does not mention anything like the southern British system.

A general issue with letter-to-sound correspondence rules concerns the variety of the spoken language that is used as a basis for correspondence. This has repercussions not only for correspondence rules but also for the teaching of spelling to children and for issues of spelling reform. Albrow's analysis is based on a particular accent of British English, namely RP, having associations with the south of England and with a particular social class. There is some dispute whether this RP accent now has more than a notional existence. John Wells claims that 'anyone who has grown up in England knows when he hears a typical instance of it' (Wells 1982: 301); such stereotyping may be endemic amongst those who live in England but it hardly provides a scientific foundation for RP. In as much as Venezky defines American English, he talks of the vowels of 'General American speech, a dialect spoken through a wide area of the country outside of eastern New England and the South' (Venezky, 1999: 60).

Albrow insists that it is not the word as such that belongs to a system but the orthographic symbol. Although it is convenient to refer to words, a single word may contain orthographic symbols with correspondences within different systems. The word 'mice' for example has an <m> that corresponds to /m/ under System 1 but a <c> that corresponds to /s/ under System 2.

Rule Box Box 12 contrasts some of the consonant correspondences covered by each system. The correspondences for <c> are /k/ 'cab' in System 1, /s/ 'cede' in System 2 and /tʃ/ 'cello' in System 3. The correspondences for <ch> are /tʃ/ 'chip' in System 1, /k/ 'chorus' in System 2 and /ʃ/ 'machine' in System 3.

Rule Box 12. Consonant correspondences in Albrow's three systems

	System 1 basic English	System 2 'Romance'	System 3 'exotic'
<c>	'cab' /k/	'cede' /s/	'cello' /tʃ/
<ch>	'chip' /tʃ/	'chorus' /k/	'machine' /ʃ/
<g>	'get' /g/	'gem' /dʒ/	'genre' /ʒ/
<k, ck, qu>	'mock' /k/	'baroque' /k/	'amok' /k/
<gh>	'right' /ø/	'ghost' /g/	
<sc>	'scum' /sk/	'science' /s/	
<th>	'think' /θ/	'Thames' /t/	
<w>	'want' /w/		'Wagner' /v/

These examples soon demonstrate that words that belong to the same system have other things in common:

- System 1 words tend to be short and derived from Old English pre-1066, like 'get' or 'man'. Albrow calls this the 'basic English' system, though he cautions against the implication that it is therefore any more important than the others.
- System 2 words tend to have entered the language from Latin or French, like 'chorus' or 'cede'. To some extent they represent a later layer of vocabulary laid down after the Norman Conquest, and hence are often associated with formal learnt language rather than everyday speech. System 2 can therefore be loosely labelled the 'Romance' system.
- System 3 words have come from a variety of languages and have to some extent carried with them the spellings from their original languages, like 'cello'; that is to say, they are often comparatively new words in English. They are, in Albrow's term, in a 'borderland' between English and foreign spelling. His label for System 3 is 'exotic'. The reservation about System 3 is whether it is not so much a system as a waste-bin for isolated foreign words that have not been fully assimilated into English.

Albrow uses the labels 'basic' (System 1), 'Romance' (System 2) and 'exotic' (System 3) with caution. He points out that some words like 'grand' have correspondences that are system 1, though clearly French in origin.

We can now take up Venezky's Principle 4 that 'Etymology is honoured' that was mentioned earlier in Part 3.2. This means that spelling is linked to the history of English: a word that was borrowed from French at an early period will have a /tʃ/ correspondence for <ch> as in 'chief'; a word that was borrowed from French at a later period will have a /ʃ/ correspondence as in 'chef' – in other words Albrow's systems 1 and 3. Few readers are consciously aware of the historical layers of English vocabulary. At best people probably have an awareness of groups of words with similar spellings, say those where <ch> corresponds to /tʃ/ 'china' or to /ʃ/ 'chiffon' or to /k/ 'choir', with no real idea of the history of a word or indeed of the languages which are involved.

The alternative favoured by Carney (1994: 100–1) is to treat words as belonging to groups labelled by source languages, prefixed by the sign '§' to indicate that they are spelling subsystems, not languages. The terms do not imply that the reader recognizes them as coming from a particular foreign language or that they resemble any word in that language today. A statement such as 'chauffeur is a French word' according to him 'is not merely absurd, it is unhelpful'.

Carney's subsystems are set out in Rule Box 13. His §Basic subsystem is equivalent to Albrow's System 1. In addition Carney postulates a §Latinate subsystem to deal with typical Latin-derived prefixes in words such as 'appropriate'. French-related words are subdivided into the §French subsystem, which includes correspondences such as <et> and /eɪ/ in 'buffet', 'chalet', etc., and the §Romance subsystem, which deals with older-established words, such as the correspondence between <-sure> and /ʒə/ in 'measure'. The §Greek subsystem covers correspondences such as <ph> and /f/ in 'philosophy'. Lastly, the §Exotic subsystem deals with correspondences such as <dh> and /d/ 'dhobi' similar to those in Albrow's System 3. Other examples are given in Rule Box 13. As these show, Carney's rules specify the correspondences for pairs and groupings of letters, not all of which would be considered orthographic units by Albrow, for example <-ium> corresponding to /ɪəm/ 'atrium'. That is to say, the correspondence rule relies on the context for the orthographic symbol as well as on the symbol itself.

While Carney's subsystems tidy up Albrow's three systems, they are not really isolatable as separate subsystems, since he treats the correspondences for letters as primary. His comprehensive listing of correspondence rules in the Venezky style only alludes to the subsystems in passing.

Rule Box 13. Carney's subsystems

§Basic	**<CCy>**	≡ /CCɪ/ 'bully'
	<er>	≡ /ə/ 'after'
§Latinate	**<ar>**	≡ /ə/ 'popular'
	<ium>	≡ /ɪəm/ 'medium'
§French	**<a>**	≡ /ɑː/ 'corsage'
	<ges>	≡ /ʒ/ 'Bruges'
§Romance	**<ture>**	≡ /tʃə/ 'adventure'
	<mm>	≡ /m/ 'command'
§Greek	**<rh>**	≡ /r/ 'rhino'
	<x>	≡ /z/ 'Xena'
§Exotic	**<kh>**	≡ /k/ 'khaki'
	<q>	≡ /k/ 'Iraq'

Grammar and spelling

So far the discussion has only concerned content words. Albrow's systems, however, work differently for function words. Partly this is a matter of incorporating the three-letter rule that only function words can have two letters, 'so'/'sow'/'sew', 'no'/'know' and a single consonant, 'an'/'Ann', 'in'/'inn'.

Turning to inflections, English has fairly few inflected forms of the verb, or indeed the noun, compared with other languages of Europe. Verb inflections are restricted to the third-person 's' in 'walks', the past tense 'ed' in 'walked', the progressive 'ing' in 'walking' and the past participle 'en' in some verbs such as 'seen'. The past tense 'ed' is a useful example of an inflection, which will recur in several later chapters. Within the last decade, past tense inflections have been at the centre of much research into English syntax and language acquisition because of their interesting properties. For example they formed a test case for Pinker's dual theory of language processing (Pinker 1994) because they involve both a knowledge of regular rules for forming 'ed' past tense forms and a knowledge of idiosyncratic examples such as 'went' and 'flew' – a variant of the rules versus items discussion of Chapter 1.

In spoken English the past tense 'ed' inflection takes several different forms according to the final phoneme of the verb stem:

- following an unvoiced consonant such as /p/ or /s/, the 'ed' inflection corresponds to /t/; that is to say, 'walked' is /wɔːkt/ and 'passed' /pɑːst/
- following a voiced consonant such as /b/ or /z/ or a vowel, the 'ed' inflection corresponds to /d/, that is say, 'clubbed' is /klʌbd/, 'lazed' is /leɪzd/, 'played' is /pleɪd/
- after a /t/ or /d/, the 'ed' inflection corresponds to a syllabic /ɪd/; that is to say, 'waited' is /weɪtɪd/, 'needed' /niːdɪd/. The two consonants /t/ and /d/ override the first two rules about voiced versus voiceless.

In addition, English has several groups of irregular past tense forms, some with a vowel change 'ring'/'rang', some with a vowel and a consonant change 'leave'/'left', some with no change at all 'hit'/'hit'.

Rule Box 14. Written past tense inflection

1 Past tense <ed> ≡ /t/ following a voiceless consonant: 'missed', 'picked'
2 Past tense <ed> ≡ /d/ following a voiced sound: 'weighed', 'planned'
3 Past tense <ed> ≡ /ɪd/ following <t>/<d>: 'plotted', 'raided'
4 Irregular past tenses: 'came', 'rang', 'said', 'hung', 'swam', 'left', 'went', 'knew', etc.

The System 1 rules for past tense inflection are displayed in Rule Box 14 above. Rule 1 states that written past tense <ed> corresponds to /t/ after any consonant with a voiceless correspondence, thus including not only voiceless plosives such as /p/ 'stopped' but also voiceless fricatives such as /ʃ/ 'rushed' and affricates such as /tʃ/ 'matched'. Rule 2 states that <ed> corresponds to /d/ after any voiced sound, covering not only vowels such as /aɪ/ 'died' and voiced plosives, fricatives and affricates such as /b/ 'grabbed', /v/ 'loved' and /dʒ/ 'nudged' but also nasals such as /m/ 'hummed' and the lateral /l/ 'ruled'. Rule 3 takes care of the case when the final consonants are themselves /t/ or /d/ by making <ed> correspond to a whole syllable /ɪd/ as in 'insisted' and 'waded'.

Albrow points out that there are other ways of spelling the past tense morpheme. One notorious trap is the word 'paid'. Usually a verb ending in <y> adds <ed> to form the past tense as in 'played' or 'stayed'. A small group of verbs, however, changes <y> to <i> and uses <d> as the ending, for example 'paid' and 'laid'. Hence a common spelling mistake – 7.6% of all past tenses for 'pay' on the web – is 'payed'. So far as the spoken language is concerned, 'paid' and 'laid' are regular examples of past tense formation with /d/, something which is usually misrepresented in textbooks for teaching English. Other pitfalls are the use of <t> in irregular verbs that have a vowel change plus 'ed', for example 'keep'/'kept', a few verbs with no vowel change 'lend'/'lent', and some verbs in which both vowel and consonant change 'leave'/'left'. Beyond this, there lie specific one-off irregular verbs which are difficult to square with any system, for example 'go'/'went'.

The main correspondence rules for written <ed> appear complex because they essentially describe a morphemic correspondence rather than a letter-to-sound correspondence. They indicate that there is a past tense 'ed' without specifying which of the three spoken possibilities it conforms to: you have to know the phonology of the spoken language to be able to work it out. Rather like a Chinese character, it is the meaning of the past tense morpheme that is important, not its spoken correspondence. In this area of spelling, Modern English breaks the alphabetic principle that letters correspond to phonemes. The correspondence is between a pair of orthographic symbols and a morpheme, not a sound: the verb ending <ed> corresponds to 'past tense', not to /t/, /d/ or /ɪd/. This emphasis on morphemes will be taken up in the next section.

Albrow's analysis of <ed> therefore depends crucially on the grammar. Alongside past tense 'ed' in System 1 are the noun plural morpheme <s> 'books' and third-person morpheme <s> 'likes'; these too have three regular forms, as will be seen in the next section. The only grammatical aspects assigned to System 2 are the occasional Latinate plural forms – /aɪ/ 'foci', /iːz/ 'crises' and /ɪm/ 'cherubim'. Presumably the grounds for assigning them to System 2 are their long existence in the language, compared with the parvenus of System 3.

Overall, Albrow provides a more comprehensive account of English spelling through the notion of multiple systems (*see* Table 3.2). Even if the actual systems he proposes may not be watertight, nevertheless they are a useful reminder that the whole of English spelling cannot be straitjacketed into a single system but is a composite of several systems working both together and against each other. Furthermore the concept of discontinuous elements is an ingenious solution to the problems of silent letters and of marking vowels by letters that follow them.

Table 3.2 Albrow's approach

Aim: a description of the English writing system for teachers

Units: orthographic symbols; simple <b>, complex <ng>, discontinuous <i_e>

Systems: basic <c> ≡ /k/ 'café'
Romance <c> ≡ /s/ 'cell'
exotic <kh> ≡ /k/ 'khaki'

(Source: Albrow 1972)

3.4 NOAM AND CAROL CHOMSKY: LEXICAL REPRESENTATION

Focusing questions

- What is the point of the <g> in 'sign'?
- How bad or good is English as a spelling system? Why?

Key words

lexical item: the mental lexicon consists of lexical items that may be one word, 'sit', more than one word, 'sit up', or less than a word, 's' in 'sits'.

lexical entry: each lexical item in the mental lexicon has an entry that specifies information about its grammatical properties, its form, its meaning and so on.

lexical spelling: the underlying form of the lexical item is represented in Chomsky's approach, rather than its phonetic form.

rhotic and non-rhotic: non-rhotic dialects of English such as British RP have zero correspondence for written <r> before consonants, e.g. 'bird' corresponds to /bɜːd/, and before silence, e.g. 'fur' corresponds to /fɜː/; in rhotic dialects like standard American <r> corresponds to /r/ in all positions.

One of the powerful voices on English spelling is that of Noam Chomsky. The influential theory of generative phonology that he developed during the late 1960s led to spin-offs for English orthography. He himself mentioned this first as asides in the monumental *Sound Pattern of English* he wrote with Morris Halle (Chomsky and Halle 1968), then as an independent article (Chomsky 1972). The educational implications were developed by Carol Chomsky, his wife, using an approach called 'lexical spelling' (Chomsky 1970). Representative quotations are given in the box below and will be used during the discussion.

Chomsky's aim in linguistics has always been to describe how the human mind bridges the gap between the actual sounds of speech and the complex abstract meanings of sentences. A crucial element in this bridge is the lexicon – the knowledge of the individual lexical items of the language that every speaker has in their mind. In the current version of Chomsky's theory, known as the Minimalist Program, the properties of lexical items determine how the sentence is put together and how it is pronounced (Cook and Newson 1996). The description of the sentence is driven by the choice of lexical items from the mental lexicon.

Views on the lexical representation approach to spelling

. . . conventional orthography is . . . a near optimal system for the lexical representation of English words (N. Chomsky and M. Halle 1968: 49)

In short, conventional orthography is much closer than one might guess to an optimal orthography, an orthography that presents no redundant information and that indicates directly, by direct letter-to-segment correspondence, the underlying lexical form of the spoken language (N. Chomsky 1972: 12)

What the foreigner lacks is just what the child already possesses, a knowledge of the phonological rules of English that relate underlying representations to sounds (C. Chomsky 1970: 299)

It frequently happens, especially in derivative languages, that there are some letters, which are not pronounced, and consequently are useless with regard to the sound; and yet are of some service in leading us to the knowledge of the thing signified by the words (*Port Royal Grammar* 1660, trans. 1753)

The mental lexicon consists of lexical entries specifying a variety of information about a word. A lexical item might be a word like ‘wasp’ or it might be a grammatical inflection like past tense ‘ed’. As well as giving its meaning, the lexical entry for ‘wasp’ specifies that it is a countable animate noun pronounced /wɒsp/, meaning ‘any insect of the genus *Vespa*’. So in a sentence ‘wasp’ can have an indefinite article ‘a wasp’ (countable); it can go with adjectives that are marked for animacy ‘a lively wasp’ (animate); and it obeys the normal rules for forming plural ‘wasps’ /wɒsps/. In the Minimalist Program the ‘computational system’ works out how the properties of all the lexical items combine to generate the actual sentence, complete with meaning and pronunciation.

One aspect of this is how the sounds in the word are pronounced. Some aspects of the sounds may be specific to that word, some parts may be elements common to many others. Chomsky’s contribution to phonology was in part to claim that the actual speech sounds that are heard are derived by a series of phonological rules acting on the forms provided in lexical entries. Words have an abstract mental form that differs in many ways from the sounds that are produced or heard. Much of the information about how words are pronounced is predictable from the general phonological rules of English rather than stored with each word. If nothing more, it would be uneconomic to duplicate such information in the entries for many thousands of items.

So how does the mental lexicon actually store the lexical item? There has to be a way of representing lexical items in our minds that can be used as a basis for the phonological rules so that we can actually pronounce them. Chomsky claims that the role of English spelling is in fact to show the abstract form of lexical items in the mental lexicon. The spelling of a word shows what is needed to access its lexical form, not its actual pronunciation. Hence the term 'lexical spelling' was coined by Carol Chomsky: 'Letters represent segments in lexical spelling, not sounds' (C. Chomsky 1970: 296). Many elements of lexical spelling appear unnecessary in terms of phonological correspondences. For example the <n> of 'autumn' may well be 'silent' in terms of correspondences but is relevant to the lexical entry because it links together the lexical entry derived from 'autumn' in which the <n> indeed corresponds to /n/ – 'autumnal'. The <a> in 'nature' corresponds to /eɪ/, the <a> in 'natural' to /æ/. At one level this breaches the one-to-one principle since <a> corresponds to two phonemes; at another level, preserving the same written vowel <a> maintains the link to the same lexical entry 'nature' despite the different sound correspondences. Spelling can show links between related words or morphemes which are lost in the actual spoken forms.

Most claims that English spelling is deficient are based on the view that English spelling corresponds to the sounds of speech. The purpose of English spelling is instead to link to the underlying lexical representation. However bad English writing may be as a sound-based system, it is efficient at showing the underlying forms of words stripped of the accidental features attached to them by phonological rules. Its purpose is not the representation of sounds but the representation of word forms. Looked at in this light, 'conventional orthography is . . . a near optimal system for the lexical representation of English words' (Chomsky and Halle 1968: 49).

The main requirement for a lexical representation system is to keep the form of the word constant: one spelling corresponds to one morpheme, whatever the permutations of pronunciation: 'an optimal orthography would have one representation for each lexical entry' (Chomsky and Halle 1968: 49). In English the forms of spoken words vary in at least three ways:

- Grammatical inflection. The ending of the word changes to show grammatical properties, say plural 'book'/'books' or tense 'like'/'liked'/'likes'.
- Derivation. One word is changed to another by adding other morphemes; 'cook' plus 'er' becomes 'cooker', 'cook' plus 'ery' becomes 'cookery', 'cook' plus 'book' becomes 'cookbook' and so on.
- Strong and weak forms. Many function words have a stressed ('strong') form and an unstressed ('weak') form; 'will' /wɪl/ and ''ll' /l/, 'have' /hæv/, /əv/ and ''ve' /v/ or 'can' /kæn/ and /kən/.

Lexical representation preserves grammatical inflections across divergent pronunciations

The spelling correspondences of some English grammatical inflections are shown in Rule Box 15. The last section discussed how the past tense 'ed' morpheme can be spelled as <ed> regardless of which of the three regular correspondences is involved: /d/ 'aimed', /t/ 'dressed' and /ɪd/ 'waited'; <ed> corresponds to the underlying lexical form of the past tense 'ed'. The different pronunciations of <ed> with particular verbs are specified in phonological rules that apply to all verbs rather than being given in each lexical entry. The underlying form is <ed>, which gets changed to suit the sounds of the particular lexical item.

Rule Box 15. Inflectional endings in English

	Underlying lexical form	Phonetic form	Examples
Past tense	**'ed'**	/t/ /d/ /ɪd/	'looked' /t/, 'opened' /d/, 'insisted' /ɪd/
Present tense third-person	**'s'**	/s/ /z/ /ɪz/	'looks' /s/, 'opens' /z/, 'matches' /ɪz/
Plural	**'s'**	/s/ /z/ /ɪz/	'cups' /s/, 'miles' /z/, 'pages' /ɪz/
Possessive	**'s'**	/s/ /z/ /ɪz/	'patient's' /s/, 'team's' /z/, 'judge's' /ɪz/

The <ed> form of the written verb 'liked' or 'waded' omits information that is not needed by the reader, who possesses a general phonological rule that leads to /t/ or /ɪd/. If the information about how 'ed' was pronounced was solely in the lexical entry, readers would not be able to read out loud nonsense words with appropriate past tense pronunciations. The fact that everyone knows that the past form of 'vatch' is /vætʃt/ with a /t/ or of 'blig' is /blɪgd/ with a /d/ shows they have a phonological rule, not just a knowledge of separate entries. Hence the lexical representation only needs to be 'ed'.

A similar argument applies to the various 's' inflections in English. In the spoken language the morpheme 's' for present tense third-person seen in 'bites' can be pronounced in three ways:

- /s/ after voiceless phonemes, 'starts', 'picks', etc.
- /z/ after voiced phonemes, 'plays', 'dines', etc.
- /ɪz/ after affricates and sibilant phonemes, 'misses', 'watches', 'washes', etc.

The written third person <s> therefore corresponds to three distinct spoken forms /s/, /z/ and /ɪz/. In terms of underlying lexical representation, it corresponds to the present tense morpheme 's'; its different pronunciations are derived from this by phonological rules. Seeing a verb with an 's' alerts the reader that it is third-person present tense, not how the inflection is pronounced.

The plural morpheme 's' attached to nouns also has the same three surface pronunciations /s/ 'books', /z/ 'days' and /ɪz/ 'matches', all corresponding to the same underlying lexical form. The possessive ''s' inflection for nouns again has the same surface forms: /z/ 'John's', /s/ 'Pete's' and /ɪz/ 'Chris's'.

So some major verb and noun inflections in English are always spelled in the same way. It is irrelevant to the reader how they are said as they link primarily to the lexical representation, not to the sounds of speech. English is exploiting a visual orthographic feature to show a morphemic level of representation rather than a phonological one.

A minor flaw in the argument is that, if it is useful to have the same representation for the same morpheme, it is odd that there are three different morphemes – noun plural, possessive and third-person present tense verb – with the same representation 's'. Presumably in context this is unlikely to cause difficulty since third-person 's' belongs to verbs and plural and possessive 's' to nouns. Some possible confusion between the identical written forms of plural 's' and possessive 's' is averted by the use of apostrophe ''s', 'cat's' versus 'cats', though this itself leads to confusions, particularly with the so-called greengrocer's apostrophe, 'hotdog's' and 'photo's', as will be seen in Chapter 4.

Lexical representation preserves content words across diverse word-formation

As well as preserving the form of inflectional endings, spelling can also maintain the word itself in a constant form despite changes in pronunciation.

Silent letters

This approach claims that many so-called 'silent' letters are needed in the underlying lexical representation because they occur in other forms of the same word. Silent <g> may be redundant so far as the sound correspondence rules are concerned in 'sign' but it is pronounced in the derived forms 'signature', 'assignation', 'resignation', etc. The underlying lexical representation needs a <g> because this unifies the different forms of the word, even if it is superfluous in the form 'sign'. Similarly <b> may be 'silent' in 'bomb' but it corresponds to /b/ quite normally in 'bombardier', 'bombastic' and 'bombazine'; 'silent' <k> in 'know' corresponds to /k/ in 'acknowledge'; even the 'silent' <w> in 'two' corresponds to /w/ in 'twin'. In all these cases preserving the written consonant in the related words means the reader can link them to a single underlying lexical form; changing the spelling to suit the pronunciation would destroy these mental links. Rule Box 16 displays some pairs of words that fit this idea, mostly taken from Carol Chomsky (1970).

Rule Box 16. Some 'silent' consonants

	'Silent'	Not 'silent'
<g>	'paradigm'	'paradigmatic'
<b>	'bomb'	'bombard'
<k>	'know'	'acknowledge'
<n>	'solemn'	'solemnity'
<t>	'soften'	'soft'
<c>	'muscle'	'muscular'
<d>	'handkerchief'	'hand'
<p>	'cupboard'	'cup'

Vowels

A complicated area of English phonology concerns the assignment of stress. In particular, spoken vowels often vary in derived words because of the resultant stress change. The <a> of 'nation' corresponds to /eɪ/ but the <a> of 'national' to /æ/. The second <e> of 'extreme' corresponds to /iː/, whereas that in 'extremity' corresponds to /e/. The letter <a> corresponds to three different spoken vowels in 'telegraph' /ɑː/, 'telegraphic' /æ/ and 'telegraphy' /ə/. The second <o> of 'compose' corresponds to /əʊ/, that of 'compositor' to /ɒ/. Keeping the written vowel constant allows the reader access to a single lexical entry. The written vowel does not need to be specified in more detail as the changes in the spoken vowel can be predicted from the phonological rules of English.

Preserving the same consonant

Sometimes derived forms of the same word differ in their spoken consonants, as seen in Rule Box 17. There is for example an alternation of correspondences for <c> seen in 'critic' /k/ and 'criticize' /s/, and in 'medicate' /k/ versus 'medicine' /s/. The correspondences of <g> also alternate between /g/ 'sagacity' and /dʒ/ 'sage'. Other variable correspondences are <t> to /t/ in 'right' but to /tʃ/ in 'righteous', and <s> to /z/ in 'revise' but to /ʒ/ in 'revision'. By ignoring the different spoken consonants, writing unites the different forms of the same word.

Rule Box 17. Some alternative consonant correspondences

<c>	≡	/k/	**'critic'**
	≡	/s/	**'criticize'**
<g>	≡	/g/	**'sagacity'**
	≡	/dʒ/	**'sage'**
<s>	≡	/z/	**'revise'**
	≡	/ʒ/	**'revision'**

Yule (1991) points out that the principle 'Related words should retain their visual similarity' has the corollary that unrelated words should look dissimilar. Hence, English is justified in having pairs of homophones with different spellings. It is an asset for English that 'whole' is spelled differently from 'hole', despite both having the pronunciation /həʊl/, and the same goes for pairs such as 'there'/'their', 'for'/'four' or 'write'/'right'. Treated as lexical representation, these diverse spellings for the same sound are logical.

The English spelling system then is not a poor approximation to spoken English but an accurate lexical representation, justifying Venezky's principle 6 'Visual identity of meaningful word parts takes precedence over letter-sound simplicity'. The system relies on the reader already knowing the phonology of English. Provided readers know the underlying lexical form, the rest can be predicted by phonological rules and does not need to be stated: 'It provides . . . just the information about the item in question that is needed by a person who knows the language and wishes to use this item properly' (Chomsky 1972: 7). Hence the spelling system assumes in a sense that the reader is an adult native speaker of standard English; this creates considerable difficulties for people who do not have such knowledge. One such group is made up of people learning English as a second language; 'What the foreigner lacks is just what the child already possesses, a knowledge of the phonological rules of English that relate underlying representations to sound' (Chomsky 1970: 299).

Indeed there may be aspects of English phonology that native children have still not mastered by the time they learn to read, as will be seen in Chapter 5. For instance many of the derived words that crop up in the discussion come from a Latinate level of the vocabulary that children acquire comparatively late: few seven-year-olds are using words like 'assignation', 'telegraphic' or 'sagacity', all needed here. Children may have problems with acquiring the system because they have not yet acquired some of the phonological rules that link the lexical representation to its surface form; it is not the spelling that is the problem but their immature phonology.

Task 5. Spelling exercises

Here are some exercises for improving children's spelling, adapted from Carol Chomsky (1970). First try them for yourself and then consider how useful they may be for children.

	1	2
1. Fill in the missing reduced vowel in column 1 and then justify the choice by thinking of related words that retain vowel quality leading to column 2.	**dem_cratic** **pres_dent** **prec_dent** . . .	**democracy** **preside** **precede** . . .
2. Cover column 1, look at column 2 and think of related words in which the underlined consonant becomes silent.	**muscle** **sign** **bomb** . . .	**muscular** **signature** **bombard** . . .
3. Cover column 2: can you think of a word where the <t> is not said as /t/ but written <c> and pronounced as /s/?	**coincidental** **pirate** **present** . . .	**coincidence** **piracy** **presence** . . .

One advantage of lexical representation is that it allows English speakers with different accents to understand each other, just as speakers of different Chinese dialects share a common written language. The underlying representations of the lexical items are common to speakers of English regardless of their dialect and change little over time.

The same lexical representation can then accommodate many dialects of English. According to Chomsky, this explains the ease with which English speakers from different parts of the world can understand each other's writings. For example, a major difference between British and American English is that non-rhotic British English does not allow /r/ before a spoken consonant or silence, whereas rhotic American English does. In words like 'car' and 'bird', written <r> corresponds to spoken /ø/ in British RP English and to /r/ in General American English, which is therefore a 'rhotic dialect'. The fact that <r> is 'silent' in 'non-rhotic' dialects like RP except in the onset of the syllable does not affect the spelling of English and hence written forms like 'bear', 'third' or 'there' are intelligible in England or Scotland, India or the USA, regardless of whether the local correspondence is /r/ or /ø/. Although there are indeed differences between British and American styles of spelling, these are not related to differences of pronunciation, as will be seen in Chapter 7.

The vowel systems of different dialects are similarly no barrier to comprehension in the written form. Accepting the written language as the basis for analysis, as in the definition of Chinese, would show that there was essentially one form of English with slight variation, except in the correspondence to spoken sounds. 'Although the dialects of English differ enormously in their "phonemic" structure, they seem quite similar, so far as is known, at the level of lexical representation that is directly related to orthography' (Chomsky 1972: 14). If linguists who investigated global varieties of English had started from the written language rather than the spoken language, they would have had rather little to say.

Furthermore, a constant lexical representation has the advantage of uniting different realizations of the same word, whose spelling would otherwise vary from one instance to another. The word 'have' has the same spelling <have> even if a speaker varies between the stressed /hæv/, the unstressed /həv/ or /hæf/ ('have to'); 'man' is spelled <man> even if it is said as /mæn/ or /mən/ ('gentleman'). Being part of the stress patterns of English these correspondences do not need to be shown in the spelling. These issues obviously have a strong bearing on the arguments for making English spelling more sound-based, as will be seen in Chapter 6.

For the adult native speaker of English therefore the writing system works very well: 'conventional orthography is much closer than one might guess to an optimal orthography, an orthography that presents no redundant information and that indicates directly, by direct letter-to-segment correspondence, the underlying lexical form of the spoken language' (Chomsky 1972: 12).

English is not alone in using lexical representation. Other languages keep the same spelling for a word despite its different pronunciations. In German for instance the forms of the word 'König' ('king') are spelled the same, although in 'König' the <g> corresponds to /ç/, in 'königlich' ('royal') to /k/, and in 'Könige' ('kings') to /g/. French too uses silent letters to distinguish words with the same pronunciation, for example 'champs' ('field') versus 'chants' ('songs') (*Port Royal Grammar* 1660); according to Catach (1993) 12.47% of French graphemes are silent letters. The main question for English is really whether the lexical representation approach works outside a small set of carefully chosen words. Yule (1978, 1991) looked in detail at the spelling of related words taken from the 6000 set for children in the State of Victoria Education Department in Australia. She divided the words into those that directly supported the lexical representation hypothesis by keeping the same letters despite having different sounds, such as 'child' /aɪ/ versus 'children' /ɪ/; a sample of these words is given in Rule Box 18. Then she looked at those that did the opposite of what was predicted by having different spelling although the sounds were the same, for example /ɔː/ corresponding to <our> in 'four' but to <or> in 'forty'. Finally, she looked at those where both the sound and spelling of different forms of the same word varied in parallel, for instance 'began' versus 'begin'; this group of words have an almost straightforward correspondence between sounds and letters with no attempt to keep morphemic identity.

Yule's results were that 'under 3% could be considered to be in this category'. In other words the principle of preserving lexical form at the expense of sound correspondences is a poor guide to most English spelling. Hence Yule (1978: 10) claims 'there appears to be negligible practical value in the maintenance of orthographic similarities overriding major sound changes, since usually adequate clues remain'.

Rule Box 18. Yule's test words for lexical spelling (partial list)
An asterisk shows examples that do not work completely for British English.

Words that fit	Words that do not fit	
Sound changes: spelling constant	*Spelling changes: sound constant*	*Spelling and sound changes*
bath/bathe	fire/fiery	began/begin
decide/decision	four/forty	bring/brought
family/familiar	high/height	five/fifth/fifty
image/imagine	speak/speech	man/men/women
meaning/meant	strategy/stratagem	process/proceed
pleasant/please	*honour/honorable	retain/retention
reader/read	*favour/favorite	success/succeed
use (verb)/useful	*labour/laboring	was/were/is

**Different in American and British English style.*

The overall importance of the lexical representation approach to spelling is its recognition of different levels beneath the surface of the sentence. Other approaches had operated essentially with a single level of letters matched against a single level of sounds. Even if some details of the Chomskyan approach (*see* Table 3.3) may be doubtful, lexical representation gives a new depth to the discussion of spelling and reminds us that written language is not just the representation of surface speech but links to the mental lexicon and to the grammar of English. Its other value was perhaps in bringing into spelling research the concept of word families, familiar from studies of lexis and from traditional syllabuses for teaching spelling, as will be seen in Chapter 5, but little mentioned in other approaches. The relationships between words shown through their spelling has to be accounted for somewhere in an overall approach to English spelling.

Table 3.3 Noam and Carol Chomsky's lexical representation approach

Aim: description of 'conventional orthography'

Units: lexical entries; letters

System: surface sounds are derived from the underlying lexical form, which is close to the actual spelling, that is, the /s/ of 'thinks' and the /z/ of 'plays' both correspond to the same third-person <s>

Main sources: C. Chomsky (1970), N. Chomsky (1972)

CONCLUSIONS

Let us briefly try to sum up these disparate accounts of English spelling.

English is not just a sound-based system in which letters correspond directly to phonemes

None of these approaches to English spelling treats it as a straightforward alphabetic system in which letters correspond directly to sounds; the English system is far from shallow. All of the approaches recognize factors that intervene between the two levels of letters and sounds. Venezky postulates relational units and markers; Albrow orthographic symbols and alternative systems; Chomsky an underlying lexical representation. Criticisms of English spelling on the grounds of illogical correspondences between letters and sounds are misguided since they fail to take into account the many other factors involved.

'Silent' letters have a variety of roles in the system

The bugbear of interpreting English as a sound-based system is its use of 'silent' letters that have no direct correspondences in the spoken form. Venezky treats them as markers showing the correspondence at some other point in the word; Albrow as part of complex, sometimes discontinuous, orthographic symbols with sound correspondences of their own; the Chomskyan approach as signs of the underlying lexical representation. None of them manage to accommodate exceptions like the <b> in 'doubt' and 'debt', which seems truly silent in not having a correspondence in any derived forms, as we shall see in Chapter 6. These are largely the products of sixteenth century meddling with English spelling and may have to be classed as one-off lexical items processed by the lexical route.

Grammar is important to the spelling system, particularly morphology

Finding the correspondences between letters and sounds requires a knowledge of the grammar of English. Partly this concerns the representation of function words, which need to be dealt with separately in Albrow's approach, and grammatical inflections, which are a main plank in the lexical representation approach. Partly it is a matter of the word-formation rules of English, featuring most prominently in the Chomskyan account because of the related issues of stress patterning.

English uses different types of correspondence rules for different groups of words

In general all the accounts accept that not all English words behave in the same way, in particular Albrow's three systems. To those who know the history of English, these groups roughly correspond to the periods at which the words entered the language, say pre-Norman Conquest, Middle Ages or Modern English, as will be seen in Chapter 6. But, of course, the vast majority of readers are unaware of the history of English and treat these as groups within the contemporary language, as Carney (1994) suggests. One way of comparing the relative success of the three approaches is to look at the extent to which they explain everyday mistakes with English spelling. Task 6 gives a selection of mistakes from adult native speakers of English.

Task 6. Native speaker mistakes

Here is a selection of spelling mistakes collected from students who are native speakers of English. Decide which ones are better explained as problems with Venezky-style correspondence rules, which as confusions between Albrow-style systems, and which as issues of Chomsky-style lexical representation, or whether in fact the 'basic' rules of consonant-doubling, etc. given in Part 3.1 are all that is needed.

1. definately	2. knew (new)	3. bare (bear)	4. baring (barring)
5. demeening	6. tradditional	7. detatchment	8. finnished
9. grater (greater)	10. senario	11. compulsary	12. relevent (relevant)
13 illicit (elicit)	14. pronounciation	15. booring (boring)	16. layed out
17. pysche	18. embarassing	19. accomodate	20. quite (quiet)
21. syllubus	22. their (there)	23. sited (cited)	24. where (were)
25. to (too)	26. usefull	27. vocabularly	28. affect (effect)
29. percieved	30. principle (principal)	31. sence (sense)	

DISCUSSION TOPICS

1. Do you think it *is* possible to describe English spelling systematically or that it is simply a collection of idiosyncratic rules and words?
2. What do you think are the values of silent letters in English, or should they be eliminated?
3. In the light of the three approaches in this chapter, what types of reform do you think could be made to English spelling, if any?
4. If you had to give rules to someone learning English, which would be most useful to explain?
5. To what extent do you think English deals systematically with foreign words that enter it or simply puts them in an 'exotic' ghetto?
6. How important do you feel a knowledge of grammar is to the use of spelling?

7. Is English spelling really ‘near optimal’?
8. What implications do the three approaches described here have for the teaching of English spelling to children?

ANSWERS TO TASKS

Task 1. <ie> rule

Teaching accounts phrase the rule as:

> ‘After the letter “c” write “ei” to give the sound of the long vowel “e”’
> (J. Davis, *Handling Spelling*)

> ‘“i” before “e” except after “c” but only when these letters sound like long “e”.’
> (V. Parker, *Test Your Spelling*)

That is to say the crucial qualification to the rule which excludes ‘weight’, ‘sleigh’ and ‘either’ (for those who pronounce it /aɪðə/ not /iːðə/) is that <ei> ≡ /iː/. Exceptions: ‘ceiling’, ‘species’, ‘caffeine’ (<ei> ≡ /iː/), ‘leisure’ (<ei> ≡ /e/).

Task 2. Function words

Function words may have one or two letters, content words must have more than two; in function words <th> ≡ /ð/ ‘this’, in content words initial <th> ≡ /θ/ ‘thistle’.

Task 3. Consonant doubling

Right answers, British style spelling.

accommodate	☑	beautifull	☐
beginning	☑	developping	☐
disappointedly	☑	dissappear	☐
embarrass	☑	equipped	☑
harrass	☐	inferred	☑
milennium	☐	neccessarily	☐
nonproffessional	☐	occurrence	☑
offerred	☐	opperating	☐
personnel	☑	presupposes	☑
successfull	☐	till	☑

Task 4. Checked vowels and doubling

The following words have free vowels before double consonants that do not fit the rules: ‘all’ /ɔː/, ‘’ll’ syllabic /l/, ‘staff’ /ɑː/. Others have schwa /ə/ rather than the usual checked vowel, for example ‘across’, ‘according to’, ‘account’, ‘approach’, ‘appropriate’, ‘committee’, ‘community’, ‘effect’, ‘success’, ‘support’

FURTHER READING

The main references for the three approaches are:

- Venezky, R.L. (1970) *The Structure of English Orthography*. The Hague: Mouton.
- Venezky, R.L. (1999) *The American Way of Spelling*. New York: NY: Guilford Press. Far more entertaining and interesting than its 1970 version.
- Albrow, K.H. (1972) *The English Writing System: Notes towards a Description*. London: Longman. Difficult to obtain as it was published in a pamphlet-like form.
- Chomsky, C. (1970) Reading, writing and phonology. *Harvard Educational Review* 40, 287–309.
- Chomsky, N. (1972) Phonology and reading. In H. Levin (ed.), *Basic Processes in Reading*. London: Harper & Row, 3–18.
- Carney, E. (1994) *A Survey of English Spelling*. London: Routledge. This contains useful discussion of the three approaches as well as being an extraordinarily comprehensive account of English spelling.

4 Punctuation and typography

INTRODUCTION

This chapter brings together some of the features of written English that do not depend upon spoken English, ranging from the linguistics level of grammar to the typographical level of layout, all part of the English writing system. This chapter moves towards writing produced by mechanical means, that is, keyboards, whether typewriter, computer or printing proper, rather than handwriting. Much of the discussion is about professional presentation by 'experts' – journalists, editors, novelists and the like. The punctuation and layout of informal 'amateur' writing has been little studied or commented on.

> **Why punctuation matters**
> You don't want to look stupid! (VanDyck 1996)
>
> The problem with poor punctuation is that it makes life difficult for the reader who needs to read what you've written (Trask 1997)
>
> Intellectually, stops matter a great deal. If you are getting your commas, semicolons, and full stops wrong, it means that you are not getting your thoughts right, and your mind is muddled (Archbishop William Temple)
>
> Good punctuation, we feel, makes for clean thought (Robinson 1980)
>
> Punctuation is cold notation; it is not frustrated speech; it is typographic code (Bringhurst 1992: 84)

Hence most description and discussion takes the form of guidance manuals that tell students how to punctuate, printers how to hyphenate and authors how to present lists of references. In other words they do not describe what happens but proscribe what should not happen. For example the greengrocer's apostrophe, seen in the plural 'Taxi's', is universally held to be a mistake on a par with 'split' infinitives, rather than accepted as something which occurs with high frequency in the genre of shop notices – I see at least two examples every time I visit my local shops, ranging from 'Universal Studio's Ticket Offer' to 'Lunchtime Home-made Special's'.

Punctuation in particular is treated as a matter of good manners, intelligence or even morality, as seen in the box above: the emphasis is on getting it right because there *is* a right and a wrong. It is hard to imagine similar advice addressed to native speakers on, say, the correct intonation patterns to use in speech. Usually linguistics follows usage, rather than prescribes it. Only in spelling and punctuation is it felt allowable to dictate what people *should* do (*see* Task 1).

Task 1. Punctuation

Insert the appropriate punctuation marks into these two texts.

1 but now there were things that were not being talked of a wall of silence being built around the unspoken sadnesses silently day by day partitioning off parts of him places that became the more taboo with time building a wall that would become a part of them taken for granted hardly noticed at all a wall that once built would be breachable only by the unthinkable by assault and destruction or it would never be breached at all so that only a part of themselves was contiguous open plan until they could no longer see each other whole note the origins of act and word

2 before them in the west the world lay still formless and grey but even as they looked the shadows of night melted the colours of the waking earth returned green flowed over the wide meads of roha the white mists shimmered in the water vales and far off to the left thirty leagues or more blue and purple stood the white mountains rising into peaks of jet tipped with glimmering snows flushed with the rose of morning

The original punctuation is seen in Text 2 and Text 3.

Almost every publishing house produces a guide to punctuation featuring the publishers' name in the title, whether *Chambers Good Punctuation Guide* (Jarvie 1992), *The Cassell Guide to Punctuation* (Todd 1995), *The Penguin Guide to Punctuation* (Trask 1997), *Collins Wordpower: Punctuation* (King 2000) or *Merriam-Webster's Guide to Punctuation and Style* (2002), at least two of these written by linguists well-known in other areas. Even NASA feels it has to provide its own on-line *Grammar, Punctuation, and Capitalization: A Handbook for Technical Writers and Editors* (McCaskill 1998). Publishers want their names to be associated with punctuation as conferring some seal of respectability and authority: there do not seem to be similar titles in other genres, say, correct pronunciation or proper driving. These manuals arise partly out of the tradition of publishing houses providing printer's guides, say *Hart's Rules* (1983) or Collins *Authors' and Printers' Dictionary* (1973). While it may be legitimate for publishers to maintain a consistent style in their own books, there is no reason why their opinion should count for other publications, let alone for 'amateurs' not aiming at print. Cameron (1995) provides an illuminating discussion of the ideology of such attempts to impose a 'standard' on English.

4.1 GRAMMATICAL AND CORRESPONDENCE PUNCTUATION

Focusing questions

- Why do *you* think punctuation matters?
- What difficulties have you yourself had with English punctuation?
- Is punctuation primarily to do with reading aloud or is it something of its own?

Key words

punctuation: 'the rules for graphically structuring written language by means of a set of conventional marks' (Coulmas 1996: 421).

grammatical punctuation: relates the written text to the grammar of the written language.

correspondence punctuation: relates the written text to the spoken language, as in reading aloud.

Punctuation consists of the use of additional marks to the letters of the alphabet, such as the full stop <.>, the comma <,> and so on. Modern English uses more or less the same set of punctuation marks as other languages. Nunberg (1990: 10) goes so far as to say that 'there is only one system of punctuation . . . which is used in all developed Western, alphabetic languages, subject to the fixing of a few parameters and the establishment of various local conventions and constraints'. Even Chinese and Japanese character-based writing has adopted versions of full stops and commas, as can be seen in Text 1 and Text 2 in Chapter 1.

Within Europe there is some variation in the actual form of the punctuation marks. Double quotation marks for example are <“ ”> in England, <″ ″> in Germany and goosefeet <« »> in Italy and Greece (but <» «> in Switzerland) (Bringhurst 1992; Tschichold 1991); Spanish uses sentence-initial inverted question marks <¿> and exclamation marks <¡>, following a decision by the Spanish Royal Academy in 1754, based on the convenience of knowing the sentence-type from the very beginning of the sentence; Catalan uses a raised mid full stop. Details of the variation between languages can be found in *Punctuation Design Standards* (www.microsoft.com/typography/ developers/fdsspec/punc.htm).

English perhaps makes less use of accents, umlauts and so on than most other languages in Europe, say French or German. The frequencies of the punctuation marks for English are given in the box below, based on Meyer's analysis of the Brown million-word corpus (Meyer 1987). Ninety-one per cent are commas and full stops; the others all have low frequencies. You could get most English punctuation right if you mastered full stops and commas.

Frequencies of punctuation marks (%)

Commas	47
Full stops	45
Dashes	2
Parentheses	2
Semi-colons	2
Question marks	1
Colons	1
Exclamation marks	1

(Source: Meyer (1987): analysis of the Brown Corpus)

Grammatical punctuation

What is punctuation for? And to what extent is it peculiar to writing or a servant to reading aloud? Halliday (1985) divides punctuation into three main categories:

- ***boundary markers***, which show grammatical units, for example word spaces:

  Air tragedy city in mourning

  versus:

  Airtragedycityinmourning

- ***status markers***, which show the function of units, for instance question marks:

  How could this happen again?

- ***relation markers*** that show links between units, for example apostrophes:

  At 95 he's gardening's grand old man.

None of these categories directly corresponds to spoken language: word spaces seldom correspond to pauses; the intonation of spoken English questions varies according to the type of question, rather than <?> invariably corresponding with a rising intonation; the <'> in 'he's' corresponds to no part of the spoken form /hi:z/.

This section makes a slightly different division between *grammatical* punctuation, which relates the text to the grammar of the written language and thus includes most of Halliday's categories, and *correspondence* punctuation, which relates the text to the spoken language, as in reading aloud. It concentrates on grammatical punctuation as the unique property of writing, and it takes in only major characteristics rather than exhausting all the possibilities. Actual examples of punctuation are mostly taken from one edition of a local newspaper, the *East Anglian Daily Times* (henceforth *East Anglian*), and one of a national paper, The *Guardian*.

Let us start with the concocted sentence:

When Brown's plan collapsed, the spin-doctor resigned.

A conventional phrase structure tree breaks this sentence into smaller and smaller grammatical constituents until no more splits are possible, as seen in Figure 4.1. The grammatical analysis is intended to be illustrative rather than to conform to any particular syntactic theory. The type of grammatical unit involved at each branching level in the tree is specified on the left.

Grammatical unit

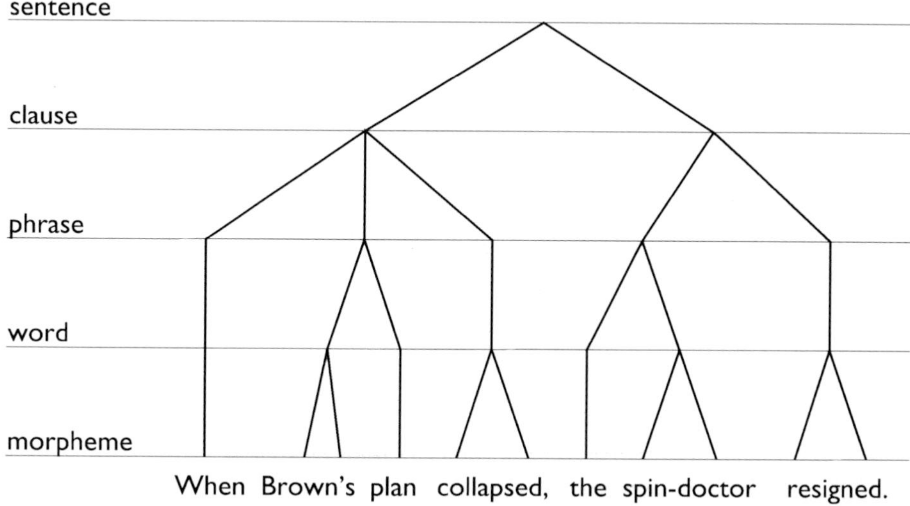

Fig. 4.1. Phrase structure of 'When Brown's plan collapsed, the spin-doctor resigned'.

So this tree claims that the *sentence* 'When Brown's plan collapsed, the spin-doctor resigned' consists of two *clauses* 'When Brown's plan collapsed' and 'the spin-doctor resigned'. The former clause has two main *phrases* 'Brown's plan' and 'collapsed'; the phrase 'Brown's plan' consists of two *words* 'Brown's' and 'plan'. The word 'Brown's' has two *morphemes* 'Brown' and ''s'; the word 'collapsed' has two morphemes 'collapse' and 'ed'. And so on for the other clause in the sentence. Grammatical punctuation is then one way of signalling the phrase structure of the sentence to the reader.

Morpheme punctuation

Starting at the bottom of the tree in Figure 4.1, the relations between morphemes can be shown through punctuation. One link is the apostrophe <'> in 'Brown's', which indicates that the final 's' is a singular possessive morpheme, thus distinguishing it from plural 'Browns' or plural possessive 'Browns' '. One issue with the apostrophe <'s> is its use in shop notices and small ads with ordinary plural nouns <taxi's>, known as the greengrocer's apostrophe. Some real-life examples are given in Text 1. Many more can be seen on websites such as *The Greengrocer's Apostrophe* (http://homepage.ntlworld.com/vivian.c/ApostGrocers.htm) and *The Golden Apostrophe Awards* (www.sharoncolon.com/). While Todd (1995) claimed the greengrocer's apostrophe occurred primarily after vowels as in 'tomato's', examples are now found after consonants 'hotel's' and 'dog's'. In fact, the <'s> is occasionally found for some plurals such as dates 'the 1990's', letters of the alphabet 'he got five A's', and words not normally found in the plural 'there were eight King Henry's'.

Text 1. Greengrocer's apostrophes, taken from street notices

CAPITAL TAXI'S
1 HOUR PHOTO'S
Burger's Chips Hot Dog's
Paper Boy's/Girls WANTED
Airport Hotel's from £23
NEW'S FOOD BOOZE
FRI. and SAT. night's
THE CURRY NIGHT'S

A second type of morpheme link is made by the hyphen <-> of 'spin-doctor', which connects 'spin' and 'doctor' together as one compound word. The problem with this compounding use of the hyphen is its arbitrariness. Should it be 'time table', 'time-table' or 'timetable'? The *OED* (1994) sources 'time-table' in 1820, 'time table' in 1838 and has no example of 'timetable' (except as a verb): 'timetable' is the only form in the *COBUILD* dictionary (1995). Similarly the *OED* has 'Time-Keeper' in 1686, 'timekeeper' in 1878, while *COBUILD* gives both spellings. The advice almost invariably given in manuals is that it is 'a matter of taste' (Todd 1995). A rule of thumb is that the longer the word has been in English the more likely it is to have lost its space and its hyphen: *OED* 'tea bag' 1898 becomes 'tea-bag' in 1936 and 'teabag' in 1977. Hyphens can be used to make a single compound word out of any number of words. The longest example in the *BNC* is 'oral-aggressive-anal-retentive-come-and-see-me-five-times-a-week-for-years-at-vast-expense-or-how-do-I-know-you're-really-committed' (Leech *et al.* 2002).

Other uses of the apostrophe and hyphen are discussed later.

Word punctuation

The separate words in the sentence:

When Brown's plan collapsed, the spin-doctor resigned.

can be immediately distinguished because they are separated by word spaces: a word is sometimes defined as a 'sequence of letters without any spaces' (Hurford 1994), that is, an orthographic word. Without the spaces, reading becomes extremely difficult for a modern reader. Word-processing jargon indeed calls a word space a 'character'. Though word spaces seem so natural that people are unaware of them as punctuation, they only became widespread from the eighth century AD, as we see in Chapter 6, and they are not used in Chinese character writing and in some alphabetic languages such as Inuktituit. They are also important to children's acquisition of spelling, as we shall see in Chapter 5, and are closely linked to theories of grammar developed in countries where spaces are used.

Spaces have led to problems with computer files. A space is simply another 'character' to a computer, rather than the absence of a character. In forms like e-mail addresses, they need to be underlined 'dave_cook@hotmail.com' or omitted 'lastminute.com' or 'natwestonline.com'.

Spaces are also sometimes omitted for literary effect. The speech of the character called the Sheepman in Hiroko Murakami's novel *Dance Dance Dance* is written without spaces in the English translation, made more comprehensible perhaps by the presence of ordinary punctuation marks: 'Youlostyourway. Yourconnectionscomeundone. Yougotconfused, thinkingyougotnoties. Butthere'swhereitalltiestogether'.

Phrase punctuation

Sometimes, though not in our specimen sentence, there is a need to separate elements within a phrase, chiefly with a comma. One use is lists:

> The Lucas family from Manningtree took first, second and third place.

There is variation about whether the final item with 'and' should have a preceding comma, particularly between the UK, where it is shunned, and North America, where it is recommended.

Another use of the comma is to separate initial elements from the rest of the sentence:

> Thankfully, he was not more seriously hurt.

This applies particularly to elements that have been 'fronted' to the beginning of the clause:

> God and my wife and the kids, they were the only things that got me through.

This may also happen to final elements whether words or phrases:

> . . . the British Crabbing Championships in Walberswick, near Southwold.

When such elements occur within the clause rather than at the beginning or end, they are usually delimited by a pair of commas:

> . . . but, hopefully, we will still be able to operate without going bust.

Text 2 illustrates how commas may be built-in to a highly complex text-sentence, 15 in all.

Text 2. Sentence from Adamson (2000) *The Tuscan Master*. London: Sceptre, 48.

> But now there were things that were not being talked of, a wall of silence being built around the unspoken sadnesses, silently, day by day, partitioning off parts of him, places that became the more taboo with time, building a wall that would become a part of them, taken for granted, hardly noticed at all, a wall that, once built, would be breachable only by the unthinkable, by assault and destruction; or it would never be breached at all, so that only a part of themselves was contiguous open plan, until they could no longer see each other whole, note the origins of act and word.

Clause punctuation

Another use of the comma is to separate subordinate clauses, in our example the initial subordinate clause 'When Brown's plan collapsed' from the main clause 'the spin-doctor resigned'. When the subordinate clause occurs within the sentence rather than at its beginning or end, two commas may mark it out:

> Abbas, who rode with the Honda Imps team for three years, was classed as senior and a skilled rider.

Use or non-use of such commas is sometimes meaningful, as in the old chestnut of the non-restrictive relative clause:

> My wife, who lives in New York, is called Sarah.

implying monogamy, versus the restrictive clause:

> My wife who lives in New York is called Sarah.

implying polygamy. Dashes can also be used for similar purposes, seen grammatically as 'apposition':

> Almost 500 readers took part in the vote – the first test of public opinion on the proposals – with 411 opposing the expansion plans and 88 in favour.

The box below gives the frequencies for the different uses of the comma, taken from a study of the *Wall Street Journal* by Bayraktar *et al.* (1998). Lists, sentence-initial elements and apposition add up to the majority of uses, followed by non-restrictive clauses; sentence-final elements, interrupters and quotations nevertheless each occur around 4% to 6% of the time.

Frequencies for comma distribution (%)	
Elements in a series (words, phrases, clauses, etc.)	20.3
Sentence-initial elements (words phrases, clauses, etc.)	20.2
Sentence-final elements (phrases, clauses)	5.0
Non-restrictive phrases or clauses	17.3
Appositives	26.1
Interrupters	6.6
Quotations	4.5

(Source: Bayraktar *et al.* 1998)

Sentence punctuation

Some punctuation marks proclaim that a sentence has ended, whether with a full stop <.> (known in the USA as a 'period'), exclamation mark <!> or question mark <?>, paired with an initial capital letter for the first word. Indeed, just as the unit of word is sometimes defined by the word spaces that surround it, a sentence can be defined as 'a stretch of language beginning with a capital letter and ending in a full stop' (Fries 1952: 9), which may be considerably more extensive than a typical spoken sentence, as seen below. The difference between these three marks shows crudely whether the sentence is a question 'John?', an exclamation or call 'John!' or an unmarked declarative statement 'John.'.

Thus the phrase structure of the sentence is largely indicated through its punctuation from morpheme up to sentence. Figure 4.2 links the punctuation marks roughly to the phrase structure tree of the sentence. Indeed it is possible to go one step higher and to look at the punctuation of the paragraph, shown either by extra spacing before the first line or by indenting the first line, but not, according to the manuals, by both.

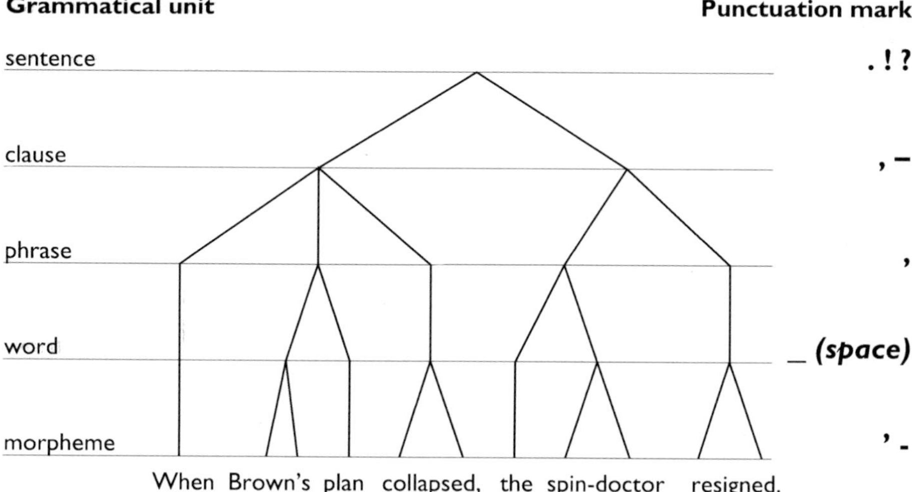

Fig. 4.2. Punctuation marks and grammatical units.

A commonly made distinction is between punctuation marks that divide elements of the sentence from punctuation marks that bring elements together. Thus, commas divide lists up into separate items:

> Italy, Spain, Greece and France are all members of the European Union.

And commas bring together words into a single element as well as, in a sense, separating the element from the rest:

> They had demonstrated, quite frankly, the wisdom of Jade but without her charm.

The two commas around 'quite frankly' show it is acting as an element as well as showing it is not part of the elements that come before and after it.

Punctuation marks for bringing words together therefore often come in pairs, as in the commas above, or in pairs of dashes:

> Former fireman Eric Southgate's mantra – 'Fireman Southgate is dead and buried, Eric Southgate lives on' – has helped him to rebuild his life.

or pairs of brackets:

> Persist until something (however little) is done . . .

At the beginning or end of the sentence, the outlying member of the pair is not then needed:

> In Suffolk, minor falls in the claimant count left the unemployment rate unchanged . . .

except in the case of pairs of brackets.

Text-sentence punctuation

The analyses of spoken and written language differ over what constitutes a sentence, as seen in Chapter 2. Most familiar definitions of the written sentence emphasize its grammatical or semantic completeness in some sense, not just the capital letter and full stop. The NASA handbook (McCaskill 1998), for example, says the full stop's 'primary purpose is to separate complete thoughts, . . . The key word here is *complete*; a period should be used only after a sentence complete with subject and predicate.'

How would such definitions apply to Text 3 below? This contains at least five sentence-like elements with subjects and predicates. Two are linked with 'but', as they might be in the spoken language. The rest, however, are linked with colons <:> or semi-colons <;>. The flow of ideas through the sentences is shown through punctuation. Or perhaps one should say *may* be shown, as this is not done in all styles of writing nor by all writers, but confined to certain genres of academic or literary writing. In other contexts the sentence could have been split into four or five separate sentences with full stops.

Text 3. Sentence from J.R. Tolkien (1954) *The Two Towers*. London: Allen & Unwin, 24.

> Before them in the West the world lay still, formless and grey; but even as they looked, the shadows of night melted, the colours of the waking earth returned: green flowed over the wide meads of Rohan; the white mists shimmered in the water-vales; and far off to the left, thirty leagues or more, blue and purple stood the White Mountains, rising into peaks of jet, tipped with glimmering snows, flushed with the rose of morning.

At this point we need to fall back on Nunberg's useful distinction between lexical sentences and text-sentences (Nunberg 1990), outlined in Chapter 2. Text-sentences may consist of more than one lexical sentence, as in the example above. Written English can combine an indefinite number of lexical sentences into a single text-sentence by using commas, dashes, semi-colons and colons. One reason for the subjective impression that writing is grammatically more complex than spoken language may be its use of extended text-sentences rather than 'complete' lexical sentences, typically taken from continuous prose rather than notices, e-mails and other written registers.

However, text-sentences may also fail to meet the classic 'completeness' definition for the lexical sentence, as in the small ad example in Chapter 2 and in the following dialogue sentences from the *Two Towers*:

On foot?
The horses!
Your bow, Legolas.
Why alive?
To Isengard!
Five nights ago.

The punctuation of text-sentences concerns which marks to use and how to combine them together. The *Two Towers* sentence in Text 3 above shows the hierarchy:

- colons are used for major divisions: '. . . the world lay still . . .: green flowed over the wide meads . . .'
- semi-colons for less major divisions: 'green flowed . . .; the white mists shimmered . . .'
- commas for minor divisions: 'the shadows of night melted, the colours of the waking earth returned . . .'.

Punctuation manuals expend much energy on the intricacies of this system. For 100 years their writers have been fighting against the trend in most registers to make text-sentences closer to lexical sentences and to get rid of colons and semi-colons – so-called 'light' punctuation. The *East Anglian* for instance uses the colon only for reporting speech:

> Chris Mole the Labour MP for Ipswich said: "There have been concerns for some time about . . ."

One variation in punctuation is whether to use a capital letter after the colon, preferred in American-style spelling, decried in British style, as shown in Text 3 above:

> . . . the colours of the waking earth returned: green flowed over the wide meads of Rohan; . . .

A distinctive use of the colon is to introduce an elaboration or enumeration of the main part of the sentence, called by Nunberg (1990) the 'colon-expansion'. Thus, the *Two Towers* sentence proclaims '. . . the colours of the waking earth returned', inserts a colon and then lists the colours 'green . . . white . . . blue and purple . . .'. This usage also occurs sporadically in the *Guardian*:

> the same imperfect triad of treatments that have been used for generations: chemotherapy, radiotherapy and, . . . surgery

A more dramatic use of the colon to introduce more specific information is seen in Churchill's epigraph to his book on the Second World War:

> In war: resolution. In defeat: defiance. In victory: magnanimity. In peace: goodwill.

Here the colon almost functions as a subject and verb: 'In war (we must have) resolution'.

Task 2. Reading aloud
Go back to your attempt at punctuating the two sentences in Task 1. Read your versions aloud; then read the versions in Text 2 and Text 3 aloud (if different from yours). Do you think the punctuation marks you inserted were based on how you read aloud or based on the grammar of the written sentence?

The semi-colon is therefore used to combine several lexical sentences into a single text-sentence without the connecting implications of the colon, as in the only *East Anglian* example:

> Now you see it; now you don't. Glass.

The *Guardian* also uses semi-colons sparingly, mostly in think-pieces such as editorials. A lexical sentence that has a main clause with a verb and a subject can be linked to a fellow lexical sentence with a semi-colon. Commas are reserved for subordinate clauses, phrases, etc., that do not meet the lexical sentence criteria, the exception being lexical sentences starting with 'and', 'but' and other co-ordinators:

> Alan Bloom is 95, but you'd never think it.

Reporting speech

Lastly, several punctuation marks combine to mark out elements of the text-sentence as being reports of speech. Both the *Guardian* and the *East Anglian* use a colon followed by double quotation marks before the reporting clause:

> Mr Jenkin said: "I'm really shocked by the news . . ."

And commas with double quotations for internal reporting clause:

> "I can't stand people who boast," she says, "but that night I was being really proud . . ."

According to the punctuation manuals, British style prefers single quotation marks and uses double quotation marks for quotations within quotations:

> 'The physiotherapist took one look at me and said: "You must be in agony" . . .'

rather than:

> "The physiotherapist took one look at me and said: 'You must be in agony' . . ."

though in fact the sentence appeared in the latter form in the *East Anglian*. The *Guardian*'s on-line style sheet recommends 'Use double quotes at start and end of quoted section, with single quotes for quoted words within that section' (www.guardian.co.uk/styleguide).

An interesting minor use of the single quotation mark is to separate writers from their own statements, by in a sense distancing themselves from the vagueness of the words they are forced to use:

> the reader whose educational background, like my own is more in the 'humanities' than in mathematics and 'science' . . .

These are known as 'apologetic quotation marks', and are particularly common in some academic texts.

Correspondence punctuation

Although punctuation has been treated here as a subsystem of the English writing system in its own right, historically it arose as an aid to reading aloud, as will be seen in Chapter 6. Punctuation marks have often been considered instructions for reading aloud aspects of the sentence that would not be transparent from the letters alone. Partly this has been interpreted as different lengths of spoken pause. A sentence-final marker indicates a longer pause in reading aloud than a comma, as punctuation manuals usually recommend – 'Well, basically, a comma means a slight pause in the sentence' (VanDyck 1996: 35) – with colons coming in between in length. Elaborate timing schemes have been devised for pauses at punctuation marks, the most famous being in Lowth's *A Short Introduction to English Grammar* in 1775 (*see* box below), though such schemes go back at least to Puttenham (1589) who recommended one pause for the comma, two for the colon or semi-colon, three for the full stop (cited in Partridge 1964: 187).

Pauses and punctuation

> The proportional quantity or time of the points, with reſpect to one another, is determined by the following general rule: The Period is a pauſe in quantity or duration double of the colon; the colon is double of the ſemi-colon; and the ſemicolon is double of the comma. So that they are in the ſame proportion to one another, as is the ſemibref, the minim, and the crotchet, and the quaver, in muſic.

(Source: Lowth R. (1775) *A Short Introduction to English Grammar*)

The choice of sentence-final punctuation marks may signal one of the possible sentence-final intonation patterns, say a falling tone for <.>, a declarative ‘He went on `Tuesday.’, a rise–fall for <!>, an exclamation ‘He went on ˆTuesday!’ or a low–rise tone for <?> for some types of question, ‘He went on ˏTuesday?’. Punctuation also conveys sentence-internal intonation patterns. Listing commas can correspond to low rising intonation, followed by a final fall. Keats’ phrase:

a sleep full of sweet dreams, and health, and quiet breathing.

is probably read as a succession of low rises on ‘dreams’ and ‘health’ followed by a fall on ‘breathing’. Danielewicz and Chafe (1985) indeed speak of ‘comma intonation’ and ‘period intonation’.

While punctuation separating clauses may well often correspond to possible tones and pauses, Halliday (1985) feels this association reflects only the statistical tendency for a clause to correspond to a tone-group (the phonological unit of intonation, usually containing a single tone) and obscures the speaker’s freedom to convey meaning through any length of tone-group they want. It is hard to imagine:

Friends, Romans, countrymen, lend me your ears;

as anything other than four tone-groups, using the sign </> to mark tone-group boundaries:

Friends/ Romans/ countrymen/ lend me your ears/

or:

red, white and blue

as anything but one tone-group:

/red, white and blue/

not:

/red/ white/ and blue/

Nevertheless in both cases the speaker has the freedom to choose unusual tone-groups to signal particular meanings.

The correspondences between punctuation and the non-phonemic aspects of phonology are hardly extensive. In a sense grammatical punctuation does not dictate how to read a text aloud so much as give clues to the meaning of the sentence so that the person reading aloud can assign tone-groups and other features to the text. The spoken correspondences of some aspects of punctuation are misleading. Word divisions for instance seldom correspond to anything in speech, except in fictional robots, Daleks, and computer-generated announcements in lifts and on Underground trains. Some elements of punctuation have no spoken correspondence, for instance capital letters and line-breaks in lists and in much poetry.

Nevertheless, Chafe (1988) insists that the main function of punctuation 'is to tell us something about a writer's intentions with regard to the prosody of that inner voice'. He argues that commas in particular are inherently flexible in showing the divisions into tone-groups and indicating non-rising intonation. Part of his evidence comes from the tone-groups that people used when reading aloud a set of passages and the punctuation marks they inserted into unpunctuated versions of the same passages. Almost invariably there were more tone-groups when reading aloud than punctuation groups; yet they divided the written passage into about the same number of punctuation groups. His explanation is that written English may show tone-groups in other ways than through punctuation: 'perhaps learning to deal with written language involves learning to give prosodic interpretations to specific syntactic patterns, even when punctuation is not involved'.

Occasionally there are conflicts between grammatical and correspondence punctuation. Manuals are highly prescriptive about commas between the subject phrase and verb phrase, as in, say, the commas after the subject in this sentence from the *East Anglian*:

> However, Mrs Chapman, said the events had been like "getting stuck between two gangs of fighting kids . . .".

'a comma between subject and verb – for me the most offensive of all punctuation error' (Robinson 1980) and 'the rule is clear enough and is strictly observed in print' (Quirk *et al.* 1972: 1619). Yet this corresponds to the spoken usage of television newsreaders who often pause at this point or use a separate tone-group (Brown 1977). In Chafe's reading aloud test (Chafe 1988), 85% of the people put a tone-group break between subject and verb in the sentence:

> The car ahead with the 'I brake for squirrels' bumper sticker / really does brake for squirrels.

perhaps because of the length of the subject. This type of comma use is felt to introduce an unnecessary break in the sentence (Carey 1960: 45), though indicating the main division in the main sentence seems little different from indicating the division into clauses or phrases. Indeed, early seventeenth century grammarians suggested putting commas not only between the subject and verb, reflected in Shakespearean examples such as:

> To moue, is to ſtir: and to be valiant, is to ſtand. (*Romeo and Juliet*, I, i, First Folio)

but also between verb and object (reported in Partridge 1953).

Other uses

Two other uses of punctuation need to be mentioned, which do not fit tidily into the discussion above.

Apostrophe for 'contraction'

Most manuals claim that the apostrophe <'> is used to show that something has been omitted from the word, that is, that there are one or more letters in the written form that have no correspondence in the spoken form. Thus for dates one might have 'the '90s' or for 'Southampton' 'S'ton'. The omission often took place in a previous period of English 'seven o'clock' or 'will o'the wisp'. This sometimes overlaps with abbreviation shown by a full stop, 'reg.' 'registration' and 'exp.' 'experienced'. The trend in British style spelling for some time has been to omit the full stop; the *Guardian* favours 'Mr TS Eliot', 'BBC', 'mph' and 'US', not 'Mr. T. S. Eliot', 'B.B.C.', 'm.p.h.' and 'U.S.' (www.guardian.co.uk/styleguide).

Contraction seems an inappropriate term if the 'full' form does not exist – 'five of the clock'? An interesting example is the form ''em' for 'them', first recorded in the *OED* in 1380, which reflects omission of <h> from 'hem', an early form of 'them'. So what can one say is omitted today? Several words have shifted from being contracted forms to having no apostrophe: who nowadays writes ''bus' as short for 'omnibus'? Some short forms have overtaken their progenitors in frequency: ''flu' occurs 557 times in the *BNC*, 'influenza' 137: the *COBUILD Dictionary* in fact gives 'flu' without the apostrophe; ''cos' occurs 16,247 times in the *BNC* compared with 85,183 for 'because'; *COBUILD* states 'it is also spelled "'cos"'. An interesting example is ''til' as a contraction of 'until', though 'till' is a distinct word from 'until', not a contraction.

The most common group of words containing contraction apostrophes is function words, in particular auxiliaries and negatives. Function words frequently have more than one spoken form, typically 'strong', as in the auxiliary 'have' /hæv/, versus weak as in ''ve' /əv/ or /v/ and in the negative 'not' /nɒt/ versus 'n't' /nt/. Some registers of writing reflect this in the spelling by an apostrophe: 'can't', 'won't', ''d', ''s' and so on. There seems no more reason to say that these forms have omitted letters than to say the spoken forms have omitted phonemes. Written forms of many function words can be strong or weak, 'will' /wɪl/ versus ''ll' /l/. The weak forms tend to be used in less formal styles of writing, particularly when reporting speech:

> 'It's terrible . . .'

Chapter 7 will look at some of the uses of the apostrophe for showing non-standard speech, which may sometimes constitute contraction in a sense – ''Allo, 'Allo' and 'rock 'n' roll'.

Hyphens for line-breaks

Except for handwriting, most forms of writing require the lines on the page should appear to be the same length, as will be seen below. So far as punctuation is concerned, this amounts to decisions about how to break up words so that they can be divided over two lines. Most accounts of line-breaks come from manuals since the problem is most acute for professional printers. The developing awareness of this issue in modern writing is shown by its apparent lack of mention in the early twentieth century manual *A Dictionary of Modern English Usage* (Fowler 1926) and its extensive treatment in the late twentieth century book *The New Fowler's Modern English Usage* (Burchfield 1996).

The box below gives a neutral account of hyphenation by a book designer, Robert Bringhurst (1992). His rules chiefly concern letters on the page: a designer does not want odd-looking ends or beginnings of lines with too few letters 'a-broad' or 'plac-e' (rule 1) or paragraphs ending in only a few letters (rule 2); and does not want the page to look ugly or be difficult to read through having too many lines ending in hyphens (rule 3). Rule 4 is a special plea not to hyphenate proper names. Rule 5 that one should 'Hyphenate according to the conventions of the language' is the crux: what *are* the conventions of the language? The omitted rules 6–9 are technical. Rule 10 is a reminder that the overall aim of all this is to convey the meaning of the text.

Traditional 'printing craft rules' for hyphenating

1. At hyphenated line-ends, leave at least two characters behind and take three forward.
2. Avoid leaving the stub-end of a hyphenated word, or any word shorter than four letters, as the last line of a paragraph.
3. Avoid more than three consecutive hyphenated lines.
4. Hyphenate proper names only as a last resort unless they occur with the frequency of common nouns.
5. Hyphenate according to the conventions of the language.

. . .

10. Abandon any and all rules of hyphenation and pagination that fail to serve the needs of the text.

(Source: Bringhurst, R. (1992), *The Elements of Typographic Style*.)

Most manuals give a few tips on hyphenation and then urge the reader 'Consult a dictionary for syllabification' (NASA), 'check usage in an up-to-date dictionary' (Todd 1995) or 'consult a dictionary' (Trask 1997); writers would, however, seek for information about hyphenation in vain in most dictionaries whether the *OED* or the

COBUILD dictionaries. The assumption that the dictionary knows best is a breach of the usual linguists' claim that dictionaries follow usage rather than prescribe it. When I objected to the fact that the third edition of one of my books had 72 line-break hyphens in the first chapter compared with one in the second edition, I was told that they all conformed to the recommendations in *Collins*. Text 5 gives some examples of strange hyphenation.

Text 5. Odd-looking hyphens

bre-akfast mans-laughter fin-ding unself-conscious rein-stall ch-anges the-rapist male-volence pos-twar fru-ity berib-boned spi-noff pain-staking rear-ranged ever-yone da-ily se-arched af-ternoon

(Sources: mainly McIntosh 1990)

For most writers these days the question is why bother? A word-processing program will supply hyphens adequate to most needs; higher precision programs like HYPHENOLOGIST (McIntosh 1990) will take care of more specialist uses. People who are concerned about hyphens seem not to worry about other aspects of layout, such as the consequences of *not* hyphenating for spacing, demonstrated in Text 6 on page 117 below.

As usual the tension is between basing the decision on grammatical or sound correspondence criteria. Grammatical criteria here mean either the morphology of the word – 'transformational' may be split into 'trans-form-ation-al' because of its morphological structure – or etymology – 'transport' may be split into 'trans-port' rather than 'tran-sport' because 'trans' and 'port' can be traced back to their Latin roots. Some examples of alternatives are seen in the box below.

Hyphens by 'roots' and by 'sounds' (based on McIntosh 1990)

Roots	*Sounds*
pho-to-grapher	pho-tog-ra-pher
omni-potent	om-nip-o-tent
poly-gam-ist	po-lyg-a-mist

According to Quirk *et al.* (1972) 'BrE [British English] practice tends to favour morphological breaks (struct-ure), AmE [American English] syllable (struc-ture)', though McIntosh (1990) insists this 'is difficult to interpret' and points out that the British *Longman Dictionary of Contemporary English* (1978) gives 'struc-ture' despite Quirk being one of its advisors. Thus British English would tend to have 'triumph-ant', American English 'trium-phant'; British 'know-ledge', American 'knowl-edge'.

Table 4.1 provides a summary of English punctuation.

Table 4.1 English punctuation

Grammatical punctuation	
morphemes	<’> ‘Milton’s Paradise Lost’ **<->** ‘sensori-motor’
words	spaces: ‘God bless the child that’s got its own’/ ‘Godblessthechildthat’sgotitsown’
phrases	<,> ‘Policemen, like red squirrels, must be protected.’
clauses	<,> ‘An Englishman, even if he is alone, forms an orderly queue of one’. **<–>** ‘Federal work teams – split by race – finish ratchetting together a grandstand.’ **<:>** ‘Man proposes: God disposes.’
text-sentences	Capitals plus <.> ‘War is peace. Freedom is slavery. Ignorance is strength.’
Correspondence punctuation	
length of pauses (according to Lowth 1775)	comma: single pause semi-colon: 2 × pause colon: 4 × pause full stop: 8 × pause
tone-groups	clause-separating punctuation may conform to spoken tone-groups: ‘Friends, Romans, countrymen, lend me your ears.’
inner voice	Punctuation may show the ‘prosody of the inner voice’ (Chafe 1988)
‘contraction’	<’> sometimes corresponds to a weak spoken form: ‘he’s’, ‘can’t’, ‘’em’
‘line-breaks’	
words are broken by hyphens at line-breaks according to morphemes ‘trans-port’ or syllables ‘tran-sport’	

4.2 THE TYPOGRAPHY OF ENGLISH

Focusing questions

- Which fonts do you use on your computer? Why?
- When do *you* underline words?

Key words

typography: 'the structuring and arranging of visual language' (Baines and Haslam 2002: 1).
intrinsic and extrinsic typography: intrinsic typography refers to the actual letter shapes, extrinsic typography to their arrangement on the page or screen (Twyman 1982).
roman, italics, capitals: 'the three alphabets in common use for English people' (Gill 1931: 59), with different letters, lines, etc.
font: strictly a complete set of type for printing; nowadays mostly it refers to a particular design for the whole set of characters available through a computer keyboard.
serif letters: have small cross-strokes (serifs) and variable line width:

<Fred specialized in the job of making very quaint wax toys.>

(sentence with all the letters of the alphabet).
sans-serif letters: have no cross-strokes and usually constant line width:

<Fred specialized in the job of making very quaint wax toys.>

justification: text on a page may be lined up to the left ('left-justified' or 'ragged right'), or to both left and right ('fully justified').

Typography is used here in the sense of 'the structuring and arranging of visual language' (Baines and Haslam 2002: 1). Its domain is thus far wider than the design of typefaces and fonts, and covers any medium of presentation, whether a letter, a poster, a book or a web page. Some aspects of typography apply to many languages; some are specific to English.

A distinction needs to be made between *intrinsic* and *extrinsic* aspects of typography (Twyman 1982). Intrinsic typography concerns the actual shapes on the page, whether the forms of the letters, such as capitals and lower-case, the fonts used or the size of the letters. Extrinsic typography is anything to do with the arrangement of these on the page or screen, such as the space between lines, the formatting of paragraphs and the layout of the page. This section concentrates more on intrinsic elements that relate fairly directly to meaning rather than on extrinsic elements that relate to overall appearance.

Like the last section, much of this section concerns text written by keyboard rather than text written with a pen. So it again largely draws on manuals of book design or typography rather than description of what people actually do. Typography is subject to constant technological change and to movements of fashion. One lesson from the manuals is the extent to which our experience of the printed page has been designed for us by particular individuals. Yet people know more about clothes designers and chefs whose wares they will never sample than about typographers whose work they use every day, say Stanley Morison without whom there would be no Times New Roman on their PC or Matthew Carter, designer of Verdana for the web and many other current fonts.

Letter forms

Underlining

In the pre-computer era almost the only way for writers to mark words as special was to underline them with a pen or on a typewriter:

The best rosé comes from Chile.

This underlining in part corresponds to the sentence stress of spoken language, that is, 'rosé' would have a fall–rise nuclear tone showing a contrast with 'beer' or some other previously discussed noun. Underlining could be used both in handwriting and in typing, although the latter involved the cumbersome task of going back to underline letters that had already been typed.

Computer keyboards now allow ordinary people the wealth of resources for drawing attention to words that already existed for professional typesetters, for example small capitals and italics, as well as underlining. Many keyboard users are not, however, aware that printers try to avoid underlining because it cuts across the descenders of letters such as <g> and <y> which go below the line of print, and thus makes them less legible, as seen in:

'suggesting'/'suggesting' 'deputy'/'deputy' 'playing'/'playing' 'quip'/'quip' 'pig'/'pig'

Nor do printers like underlining capitals, as often happens in everyday notices:

NO ENTRY CAR FOR SALE

Crystal (2001) suggests that spam e-mails can be detected by looking for subject lines that are all in capitals. For instance the latest specimen of the million-dollar bank account scam to arrive on my computer is headed:

SINCERE ASSISTANCE NEEDED

Italics

Italic letters started as a different alphabet used for handwriting, notably by Queen Elizabeth I, and only became a partner with the roman alphabet in print in the sixteenth century. To the purist an italic alphabet is not just a slanting, slightly narrower, version of a roman alphabet but has specially designed letters, for example the roman <a> versus the italic <*a*> – sometimes a problem for children in the early stages of learning to read and write. Bringhurst (1992) says 'flow, not slope, is what really differentiates the two', italics preserving the lines that a pen would make.

Like underlining, italics are primarily utilized for making some words stand out from the rest.

This *is* the right solution.

often corresponding to the main sentence stress. Sometimes they are used for book titles:

William Faulkner wrote *Sanctuary* and *The Sound and the Fury*.

or for examples:

Now is the winter of our discontent made glorious summer shows inversion of subject and verb following initial *now*.

or for foreign words or phrases (though not in the newspapers):

He was *inter alia* a civil servant in Burma and a shop assistant in a book shop.

Other ways of distinguishing headings from text are to highlight them with italics, bold face or small capital letters:

The Life of David Gale
The Life of David Gale
THE LIFE OF DAVID GALE

Nowadays italics are rarely used for long passages or whole books, as they are considered to be less legible. They are sometimes used for poetry and for stage directions in plays:

Enter Viola and Malvolio, at several doors.

The uses of italics in the *East Anglian* are for the names of publications such as their own '*East Anglian Daily Times*' and for names of ships '*Predator*', '*Misprint*' and '*Jasba*'.

Capital letters

Despite sources such as McArthur (1992: 188) describing capitals as 'large' and lower-case as 'small', capital letters differ in shape and function from lower-case letters, not necessarily in size. A 'small' <A> is still a capital letter, a 'large' <a> is still lower-case. Hence typographers often speak of English having three alphabets; capitals, lower-case and italic (Gill 1931). Incidentally the terms 'upper' and 'lower' case refer to the boxes or 'cases' in which printers kept their supplies of letters – typically 54 characters in the lower case, 98 characters in the upper.

The shapes of many capital letters are quite different from their lower-case counterparts, even if they are historically related, as seen in <A/a>, <B/b>, <D/d>, <E/e>, <G/g>, <Q/q> and <R/r>. Capitals usually have a squared-off shape, which adversely affects their legibility: hence direction signs on roads in England deliberately mix upper- and lower-case rather than being all capitals. Only 'amateur' notices spell everything in capital letters, as seen in the 'Café Open' notice in Task 4.

Task 4. Café notices

What characteristics of hand-written street notices can you see in these examples?

TODAY SPECIAL
2 Sousege
Mashed pot
onions peas

CAFE
OPEN
TEA, COFFEE.
FISH . CHIPS
HOT DOGS
BURGERS.

The systematic difference between capitals and lower-case letters is used for a variety of reasons in English unconnected with spoken correspondences. Initial capitals on a word may show:

- *Proper nouns and adjectives.* Proper nouns, including places, countries, brand-names, etc., have an initial capital: 'London', 'Linda McCracken', 'Microsoft', as do adjectives for nationalities or groups, 'French wine' and 'Romantic poets'. Articles too have a capital when part of the name: 'The Hague' and 'The Andes'. Spelling the name of a group with a capital letter may then confer some recognition of its existence. The Gypsy Council asks people to 'show us the same respect as other ethnic groups by spelling our name with a capital G not a small g'.
- *Content words in book titles.* One convention for citing titles of books, films, etc., is to capitalize the initial letters of content words, but not function words: 'The Taming of the Shrew', 'The Education (National Curriculum) Attainment Targets and Programmes of Study in English'.
- *Grammatical divisions.* Part 4.1 dealt with initial capitals used in grammatical punctuation for text-sentences or after colons in American English. In addition, capital letters are used to start reported speech and at the beginning of lines in some poetry:

  The trees are in their autumn beauty,
  The woodland paths are dry,
  Under the October twilight the water
  Mirrors a still sky;

- *A short list of idiosyncratic words.* An eclectic list of English words has an initial capital: months 'May', days of the week 'Tuesday', 'God' and references to God 'in His name', the first person singular pronoun 'I' and nationality adjectives 'French'.

Using capitals for all the letters in a word or series of words may show among other things:

- *Acronyms*: where letters stand for whole words: 'NFU (National Farmers' Union)', 'TBA' (to be advised), 'VIP'.

- *Speech of unusual characters*. The character of Death in Terry Pratchett's *Discworld* novels always speaks in capitals: 'A HUNDRED YEARS CAN PASS LIKE INFINITY'.
- *Headings*. The front page headline in the *East Anglian* is in capitals:

  RIDER TRAGEDY

  though this is not used in other headlines in this paper or in the *Guardian*.
- *Opening of texts*. The *East Anglian* starts each news story with one word in capitals, two words if the first is an article:

  A WESTERN Ukrainian city began two days of official mourning . . .

Capital letters for continuous text have often been condemned in discussions of e-mails, as we shall see in Chapter 7. Early computers used to be happier using only capital letters. The convention in some novels is still that computers use capitals, for example Columbus, the computer cab in *Pollen* (Noon 1995):

GLAD TO HAVE YOU ON-LINE, DRIVER.

This is known in net jargon as 'shouting'.

Word-medial capitals are found in:

- *Trade names*. During the 1990s there was a fashion for companies to combine several names in one without hyphens, thus having word-medial capital letters: 'FarrVintners', 'GlaxoSmithKline', 'BSkyB', 'NatWest'. This topic will recur in Chapter 7. Some proper names also have medial capitals, such as 'MacWhinney', 'DeFrancis' and 'VanPatten'.

The conventions for capitals in the English writing system differ to some extent from those in other languages. Most non-Roman writing systems, such as Hebrew, Arabic, Urdu and Burmese, do not have capital letters. While the first-person pronoun 'I' has a capital in English, this is used for the second-person plural 'polite' 'you' form in other languages, for example German 'Sie' and Italian 'Lei', thus leading to suspicions from speakers of other languages that English speakers are egocentric. In German the nouns in the sentence are marked out by initial capitals:

Zum Frühstuck gibt es Kaffee, Tee oder Kakao nach Wahl.
(for breakfast there's coffee, tea or cocoa by choice)

as sometimes happened in English before the nineteenth century. Capitals are not used to start text-sentences in written Inuit. The choice of capitals versus lower-case is therefore in part language specific; in French for example 'un français élégant' (elegant French) has a different meaning from 'un Français élégant' (an elegant Frenchman).

Fonts and typefaces

Most people have little choice about their style of handwriting, relying on whatever they were taught in primary school, as Sassoon (1999) discusses. At best some of us can vary between an illegible scribble and a sloppy italic for public writing, say on whiteboards.

Thanks to the invention of Postscript and Truetype fonts, anybody with a computer now has many letter-forms at their disposal. The description of fonts is a vast, technical area that can only be touched on here. For those interested, *Printing Type Designs* (Glen 2001) gives a readable account of different fonts. *Type and Typography* (Baines and Haslam 2002) presents a concise outline of type classification based on Dixon (2001), which uses three main dimensions:

- *source*, that is to say, the overall historical tradition that the font belongs to, for example handwriting or roman
- *formal attributes*, the details of the font's construction, such as shape, weight or decoration
- *patterns*, such as broken letters or copperplate.

The box below shows some of the varieties of fonts in their computerized forms with their approximate date and the name of the designer (sometimes open to dispute), using the same line from Marvell. A main distinction is between serif and sans-serif fonts. Serif letters have small cross-strokes at their stems: <H> for instance has pairs of serifs at the tops and bottoms of the two vertical lines: a sans-serif <H> has no such cross-strokes. Serif letters also vary the thickness of the line, seen in <B>, compared with the even thickness of most sans-serif letters, as in <B>. These features are derived from the technology of particular times (Jackson 1981), serifs from the cutting of capitals with chisels, and from the 'finishing strokes' for letters produced by a pen, varying line thickness from the behaviour of broad-nibbed pens, as will be seen in Chapter 6.

Variations in computer fonts

Serif fonts

Bodoni (Giambattista Bodoni 1788): Had we but world enough and
Garamond (Claude Garamond 16th Century): Had we but world enough
Baskerville (John Baskerville 1752) Had we but world enough and
Century Schoolbook (Linn Benton 1895): Had we but world
Times New Roman (Stanley Morison 1931): Had we but world enough

Sans-serif fonts

Arial (Robin Nicholas and Patricia Saunders, no date): Had we but
Futura (Paul Renner 1928): Had we but world enough and time, This
Gill Sans (Eric Gill 1929): Had we but world enough and time, This
Univers (Adrian Frutiger 1957): Had we but world enough and
Verdana (Matthew Carter 1996): Had we but world enough

Calligraphic fonts

Mistral (Roger Excoffon 1956): Had we but world enough and time, This coyness, lady,
Zapf-Chancery (Herman Zapf 1979): Had we but world enough and time, This

Task 5. Legibility and preference

Read these two sections of a longer text and decide (a) which you find most legible and (b) which you would prefer to read for a short passage, which for a full-length book.

1 In one way or another most people talk about the supernatural. In its most common form this is simply a matter of superstition: what actions do we think are lucky or unlucky? In England for instance it is lucky for a black cat to cross your path.

2 A more serious form of the supernatural is the poltergeist – an invisible being that is supposed to throw objects and furniture around. Strangely enough most poltergeists have manifested themselves when a young child is living in the house.

Text 1 is in a standard modern serif font, Times New Roman, Text 2 in a standard modern sans-serif font, Univers; both are in 12 point.

The early twentieth century identified the modern age with the use of sans-serif fonts. In England the first sans-serif font was designed by Edward Johnston for the London Underground in 1916, a version of which is still used today; this was used primarily for signs rather than printed books. Sans-serif fonts became as much part of modernity in Europe as the Bauhaus and Le Corbusier; they were advocated for virtually all situations – 'sanserif is absolutely and always better' (Tschichold 1928: 74).

As the box above ('Variations in computer fonts') shows, many serif fonts are based on those invented in the classic early days of printing, or even earlier. Times New Roman (1931) for instance refers back to the column erected in Rome to celebrate Trajan's victory in AD 114.

However, the arguments in favour of sans-serif letters had not taken account of how the human eye perceives letters in reading. The lack of variation and redundancy of sans-serif letters usually makes them more difficult to read than serifs in continuous texts, as reported in experiments by Tinker (1963). I can vouch for this from the trying experience of examining a PhD dissertation produced entirely in a sans-serif font. The box below compares some fonts used on web pages, based on experiments by Bernard *et al.* (2001). The actual reading time shows little variation between the serif fonts (Times New Roman and Century) and sans-serif fonts (Arial and Verdana). When asked to rate legibility, the top-ranked of the four was Verdana, a sans-serif font that was specially designed for screen display by Matthew Carter in 1996; the lowest-ranked was Times New Roman, a serif font designed for *The Times* newspaper in 1931.

Comparison of on-screen computer fonts

	Reading time (s)	Perceived legibility (1–6)	Overall preference
Arial	290	4.7	1
Verdana	285	4.9	2
Century	285	4.4	3
Times NR	270	4.8	4

(Source: Bernard *et al.* (2001)

Overall preference went to Arial, presumably because of its familiar presence as the standard sans-serif font on personal computers. The usefulness of fonts is governed by a host of factors, not just the serif versus sans-serif debate, particularly, as we have seen, by different forms of display, whether on a screen or on a printed page.

It has become rare to see sans-serifs fonts used for long connected tests, though occasional novels buck the trend, for example *Pollen* (Noon 1995). Tschichold argued in 1928 that a well-designed sans-serif font is just as legible as a serif one, as the sans-serif text of the modern translation of his book shows very well. He claimed in 1967 (cited in Tschichold 1991: xii) 'Univers . . . is one of the best sanserifs, and is what I dreamed of in 1928'.

The box below compares the use of serif and sans-serif fonts in the *East Anglian* and the *Guardian*. A serif font is used for continuous text longer than a sentence and for most headlines. A sans-serif font is used for short pieces of language, such as running headings (sometimes 'reversed', that is, white letters on black or coloured background) and by-lines for articles. Its most prevalent use is, however, for displaying lists, charts, sports results, etc., set in small sizes, presumably for legibility reasons – telephone directories provide a good example of sans-serif fonts designed to be read in very small sizes. The main difference between the two newspapers is in the *Guardian*'s visual distinction between news pages (sans-serif headlines and interspersed headings) and comments pages (serif headlines and interspersed headings). Both papers are using a system of considerable complexity for choosing serif or sans-serif fonts, with doubtless many more ramifications.

Newspaper use of serif and sans-serif fonts

Serif	Sans-serif
continuous text (G, EADT)	headlines on news pages (G)
all headlines (EADT)	running identification head (EADT)
headlines on comment pages (G)	topic heading (reversed) (EADT, G)
running identification head (G)	interspersed headings (EADT, G: news)
interspersed headings (G: comments)	quick crossword (G)
headings (G: editorials, letters, etc.)	by-lines identifying writers (EADT, G)
crossword (G, EADT)	charts/lists/results, etc. (tiny) (EADT, G)

EADT = *East Anglian Daily Times*; G = *Guardian*.

One could speculate about the general motivations for choice of serif and sans-serif fonts. Morison (1968) believed that 'seriffed letters were considered more suitable for a revered text than unseriffed ones'. The *Guardian*'s use of serifs in comments page headings presumably means 'You should read this carefully; it's not ephemeral news'. On the other hand sans-serif fonts in print seem to have lost their appeal to modernity. They look even more dated than the traditionally based serifs in common use, which often have histories going back centuries.

Other choice of fonts go outside the scope of this book. It would be interesting to examine the use of fonts with particular text genres, for instance In Memoriam versus **BOOT SALE TODAY** versus *Invitation*.

Lines

A factor in extrinsic typography is the lines on the page. A key design issue is justification – whether lines should align to the left of the page (known as 'left justification' or 'ragged right') or to both sides ('full justification'). Left justification is based on the movement of the eye from the end of each line back to the left side of the page. Locating the next line is helped by having line beginnings aligned vertically at the left of the page, whereas an uneven left margin would make the text hard to read smoothly.

The convention for virtually all book production is full justification to both sides of the page, leading to a neat look. In the *East Anglian* the main text of most news reports is fully justified; some shorter texts under photographs are left-justified, ragged right, as are some shorter news items in a series of columns headed 'Briefing', readers' letters, comment articles by columnists and some sports news. The *Guardian* also has full justification overall, but left justification for some articles beneath photos, short items headed 'in brief' and all the comments pages including editorials, reviews and letters. Again, both papers have fairly complex schemes for distinguishing certain kinds of text.

When full justification is used, the problem is how words fit on to the line, particularly critical with short lines, as in columns. One solution is to redistribute the white space on the line. Formerly, printers handled this by varying the space between the actual letters in subtle ways so that a short line could be invisibly padded out to size, to the extent that some believe that the variation in spelling of a word reflected the need for fewer or extra letters to pad out or reduce the line. Computer programs, however, tend to vary only the amount of space between the words, producing effects like those seen in the box below, where the computer has over-compensated to get full justification. When this effect stretches for several lines, it yields 'rivers of white', a distracting element on a page. The solution is either to fiddle tediously with the placement of the line-break hyphens or to be content with left justification and 'ragged right'.

Text 6. Spaces and rivers of white in newspapers

An East Anglian Ambulance Trust spokesman said the car had rolled into a field . . .

Yet defending Commonwealth champion, Jo Wise was unable to shrug off . . .

'I have worked on my fitness with Simon Thadani. Sometimes when you come back . . .

'Its looking better. But whether they lose any more lives or not . . .

Web pages introduce a new set of conventions for handling space and line-divisions since the writer has no idea what size screen the user might be employing or how they have set the default for font and size, etc. Web pages also employ a variety of ways of highlighting and presenting text through blinking or moving characters and the use of colour.

It is by no means certain that full justification is an asset. However much a single vertical line helps reading at the left side of the page for physical reasons, there is no need for one at the right as the eye is reading from left to right and simply stops whenever it meets the end of the line. Full justification is found in most modern books and its popularity may simply be that this is what readers expect to see in a book. Even this slender support was undermined in a study that found readers preferring ragged right (Macdonald-Ross and Waller 1975).

Hartley and Burnhill (1971) argue that, since space is a character like any other, a single space < > should not be stretched to <   > any more than a single letter <o> should be stretched to <ooo>. These authors went on to conduct a series of experiments with different types of line-breaks to show that left-justified text 'can be quite markedly manipulated without affecting reading speed or comprehension'. By implication, people should not be too concerned about various ways of hyphening for line-breaks as they will not make an appreciable difference to the reader.

This chapter has described some of the conventions of printed English that are mostly below the consciousness of the average reader. Yet, as soon as people start to write, they have to make decisions about them. Fortunately for many of us the decision is taken out of our hands by the defaults of a word-processing package, which may provide us with everything from an automatic capital for a sentence to a suitable font. Table 4.2 provides a summary of typography in English.

Table 4.2 Typography in English

Letters	
underlining: that gong-tormented sea	for emphasis, quotations, headings, etc.
italics: *that gong-tormented sea*	
small caps: THAT GONG-TORMENTED SEA	
bold: **that gong-tormented sea**	
capitals: THAT GONG-TORMENTED SEA	to mark grammar, special words, abbreviations, etc.
Fonts	
serif (small cross-strokes): that gong-tormented sea	used in most continuous texts and headlines
sans-serif: that gong-tormented sea	used for short texts, some headlines, notices, display, etc.
Lines	
justification	usually in print 'fully justified', both right and left, sometimes 'ragged right' in non-printed texts

Task 6. Text management

Punctuate these two texts and then decide the appropriate typography, one for a book, one for an advertisement.

1 Abbey Road (01483) 256978 226 Hills Road Norwich all new computers include five year warranty new and second user laptops second user desktops trade in your old computer repairs to most computer equipment inc laptops upgrades www.abbeyroad.com free after sales service

2 these faces four score thousand of them tilt up to seek hers out Easters forgetting bulbs seeking the feeble sun those who until this afternoon were sunk in hopeless hope too many of them swarming the shores of Jordan to get over in one go their ranks carry on swelling even as she traces their farthest edge in the convex mirror of 75000 pairs of eyes she sees herself dwarfed under monstrous columns a small dark suppliant between the knees of a white stone giant

Possible answers are given at the end of the chapter

DISCUSSION TOPICS

1 Is all punctuation really based on sounds?
2 How seriously do you think that 'mistakes' like 'hamburger's', 'it's beauty' and 'mans-laughter' should be taken?
3 To what extent have the extra facilities provided by word-processing programs such as fonts, colours, etc., actually made documents easier to read and better to look at?
4 Is the punctuation used by novelists for text-sentences relevant to the practical needs of ordinary writers of English?
5 Is it correct to say apostrophes are used for contraction?
6 On what occasions would you use a sans-serif font, all capital letters, italics, or full justification?
7 To what extent does typography matter for everyday users of word-processing?
8 How would you present an essay (a) for maximum legibility (b) for maximum elegance?

ANSWERS TO TASKS

Task 6. Text management

1 Based on an *East Anglian Daily Times* ad.

ABBEY ROAD
(01483) 256978
226 Hills Road, Norwich
All new computers include five year warranty
New and second user laptops
Second user desktops
Trade in your old computer
Repairs to most computer equipment inc laptops.
Upgrades
www.abbeyroad.com
Free after sales service

2 Text from Powers, R. (2003) *The Time of our Singing*, 46, reset:

> These faces – four score thousand of them – tilt up to seek hers out, Easter's forgetting bulbs seeking the feeble sun. Those who until this afternoon were sunk in hopeless hope: too many of them, swarming the shores of Jordan, to get over in one go. Their ranks carry on swelling, even as she traces their farthest edge. In the convex mirror of 75,000 pairs of eyes she sees herself, dwarfed under monstrous columns, a small dark suppliant between the knees of a white stone giant.

FURTHER READING

- Nunberg, G. (1990) *Linguistics of Punctuation*. Stanford, CA: CSLI. Perhaps the only serious linguistic approach to punctuation for those interested in generative grammar.
- McIntosh, R. (1990) *Hyphenation*. Halifax: Hyphen House. A delightful little book.
- Baines, P. and Haslam, A. (2002) *Type and Typography*. London: Laurence King. Authoritative, comprehensible and up-to-date.
- Bringhurst, R. (1992) *The Elements of Typographic Style*. Vancouver: Hartley & Marks. A clear account of the area.
- Tschichold, J. (1928) *The New Typography*, University of California Press edition, 1998. Classic account of the modernist approach to typography, partly disavowed in his later writings.

5 Learning the English writing system

INTRODUCTION

When children and adults learn the English writing system, they are essentially faced with all the complexities of English detailed in the previous chapters. To recap, among many other things they have to learn to use:

- the phonological route for relating letters and sounds, so that they can link written <bus> to spoken /bʌs/ and vice versa
- the lexical route to deal with individual words and meanings, so that they can link <does> with /dʌz/
- the forms and functions of written language, so that they can use the appropriate words and grammar for, say, writing an e-mail rather than making a phone-call
- the orthographic regularities and lexical spelling that distinguish content and function words ('in'/'inn'), that divide English into three spelling systems ('mock', 'baroque', 'amok'), and that show the underlying form of the word ('sign'/'signature')
- the punctuation marks that show different structural relationships in the sentence ('John's book?') and the use of typographic features such as line division and hyphens.

Some of these features are common to all languages, some peculiar to English, some 'obvious' and giving little trouble, others leaving problems that persist throughout people's lives.

The background research drawn on here comes from two main perspectives. One is studies by psychologists looking at children's development over time. The other is work by educationalists trying to devise optimum ways of teaching reading and writing. This chapter concentrates on the area of spelling rather than engaging in the debates about reading method. Nor does it deal with punctuation, partly for space reasons, partly because of the scarcity of hard evidence about children's development of punctuation; the little there is can be accessed in Hall and Robinson (1996) and in *The Punctuation Project* on-line (www.partnership.mmu.ac.uk/punctuation/punctuation.html).

Most of the examples of children's writing used here were kindly supplied by the Prettygate Infants School in Essex. While those from the early stages are scanned from the originals, those from the older children are shown here in a child-like font Kids, to take away problems in deciphering the actual letters.

Under the influence of Chomsky's ideas about language, many people have come to see children's acquisition of spoken language as an interaction between what the children's minds contribute and the samples of language they are exposed to by their parents. Children use the resources of their minds to create knowledge of English from the English sentences they hear. Their speech often bears little resemblance to that of adults but reveals language systems all of their own.

Similarly, the acquisition of writing is an interaction between children's mental development and the instruction they receive. Writing that seems wildly deviant to adult eyes, say the reversed letters 'biscuit' in Text 1 below, or the strings of letters in example 2 in Text 2 (*see* p. 126), have their own internal logic and eventually evolve into the adult forms through a series of stages and plateaux. The language environment necessarily plays a greater role in the acquisition of written language than of spoken language in that writing is taught to the child by an adult rather than picked up from spontaneous interaction. Children are not told about phonemes or intonation patterns as they learn to speak but they are taught about letters and punctuation when they learn to write.

5.1 ENGLISH-SPEAKING CHILDREN'S ACQUISITION OF SPELLING

Focusing questions

- What were the most difficult aspects of English spelling for you to acquire?
- How important is it for children to acquire the names of letters?
- Are children's spellings such as 'magnufieing glars' 'mistakes' or 'inventions'?

Key words

logographic principle: the recognition of idiosyncratic signs such as the McDonald's logo is based on the logographic principle.

alphabetic principle: the recognition that letters correspond to sounds uses the alphabetic principle.

orthographic principle: the recognition that letters have patterns and arrangements of their own is the orthographic principle.

phonological awareness: people may be 'phonologically aware' of the sounds of their language, whether phonemes, syllables or whatever.

onset/rime: the English spoken syllable can be analysed as having an *onset* and a *rime*: 'shoot' /ʃu:t/ consists of the onset /ʃ/ and rime /u:t/, the rime then consisting of a nucleus /u:/ and coda /t/.

Overall features of the English writing system

Before looking at the development of spelling, some factors need to be reviewed that tend to get ignored because of their sheer obviousness:

- *Direction of writing.* English-speaking children need to learn that writing and reading go from left to right; Hebrew and Arabic-speaking children that they go from right to left. Direction rarely proves a lasting problem.
- *Alignment of writing.* English writing goes along a straight line, rather than, for example, hanging from a line like the Devanagari script used for Hindi. Children have to make ascenders rise above the average letter height and descenders go below the line. Examples 1 and 2 in Text 1 provide examples where the child's <y> and <p> extend upwards from the line, not downwards.
- *Letter direction.* Many letters face in one direction rather than the other, a difficulty for some children. Example 3 in Text 1 shows a child reversing <b> to <d> and <s>, <k> and <t>. When this difficulty persists, it is sometimes associated with dyslexia.
- *Lower-case and capital letters.* Children's first names are written for them on their paintings by helpful adults, often in capital letters. Lower case letters, mostly coming from a handwriting tradition as will be seen in Chapter 6, may be more useful initially, particularly as they have more easily recognizable shapes than square-shaped capitals, as seen in Chapter 4, that is, <d D>, <r R>, <e E>, etc. The first letter that children write is often the first letter of their own name; the first word they write is typically their own name; the research in this area is summarized in Treiman *et al.* (2001). Children can use the letters in their name as a springboard for other words: a child called Mary has a way-in to 'ant', 'Mummy', 'rat' and so on. Or indeed they may overuse the letters in their names by adding them to other words. Children with longer names such as 'Christopher' can often spell longer words than children with shorter names such as 'Sam'.
- *Movement.* The mechanics for forming letters are a crucial element in early writing. Peters (1985: 54) typifies British practice in saying that every primary teacher knows 'All round letters are anti-clockwise. All straight letters begin at the top'. Obvious as this may seem to an English writer, in Japanese round symbols are drawn in a clockwise direction and horizontal strokes come before vertical. Other necessities are how to hold the pen and how to angle the paper, which vary across writing systems (Sassoon 1995). Example 2 in Text 1 has examples of <c>, <i> and <p> where the pencil has first gone down the letter and then back up; the reversed letters in example 3, Text 1 look, however, as if they were formed with the appropriate movements.

Text 1. Letters made by English children

1 my 2 chip 3 biscuit

Interestingly the use of the computer gets round these problems in the early stages of learning to write. Left to right direction and alignment are provided automatically on word-processing systems. Lower-case and upper-case letter shapes are pre-set, even if the keyboard shows only capitals. Movement becomes the ability to hit the appropriate key rather than to manipulate a pen. One can imagine a time when the ability to write with a pen is as unnecessary as the ability to write with a quill; many of the skills involved in using a typewriter for instance became obsolete over only about 10 years, apart from the actual keyboard.

How successful are English children at spelling?

The general question of how bad or good English children are at spelling was investigated by the National Foundation for Educational Research (NFER) (Brooks *et al.* 1993), who looked at essays written by 1492 secondary school children in England at the two ages of 11 and 15 years. One measure was how many mistakes children made in the first 10 lines of an essay. At the age of 11, only two children out of 10 had no mistakes; two out of 10 had five or more. By age 15, four children out of 10 had no mistakes; one out of 10 had five or more. To quote the report, 'A good deal of improvement occurs between the ages of 11 and 15. However, even by age 15 there is still a minority of pupils who have relatively severe problems with spelling, to the extent that their ability to communicate in writing is seriously handicapped.'

The NFER research classified spelling mistakes into five major categories, seen in the box below:

- *insertion* of extra letters, such as the <l> added to 'untill'
- *omission* of letters, such as the <r> missing from 'occuring'
- *substitution* of different letters, such as <a> instead of <i> in 'definate'
- *transposition* of two letters, such as <ei> for <ie> in 'freind'
- *grapheme substitution* involving more than two letters but only a single cause, for example when an equivalent according to sound correspondence rules is substituted for the usual form, as in 'thort' for 'thought'.

Types and proportions of 'major' spelling mistakes in English children aged 11 and 15 (NFER 1993) (%)

insertion	'untill/until'	17
omission	'occuring/occurring'	36
substitution	'definate/definite'	19
transposition	'freind/friend'	5
grapheme substitution	'thort/thought'	19
other		3

Omission is the commonest category among the children's mistakes, followed by grapheme substitution; transposition the least frequent, with the others coming in between.

This method of analysis compares children's spelling with adults' spellings in terms of the sheer letters on the page rather than taking account of any systems of spelling in children or adults. For example the doubling of <l> in 'untill' and the omission of <r> in 'occuring' probably show a general problem with letter-doubling rather than simply insertion or omission. Task 1 explores the extent to which this type of analysis can be unrevealing about the deeper properties of children's spelling. Nevertheless, the NFER research does indicate the extent of the problem that children face.

Task 1. Types of spelling mistakes

Put the following 5–7 year-old children's spellings into the NFER categories in the box above.

picnik crad (crab) wavis sawiy (sandwich) deop (deep)
isc rem poding (pudding) cefl (careful) cips (chips) tae (tea)

How useful do you think this classification is (a) in general, (b) for a child of this age?

Phases in developing spelling

Many accounts of children's development organize much the same information in slightly different ways. Three typical schemes are illustrated in the box below. These all start with a pre-writing phase, go through sound-based and orthographic phases, and finish with a complete knowledge of spelling.

The ages at which children go through the phases are not given since they vary greatly; the youngest phase is about five (that is, the age when they are first taught to read and write in England), the oldest about seven. Some five-year-olds already show signs of Phase 3, some seven-year-olds signs of Phase 1.

Phases in children's development of spelling

Phase	Example	Frith (1985)	Temple *et al.* (1993)	Nunes *et al.* (1997)
1 Pre-writing	VOMHYWƧL (cabbage)	logographic	pre-phonemic	pre-phonetic
2 Sound-based	immy ca mramy hav (Immay came round to my house)	alphabetic	early phonemic	phonetic
	DPZ anb CPs (dippers and chips)		letter-name	intermediate
3 Orthographic	kissed, played, waited	orthographic	transitional	grammatical
4 Complete			correct spelling	consistency

Pre-writing (Phase 1)

The way-in to writing for many children is to associate particular signs with meanings. The most widespread perhaps are the McDonald's golden arches, the Nike swoosh and the Coca-Cola symbol. Frith (1985) calls this stage 'logographic' as children connect a sign with a meaning – termed by her the logographic principle. Children's recognition that these signs mean something gives them a valuable clue to what writing is about, leading directly to meaning-based writing. The interpretation of such signs develops into the visual recognition of whole words. My children for instance recognized 'zoo' from early on, and, like all Londoners, the distinctive script and colour of Harrods bags and vans. Here, this overall phase is called 'pre-writing' as it does not reflect the normal characteristics of English writing, having, on the one hand, letters with no sound correspondence, on the other, meaningful signs that are not part of a writing system.

From an early stage some children make up writing of their own, such as the examples in Text 2. In example 1 in Text 2 the child has realized that writing is marks made along lines and has produced a pattern that looks like a series of <m>s. The second line has some repetitions of a <d>-like letter and vowel letters resembling <u> and <a>. The letters have no connection with the message she claims to be writing – 'I like the part when Jack is climbing down the beanstalk'. In example 2 in Text 2 a slightly more advanced child has tried to write 'chicken nuggets'. He has some idea that writing consists of letters, most of them recognizably part of the Roman alphabet. But he too has not grasped the links between letters and sounds; none of the letters relate to those involved in the spelling of 'chicken nuggets'. Nevertheless, compared with the child who wrote example 1, he has a greater variety of letter shapes and fewer pattern-like shapes.

Text 2. Pre-writing

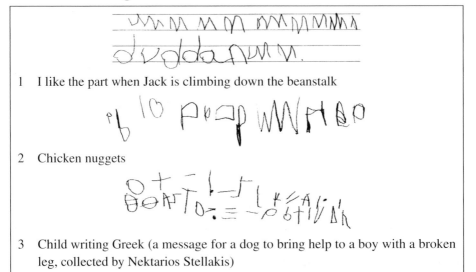

1 I like the part when Jack is climbing down the beanstalk

2 Chicken nuggets

3 Child writing Greek (a message for a dog to bring help to a boy with a broken leg, collected by Nektarios Stellakis)

This stage has been called 'pre-phonemic' and 'pre-phonetic', as well as 'pre-literate' and 'pre-communicative' because the child does not relate writing to sounds. Writing seems to be just decorative shapes on paper. Children may indeed think an adult is 'reading' the pictures on the page, not the squiggly marks below them. This phase is very widespread. Example 3 in Text 2 shows a Greek child using the same approach, except that the letters are based on the Greek alphabet.

Sound-based spelling (Phase 2)

The examples in Text 3 show children acquiring the concept that letters correspond to sounds of the spoken language – the alphabetic principle, variously called the 'early phonemic', 'phonetic' or 'alphabetic' stage. Obviously this is a general principle of correspondence between signs and sounds, linked in many languages like English to the letters of the alphabet, but in say Japanese or Cherokee to symbols that correspond to whole syllables rather than to individual phonemes, as seen in Chapter 1.

Text 3. Early spellings

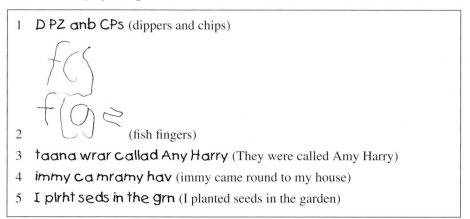

1 D PZ anb CPs (dippers and chips)

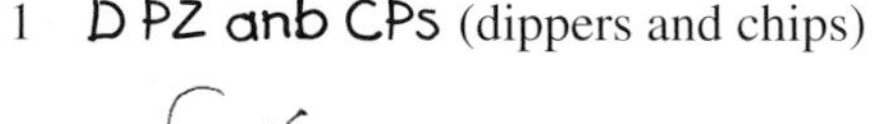

2 (fish fingers)

3 taana wrar callad Any Harry (They were called Amy Harry)

4 immy ca mramy hav (immy came round to my house)

5 I plrht seds in the grn (I planted seeds in the garden)

Letter-names

The names of the letters of the alphabet often play an important role in this sound-based phase. Children may base spelling on letter-names rather than spoken correspondences. Learning the names of the letters of the alphabet is regarded as important both by parents and by television programmes such as *Sesame Street*, even if it has been less valued in the school classroom. Recent studies have shown links between children's knowledge of letter-names and their reading progress. Once you know that <e> is called /iː/ 'seeds' can be spelled 'seds' as in example 5 in Text 3 and 'soggy' can be 'soge' as in example 4 in Text 6 (*see* p. 130). Temple *et al.* (1993) discuss at length the lovely example 'yuts a lade yet feheg ad he kot flepr' (Once a lady went fishing and she caught Flipper). The name for <y> /waɪ/ has the right sound for the /w/ of 'once' 'yuts', whereas <w> /dʌbl̩ juː/ does not. The name for <e> /iː/ fits the last sound of 'lady' 'lade'. The name for <k> /keɪ/ goes nicely with the initial /k/ of 'caught' 'kot'. The name for <r> /ɑː/ fits the ending of 'Flipper' 'flepr'.

Children prefer some letter-names such as <r> /ɑː/ for letter-name writing rather than others like <t> /tiː/, perhaps because /ɑː/ can be a nucleus for a syllable, 'farm' /fɑːm/, that is, is a free vowel (Chapter 3), while /t/ acts as an opening onset of a syllable 'tap' /tæp/ or a final coda 'pat' /pæt/, but not as a nucleus. Unluckily for children, letter-names have a confusing relationship to the letter-sound correspondences of English. None of the 'checked' vowels /æ/ 'bad', /e/ 'bed', /ɪ/ 'bid', /ɒ/ 'body' or /ʌ/ 'bud' are represented by letter-names. Names for letters introduced since Roman times such as <y> /waɪ/ and <w> /dʌbl̩ juː/ have no links to their spoken correspondences. It is only in the comparatively sophisticated language of text messages and the like that letter-names come in to their own ('C U 4 T'), as will be discussed in Chapter 7. Text 4 gives some examples for each letter, taken from Treiman (1993).

Text 4. Some letter-name spellings for vowels (from Treiman 1993)

A /eɪ/ tha (they), ran (rain)
E /iː/ hape (happy), pesue (pizza)
I /aɪ/ bik (bike), nit (night)
O /əu/ blo (blow), bot (boat)
U /juː/ flu (flew), fud (food)

To make a sound-based system work, you need to know not only the letters but also the sounds. Most North American speakers of 'rhotic' English pronounce the word 'star' as /stɑːr/ with an /r/; they have correspondence rules linking <a> with /ɑ/ and <r> with /r/. Speakers of a 'non-rhotic' standard dialect in England, however, pronounce the word 'star' as /stɑː/ with no final /r/; their correspondence rules either treat <ar> as corresponding to /ɑː/ or have a 'silent' <r>. The rules for sound–letter correspondence differ according to the phonological system of the user.

Local accents and spelling

One source of difficulty with sound-correspondence rules is the regional accents of English. The rules that are usually taught assume a standard accent of English, whether British or US, which may not necessarily be the same as that of the child, leading children to attempt to represent their own dialect accent in their spelling. Treiman (1993) found children used spellings that reflected the Hoosier dialect spoken where they lived in the USA; they spelled 'when' as 'win' and 'pen' as 'pin', showing they pronounced both vowels as /ɪ/. One of the Prettygate children spelled 'drowned' as 'drand', possibly using an Essex pronunciation.

Text 5 gives some of the dialect spellings Bromley (2002) obtained from children aged 4–7 years in East Tilbury, a town in Essex on the eastern side of London. Some of the features of the East Tilbury accent are typical of Estuary English, the accent which is developing around London and the Thames Estuary. One feature is vocalic /l/; that is to say final /l/ has become a vowel similar to /w/ so that 'wall' is pronounced /wɔːw/, not /wɔːl/. Sure enough many of the children used spellings like 'wow' and 'woo'. Another feature is fronted /θ/ and /ð/; that is to say, the sound /θ/ has become a further forward /f/ so that 'teeth' is said as /tiːf/ not as /tiːθ/. Again, many of the children spelt it as 'tef' and 'tefs'. Such dialect spellings were usually not in the majority, except for /θ/ fronting where 71% of the attempts by children in year 1 at words such as 'bath' produced spellings with <f> 'brf'.

Text 5. Dialect spelling of children in East Tilbury (Bromley 2002)

	Word	RP pronunciation	East Tilbury pronunciation	Children's spellings
Vocalic /l/	wall	/wɔːl/	/wɔːw/	wow, woo
	pool	/puːl/	/puːw/	pow, po
	towels	/taʊlz/	/taʊwz/	taw, tawe
Fronted /θ/ and /ð/	teeth	/tiːθ/	/tiːf/	tef, tefs
	feather	/feðə/	/fevə/	fevr, fevu
	thumb	/θʌm/	/fʌm/	fum, fym

Bromley (2002) also tested children's preferences with a multiple choice test. Children preferred 'fing' over 'thing' by 56% to 32%, 'nuffing' over 'nothing' by 37% to 34%. Overall they opted for the dialect spelling 30% of the time. Learning to spell English is a problem for any child who speaks English with an accent that is non-standard in a particular country, whether England or Australia. To make the spelling system work, children with non-standard accents have either to invent correspondence rules for their own dialect that are different from those they are taught, that is, <th> corresponding to /f/ or /v/ in East Tilbury, or have to imagine what a standard speaker would say rather than themselves and their parents. In other words to some extent they are in the position of second language learners, basing spelling correspondences on a phonology that is not their own.

Differences between children's and adults' phonology

But the phonology of children may also differ from that of adults. Between the age of five and eight years children's phonological systems are still sufficiently different from those of adults to affect the sound correspondences. The nasal phonemes /m/, /ŋ/ and /n/, for example, often have no corresponding letters in the child's spellings at this stage. There is an <n> missing from 'fingers' in 'figz' (example 1 in Text 3) and from 'land' in 'lad' in (example 5 in Text 6 below) and <n>s missing from 'yuts' 'once' and 'feheg' 'fishing'. The children may not perceive the /n/ as a separate phoneme of English but as a nasalized quality of the vowel, parallel to the adult pronunciation of 'genre' as /ʒɒ̃rə/ with nasalized /ɒ/ but no distinct /n/. Hence they see no need to give nasal phonemes letters of their own. Many missing <n>s occur before plosive consonants that have the same tongue position. The /ŋ/ in 'fingers' comes before a /g/ as in 'figz', both with tongue contact at the back of the mouth; the /n/ in 'land' precedes a /d/ 'lad' with the same contact at the front of the mouth, thus showing the omission is indeed related to phonology. Children also frequently omit <l> and <r>; a Prettygate child for example produced 'font' for 'front', perhaps because of a local pronunciation of /r/ using the lip and teeth that goes together with the preceding /f/. Further evidence for the phonological basis of nasal omission is given by Treiman *et al.* (1995) who found that /n/ was omitted less often than /m/ and /ŋ/. /n/ is measurably a longer sound than /n/ and /ŋ/ and so arguably easier to perceive.

Text 6. Children learning sound–letter correspondences

1 strabree yorgoat (strawberry yoghurt)
2 He drand and He last his bred and He did in his sleep (he drowned and he lost his breath and he died in his sleep)
3 He dropted his samwisch. He was biying eatin (being eaten)
4 He went to the beca and he went on a bota and he had a sawuig and he drop it and it got soge (beach, boat, sandwich, soggy)
5 The tooferee cand w bactoo tofreelad (the tooth fairy came and went back to fairyland)
6 a little girl colde Lucy she had a wobily tooth . . . and here tooth fell out an she pikt it up.

Text 6 above illustrates children's attempts to get to grips with sound-to-letter correspondences. Vowel digraphs are simplified – 'strabree' 'strawberry' reduces <aw> to <a> (example 1 Text 6), 'bred' 'breath' cuts <ea> to (example 2, Text 6) and consonant digraphs have one member of the pair missing 'eatin' 'eating' (example 3, Text 6) (though this may also represent a dialect pronunciation). Letter-names still intrude, 'biying' 'buying', 'soge' 'soggy' (example 4, Text 6) and 'did' 'died' (example 2, Text 6). Digraphs that correspond to single phonemes cause problems: the child often gives only the first letter of the pair, 'c' for <ch>' in 'chips' (example 1, Text 3 above) or 's' for <sh> in 'fish' (example 2, Text 3 above).

Orthographic regularities (Phase 3)

A mastery of the sound–letter correspondences in the sound-based Phase 2 could mislead the child who took writing to be a faithful rendering of speech, or who assumed that English was consistent – because 'tree' has <ee> so does 'strabree' (example 1, Text 6). Children have to go beyond sound–letter correspondences to tackle the complexities of English orthography – the orthographic principle that letters function in various ways not based on phonology. One sign is Treiman's claim that children spell words they frequently encounter in reading better than infrequent words. The more you see a word the better it is stored via the lexical route rather than processed by correspondence rules.

Treiman (1993) tested whether children aged 6–8 years knew orthographic 'constraints'. Children were given nonsense words that either conformed or did not conform to the orthographic patterns of English, for instance, whether doubled consonants can occur at the beginning of words 'ffeb' versus 'beff', whether <y> can occur at the beginning of words 'yb' versus 'ib', and whether <ck> can occur at the beginning of words 'ckun' versus 'nuck'. The results in Figure 5.1 show that eight-year-olds scored 83.2% on the test, whereas adults scored 94.5%. Even six-year-olds whose spelling had little developed scored above chance at 56.4%. Children soon become aware of the orthographic structure of English, which is based neither on sound–letter correspondences nor on memory for individual words. Treiman's test, in fact, was the original basis for the orthographic regularities test described in Chapter 1.

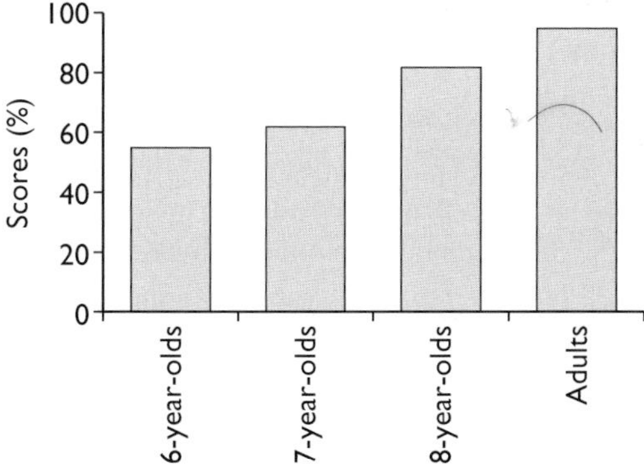

Fig. 5.1. Results for Treiman's Orthographic Constraints test.

Lexical spelling and inflections

One of the main arguments advanced for lexical spelling in Chapter 3 was that the same morpheme can be spelled in the same way regardless of how it is pronounced. So the single spelling <ed> corresponds to three pronunciations of the past tense 'ed' morpheme, /t/ following a voiceless consonant 'risked', /d/ following a voiced phoneme 'named' and /ɪd/ following /t/ or /d/ 'hinted'. Here are some examples of past tense forms taken from Text 6:

> 'colde' ('called'), 'fell', 'pikt', 'went', 'had', 'drop', 'got', 'dropted', 'was', 'drand' ('drowned'), 'last' ('lost'), 'did' ('died')

The ones that are correct are the irregular forms 'fell', 'went', 'had', 'was' and 'lost'. The regular <ed> spelling is not present. Most of the spellings for regular verbs correspond to the specific pronunciation of 'ed' in context, that is, 'co lde' ('called') has /d/ (disregarding the final <e>), 'pikt' ('picked') has /t/, 'did' ('died') has /d/ (but fails to see the need for a preceding <e>); the only word that seems to have a proper <ed> is in fact an invented past tense 'dropted'. The insight that regular past tenses end in <ed> has not yet occurred to these children.

Bryant *et al.* (1997) investigated children's spelling of past tenses between the ages of six and eight, using not only regular and irregular past tenses but also non-verbs that had the same endings, such as 'cold' and 'soft'. They found five stages:

- Stage 1. To start with, children are unsystematic in their spelling of the past 'ed' inflection.
- Stage 2. Then they use normal sound–letter correspondences rather than a consistent spelling for the 'ed' morphemes: 'kist', 'slept', 'soft'.
- Stage 3. They produce some <ed> endings 'kissed', but overgeneralize them, not only to irregular verbs 'sleped', but also to other words that are not verbs at all 'sofed'.
- Stage 4. Next they use <ed> spellings only with past verbs, 'kissed' with generalizations to irregular verbs 'sleped', but not to non-verbs 'soft'.
- Stage 5. Lastly, they use <ed> spellings only with regular past verbs, 'kissed' but not with any other forms.

Treiman (1993), however, found no examples of wrong generalizations to irregular verbs in her data. Bryant *et al.* (1997) also found clear links between children's awareness of syntax and their development of past tense spellings, seen in Figure 5.2. Not only did the stages in the development of syntactic awareness correlate with the stages in spelling but also good scores on tests of syntax predicted which children were going to do better at the next spelling stage.

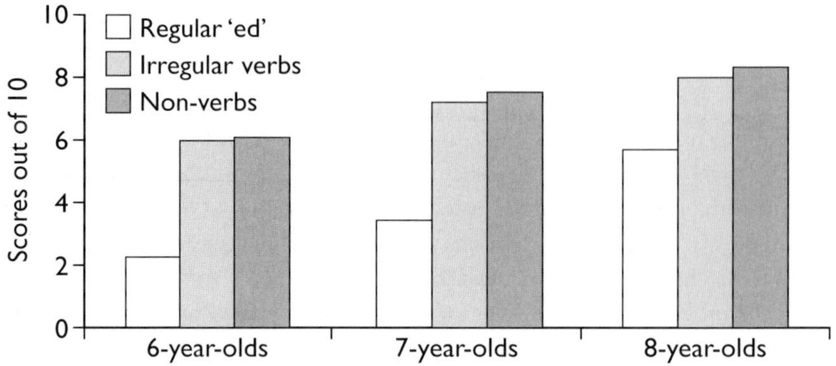

Fig. 5.2. Development of past tense spelling in English children (Bryant *et al.* 1997).

This resembles a typical pattern in the development of spoken grammar. Children first use past tense verbs as individual items, getting many irregular verbs like 'went' right; then they learn a rule for regular verbs which they overgeneralize to all verbs, including irregular 'comed', 'wented', etc.; lastly, they learn there are groups of irregular verbs to which the rule does not apply. There is no single moment when children realize that past tense 'ed' is always spelled in the same way. Indeed at Stage 3 they seem to have a general rule of sound–letter correspondence, which they apply to any word that ends in the appropriate final sounds regardless of its grammatical status.

Figure 5.2 gives the children's scores out of 10 between the ages of six and eight, not only for the regular and irregular verbs but also for the non-verbs with the same endings, such as 'gold' and 'soft'. Their ability to spell the regular and irregular verbs increases steadily between the ages of six and eight. Yet the score for regular 'ed' is only 5.68 out of 10 at the age of eight, compared with 7.9 for irregular verbs and 8.25 for non-words. Eight-year-olds still make many mistakes with the past-tense ending. Can they really be said to know the regular 'ed' spelling when they only get it right just over half the time? The claim that lexical spelling provides a convenient short-cut is far from confirmed; the uniform spelling of the regular 'ed' past morpheme is simply another problem for children to overcome where letters do not correspond in a one-to-one fashion to sounds. Treiman (1993) indeed found grammatical inflections were one of the worst spelling problems for children, not just the past tense 'ed' but also the third-person 's' and the plural 's'.

By about the age of eight most children have gone through these phases and reached 'complete' knowledge of English spelling. This does not mean that people spell everything correctly. The residual problems are mostly a matter of acquiring the spelling of individual idiosyncratic words and of orthographic regularities via the lexical route. People who have acquired the letter-doubling rule still have problems with 'accommodation' and 'millennium'; people who have mastered <c>/<s> correspondences still have difficulty with 'supersede' and 'cemetery'.

Phonological awareness and the learning of spelling

Before turning to more general models, we need to look at children's awareness of the sounds of their language. Learning a sound-based writing system relies on the child's developing phonological awareness. Primary school children in Hong Kong do not develop phoneme awareness through reading Chinese as much as English children develop it through reading English (Huang and Hanley, 1994): it only comes with an alphabetic script. In reverse, people with meaning-based writing systems have an advantage at the discrimination of abstract figures and other visually based tasks (Brown and Haynes 1985).

In one sense it is obviously impossible for children to relate letters to separate sounds if they cannot distinguish the English phonemes themselves. The ability to read and to spell seems to depend on phonological awareness in this sense. Children with better phonemic awareness usually learn to read and write more easily. Task 2 shows how learning to read affects awareness of speech.

Task 2. Awareness of speech: how many sounds are there in each of the following words?

of	☐	plant	☐	jet	☐	think	☐	sex	☐
who	☐	page	☐	edge	☐	music	☐	cost	☐
tuna	☐	ought	☐	ox	☐	judge	☐		

Answers at the end of the chapter

From another perspective, there are sounds in the adults' phonology that do not correspond to the phonemes in children's phonology, as seen in the discussion of <n> above. The child's discovery that these sounds need to be represented in speech in effect adds them as phonemes to their phonology: learning to *write* <n> makes the child *hear* /n/. In other words, phonological awareness of some adult sounds depends upon the child's ability to read and to spell.

Older children and adults indeed assume that written letters take priority over phonemes. They believe that 'ridge' /rɪdʒ/ has more sounds than 'rage' /reɪdʒ/ or 'match' /mætʃ/ more than 'chat' /tʃæt/: they 'overcount' the number of sounds. Reading has permanently changed their perception of the phonemes of English. A celebrated experiment by Bruce (1964) asked children to 'remove' sounds from words – what is 'jam' /dʒæm/ without /dʒ/, 'fork' without /k/? Children aged five years were completely unable to carry out the task; by the age of nine they still succeeded only 26.7% of the time. One of the problems with learning sound-to-letter correspondences is that children have little idea what a phoneme is.

But there is more to phonological awareness than phonemes. Children need also to be aware of the syllable as a unit since so many of the spelling patterns of English depend upon it. And they need to know its internal structure so that they can relate /k/ as the onset of a syllable to <c> 'cab' but /k/ as the coda of a syllable to <ck> 'back', or link <i> to /ɪ/ as the nucleus of a checked syllable 'sin' but to <y> as the nucleus of an open syllable 'city' (though these two sounds may be phonetically different in some British dialects or indeed some RP speakers).

Many spelling researchers have drawn on an analysis of the English syllable that breaks it down into an onset (the initial consonant or consonant cluster) plus a rime (the nuclear vowel and any following coda). So spoken 'buy' /baɪ/ splits into onset /b/ and rime /aɪ/, spoken 'stick' /stɪk/ into onset /st/ and rime /ɪk/. Spoken 'I' /aɪ/ has only a rime /aɪ/. Treiman *et al.* (1995) claim that the child's spelling 'tubol' for 'tumble' for example shows that children do not treat the <m> as a separate unit but as part of a rime <um>.

According to Goswami (1999), children become progressively aware of phonology in three stages: (1) syllables, (2) onsets and rimes, (3) phonemes. Children have mastered the first two stages at the age of four but only reach stage 3 in their first year of school. Goswami and Bryant (1990: 19) claim this shows 'explicit knowledge about syllables precedes reading while an awareness of phonemes follows it'. This raises the issue of whether phonemic awareness is the cause or effect of teaching. The first two stages of syllables and onset/rime seem part of the child's ability when he or she starts school, that is, a natural component of awareness of language; the phonemic stage comes later, after reading instruction has usually started. In other words, children may come to regard speech as phonemes because they are taught letters in school. Some linguists such as Bruce Derwing and Mark Aronoff believe indeed that the phoneme is an artifact created by linguists with a background in sound-based writing systems rather than the core of phonology (Aronoff 1992; Derwing 1992). Consequently, it does not form part of the language awareness of people who have not learnt an alphabetic writing system.

Frith's model of the acquisition of reading and writing

Having treated the phonological and lexical routes separately, they can now be reassembled in the developmental scheme proposed by Frith (1985). This neat way of conceptualizing children's development of reading and writing has been found highly useful by other researchers and educationalists, even if they do not necessarily agree with it completely. Frith uses the three principles mentioned above as an overall way of organizing development into three phases:

- *Learning logographic skills*, that is to say, learning to recognize word patterns as wholes, such as 'zoo'.
- *Learning alphabetic skills* involving matching letters with sounds, say the correspondences between <z> and /z/ or <oo> and /uː/.
- *Learning orthographic skills* involving 'instant analysis of words into orthographic units', that is, acquiring letter combinations that are not linked to phonology, such as <ck> as a spelling for a syllable coda 'back' but not for a syllable onset 'ckab'.

Although it may be convenient to relate the three principles to consecutive stages in children's development, this does not mean that particular children do not employ more than one of the principles at the same time, say for different words.

The power of Frith's insight comes from outside the area of spelling production that is concentrated on here. Extending the three principles to reading and writing means children's development has not three phases, but six steps, as shown in the box below. Each principle is learnt either in reading or in writing before it is transferred to the other medium; the principles are learnt out of step. That is to say, children acquire the logographic principle in reading before they apply it to writing: they read 'zoo' before they can write it. Then they acquire the alphabetic principle in writing before they apply it to reading: being able to write individual letters corresponding to sounds, say <a> for /æ/ in 'bat', leads them in due course to realizing the phonological basis of reading. Next they acquire the orthographic principle in reading before they can use it in writing: only by mastering the orthographic regularities of final <ck> and initial <c> can they come to spell 'cell' and 'lack' in their own writing. The development of writing dovetails into the development of reading; a principle is learnt in either reading or writing, not in both at once.

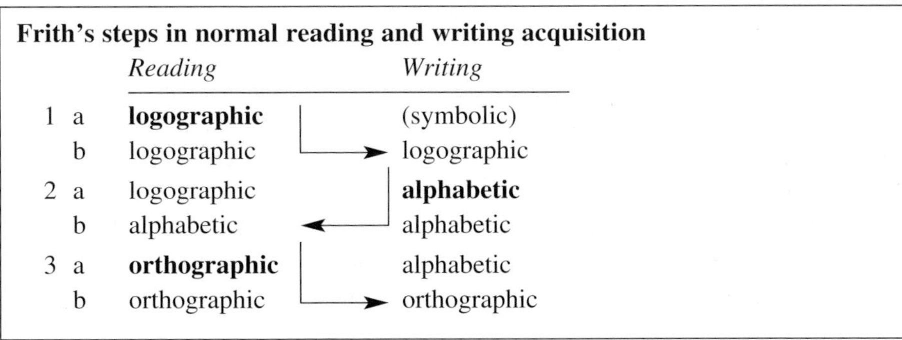

Frith's steps in normal reading and writing acquisition

		Reading		*Writing*
1	a	**logographic**		(symbolic)
	b	logographic	→	logographic
2	a	logographic		**alphabetic**
	b	alphabetic	←	alphabetic
3	a	**orthographic**		alphabetic
	b	orthographic	→	orthographic

This six-step model explains why some children do not learn to read and write adequately. Hardly any children fail to learn the logographic principle for recognizing a certain number of whole words, and so can progress through stages 1a and 1b. Some children have problems with the alphabetic principle because they cannot get hold of the idea of sound–letter correspondence, that is, they do not progress to stage 2a. This does not mean that they are necessarily unable to read logographically; Rozin *et al.* (1971) showed that Chinese characters could be taught to children who had failed to learn to read English in the normal classroom since character-writing does not involve the alphabetic principle. One type of dyslexia is marked by the failure to master the alphabetic principle, whatever the reason may be; it is not uncommon for dyslexic individuals of this type to have problems with speech as well since it is related to the phonological system.

Some children who are successful at reading and writing for several years then start dropping behind. This may be caused by their inability to grasp the orthographic principle that combinations of letters have properties of their own unlinked to sound, without which they cannot progress to steps 3a and 3b. Children with this problem have no difficulty with sound–letter correspondences, but they are bewildered by the orthographic regularities of English. Task 3 in Chapter 1 required people to cross out the <e>s in an ordinary piece of English text. This was based on Frith's test for identifying children with this problem. She distinguished two types of <e>. 'Important' <e>s are vital to the understanding of the word; for example the <e> in 'left' is important because 'l_ft' might be 'lift' or 'loft'. 'Unimportant' <e>s can be taken for granted; the <e> in 'lifted' is unimportant as there no other words that 'lift_d' could be confused with – no 'liftad' or 'liftid'.

People who do not know the orthographic principle are just as good at crossing out *important* <e>s as the rest of us, but fail to cross out the *unimportant* <e>s; in other words, they see the word primarily as sounds via the alphabetic principle rather than as letter combinations via the orthographic principle. A major additional problem for people without the orthographic principle (and for others as well) is the unstressed schwa sound /ə/ which occurs frequently in speech, but can be spelled in so many ways, leading to mistakes from adult English-speaking students such as 'syllubus', 'competance' and 'catagories'.

Spelling and the National Curriculum in England

Since children's development of spelling involves the interaction of the child's invention of spelling with the instruction provided in the classroom, we can look briefly at how the National Curriculum for England (1999) covers spelling, as presented in the box below. Key Stage 1, when children start primary school at around five years of age, emphasizes letters, sound correspondences and the spelling of common words and inflections. Key Stage 2 from the age of eight expands into syllables, 'spelling conventions' and the use of dictionary-style resources. Key Stages 3 and 4 in the secondary school aim at 'increasing knowledge', more specifically word-formation, irregular polysyllabic words and use of resources.

National Curriculum for England 1999

Spelling (extracted and shortened; some aspects, such as phonemic awareness, are dealt with in other sections of the curriculum for English).

Children should be taught to:

Key Stage 1 (5–7 years)	Key Stage 2 (8–11 years)	Key Stages 3 and 4 (12–15 years)
Write each letter of the alphabet Use sound–symbol relationships and patterns Recognize simple spelling patterns Write common letter strings Spell common words Spell words with common prefixes and inflectional endings	Sound out phonemes Analyse words into syllables and other known words Apply knowledge of spelling conventions Use knowledge of common letter strings, etc. Check spelling using word banks, dictionaries, etc. Revise and build on knowledge of words and patterns	Increase their knowledge of regular patterns, etc. Apply knowledge of word-formation Spell complex irregular polysyllabic words Check their spelling for errors with a dictionary Use different kinds of dictionary, thesaurus, etc.

Task 3 suggests comparing the National Curriculum with the account of the English writing system presented so far. This curriculum seems an ad hoc list of traditional aspects of spelling (some of which are not explained, such as 'sounding out' and 'spelling conventions') rather than building on either the descriptions of English spelling seen in earlier chapters or on the insights into children's spelling described in this chapter. Of course a curriculum has to take into account many factors other than academic research, in particular the experience of teachers and the expectations of parents. The proof of the pudding must be whether this organization of spelling into a curriculum helps teachers to teach and pupils to learn.

Task 3. Checklist for the National Curriculum

Go through the summary of the National Curriculum in (*see* box above) and decide whether it seems to pay attention at the right age to:

- Both sound and lexical routes Y ☐ N ☐
- Orthographic regularities Y ☐ N ☐
- Spelling rules (e.g. e-marking) Y ☐ N ☐
- Lexical spelling (e.g. past 'ed') Y ☐ N ☐
- Phases of development Y ☐ N ☐
- Children's inventiveness in spelling Y ☐ N ☐

It would be interesting to see how successful a curriculum would be that presented sound-correspondence rules systematically to children, that outlined a series of practical rules for English spelling like the three-letter rule, and that integrated the stages that children actually go through in developing spelling.

Table 5.1 Children's acquisition of spelling

- Children develop English spelling in broad phases:
  - (i) pre-writing
  - (ii) sound-based
  - (iii) orthographic
  - (iv) complete
- During the sound-based phase many children use letter-names. Problems include children who speak non-standard dialects who have to learn a different spoken accent and the differences between child and adult phonology
- During the orthographic phase children acquire the lexical spelling of morphemes

5.2. ACQUISITION OF ENGLISH SPELLING BY SPEAKERS OF OTHER LANGUAGES

Focusing questions

- Can you tell a person's first language by their spelling in English? (*See* Task 4 on p. 141 for a practical test.)
- What do you think are the main problems that a Chinese speaker has with the English writing system? A French speaker?

Key words

transfer: an aspect of language that is carried over from one language the person knows to another language, for example transferring the sounds of the first language to the second, creating a distinctive foreign accent.

How do people who already have one writing system cope with acquiring English? Does it make a difference what their first language is? Are their mistakes and problems the same as those of native English-speaking children and adults? This section looks at some of the issues involved in acquiring English as a second writing system.

Comparatively little research has been carried out in this area of second language acquisition (SLA) apart from the comparison of learners with sound-based or meaning-based writing systems in their L1s. This section draws partly on research I carried out in the 1990s with adult L2 learners of English that borrowed the ideas and techniques used in the L1 research described in Part 5.1. One danger in using L1 research techniques in investigating L2 acquisition is reducing L2 acquisition to just those aspects that parallel L1 acquisition in some way and hence obscuring its unique features. Another danger is that the similarities between L1 and L2 acquisition may be masked by the age differences between L1 child learners and L2 adult learners. The

L2 adults, apart from having better memory systems, are at a cognitive stage when conscious attention to explicit rules may be helpful. Furthermore they have already passed through Frith's six steps in their own language, or at any rate as many of them as apply to their first language.

Transfer across writing systems?

One of the oldest ideas in SLA research is transfer. Everyone can identify some foreign accents in English because the sounds are transferred from the first language, whether Japanese, Russian or French. The usual concept of transfer is that L2 learners carry over certain features of their first language to the second, showing up in their vocabulary, grammar or pronunciation. Some L2 researchers, however, see transfer as going in both directions and talk about the influence of the second language on the first (Cook 2003); people who know another language show signs of it even in their first language. The question here is how transfer works in terms of writing systems. This involves discussing transfer at many levels, going from letter-shapes up to the balance between the sound- and meaning-based routes.

Let us start with some of the characteristics of the English writing system, taken for granted in Part 5.1, that may well differ from other languages.

- *The actual letter shapes* can be different from those in the L2 learner's first language. Text 7A from a Greek student has transferred a Greek <α> to English. The attempt at <E> in Text 7B shows a more extreme difference in letter form from a Chinese learner.
- *The pen movements* may be different. In texts 7B, 7C and 7D the writers appear to have drawn horizontal lines before vertical, contrary to the practice taught in England, but following that taught in Japan and China.
- *Direction.* Arabic-speaking students in England have told me their children try to write English from right to left. Sassoon (1995) talks of a Japanese child who uses right to left and left to right directions on alternate lines, a system called boustrophedon not found in any contemporary writing system, although used in ancient Greek.

Text 7. Letters made by non-English-speaking adults

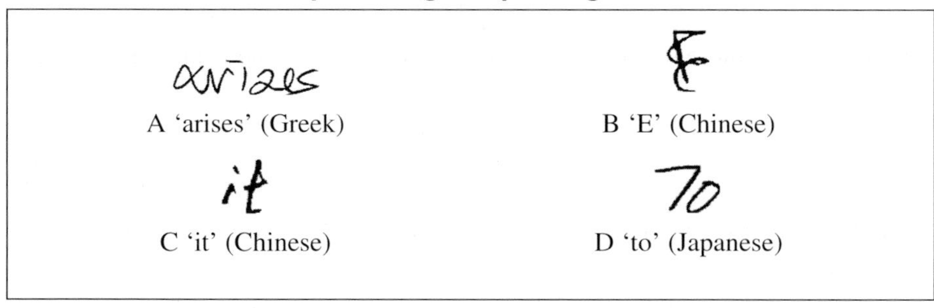
A 'arises' (Greek)
B 'E' (Chinese)
C 'it' (Chinese)
D 'to' (Japanese)

The most dramatic differences from L1 development come when a person changes from a meaning-based writing system like Chinese to the sound-based system of English, or vice versa. L2 users show many signs of transferring their L1 writing system to another language. Chinese speakers acquiring Japanese syllabic scripts rely more on visual strategies, English speakers on phonological strategies (Chikamatsu 1996), as can be predicted from their L1 writing systems.

Turning to English, Chinese university students read English at about 88 words a minute compared to the 254 words a minute of their English-speaking peers and their scores on comprehension questions were about 10% lower (Haynes and Carr 1990). Akamatsu (1998) found L2 learners with a meaning-based L1 writing system such as Japanese relied more on visual shape, such as upper- and lower-case, and were less efficient at grouping letters into corresponding phonemes. An ingenious experiment by Koda (1987) asked people to read passages containing names of fish that were either pronounceable, such as 'doffit', or unpronounceable, such as 'dfofti'. Japanese learners of English were fastest at the unpronounceable names, native English fastest at the pronounceable names, showing that the Japanese were using a lexical route, the English natives a phonological route.

How successful are L2 learners at English spelling?

Do L2 learners find English spelling as difficult as native children? To answer this means comparing L2 adults with the NFER study of L1 children described in Part 5.1 (Cook 1997). The L2 data were 375 essays supplied by overseas university students in England with a variety of first languages. Counting the mistakes in the first 10 lines of each essay as was done in the NFER study, the proportion of L2 students with no mistakes was 40.2% compared with 39% for L1 children; the proportion of L2 students with more than six mistakes was 2% compared with the children's 6%.

The L2 adults were slightly better than the children, evidenced by their average of 1.02 mistakes per 10 lines compared with the children's 1.6 (*see* Table 5.2). Despite their far superior educational level, the L2 students are still making many spelling mistakes. Yet an L2 learner of English who made only 1.2 grammatical or pronunciation mistakes per 50 words, say, might be justifiably proud; in any other area of language, most L2 learners would be pleased to use language as well as a 15-year-old child.

Table 5.2 Types and proportions of 'major' spelling mistakes (%) in non-native speakers compared with English adults and English children aged 11–15

	L2 examples	L2 adults	L1 adults	L1 children
insertion	Engilish, priemary	21	22	17
omission	bain (brain), softwar	37	43	36
substitution	privite, deligent	30	28	19
transposition	foerigners, thier	5	1	5
grapheme substitution	manshed, higher archary	6	4	19
other	boldiest, relegone	8	3	3

Table 5.2 shows the proportions of different categories of mistake from L2 learners based on a sample of 1400 mistakes (http://homepage.ntlworld.com/vivian.c/1400sample.htm), consisting of 200 errors from overseas students with seven first

languages. So that like can be compared with like, Table 5.2 also shows the proportion for L1 adults calculated from examination papers by British students (Wing and Baddeley 1980).

As can readily be seen, the highest category of mistakes for L2 learners was omission of letters, as in 'bain' ('brain') or 'softwar' ('software'), the same as for the L1 adults and children. This was followed by substitution mistakes, 'privite' ('private') and 'deligent' ('diligent'), and by insertion, 'Engilish' and 'priemary'. Next came transposition mistakes, 'foerigners' and 'thier', and grapheme substitution, 'manshed' ('mentioned') and 'higher archary' ('hierarchy').

The only category where native children had more mistakes than either group of adults is grapheme substitution, which accounted for 19% of their errors but for only 4% of the L1 adults and 6% of the L2 adults. Presumably this is because the L1 children still put too much trust in the alphabetic principle rather than the orthographic principle. While the 'other' category of mistakes was higher for the L2 adults, most examples look like attempts to create new words, such as 'boldiest' and 'relegone', where it is not entirely clear what word the writer was actually aiming at, not usually a problem in the first language.

Relationship between L1 phonological and orthographic systems and English

As well as the general effects of transfer between two writing systems, seen above, L2 learners bring along with them the phonology of their first language. In speech this manifests itself through their accent. In writing, characteristics of their first language may equally contribute a spelling 'accent' to their writing. Task 4 tests whether particular L1s are recognizable from the learners' spelling mistakes. It should be emphasized that L2 users have as many things in common as differences and so many mistakes are found from speakers of several L1s. At a less-specific level some of the characteristics of the first language are revealed – the possibility of double <kk> in 'wekk' (Dutch), the lack of a word-final voicing contrast in German in 'substitude', the use of double letters as a sign of different phonemes in Spanish 'exclussive', 'inteligent' and so on.

Task 4. L2 learners' language mistakes

What is the first language of the people who made these spelling mistakes in English?

1. bicture	2. Creek	3. boyes	4. wekk (week)
5. countery	6. materiel	7. substitude	8. thik
9. pratical	10. Grade Britain	11. finall	12. obbligation
13. monney	14. brack (black)	15. exclussive	16. cuickly
17. inteligent	18. wether	19. higher archary (hierarchy)	20. difficulity

Little study has been made of such spelling 'accents'. The box below shows a sample of L2 mistakes and possible causes, drawing on Bebout (1985), Ibrahim (1978) and the 1400 sample. As can be seen, the roots of many lie either in the properties of the L1 spelling system, say the different convention for letter doubling in Spanish, or in the L1 phonological system, whether the lack of certain phonemes found in English, such as the /l/ /r/ contrast absent from Japanese, or a different syllable structure, say the lack of final consonant clusters, as in Arabic. In many cases it is hard to tell whether L2 mistakes are a carry-over from the L1 phonological system or from the L1 writing system allied to it. Japanese for instance uses a form of Roman letters called 'romaji' which incorporates many Japanese pronunciations into the spelling; for example 'sarari' is the romaji spelling of 'salary'.

Some sample L2 mistakes

Mistake	L1	Cause?
'bicture'	Arabic	lack of /p/ /b/ contrast in Arabic
'inteligent'	Spanish	double letters correspond to a different sound than singletons in Spanish
'brack'	Japanese	no /l/ /r/ contrast in Japanese
'beginnig'	Spanish	scarcity of consonant clusters in Spanish
'subejects'	Arabic	few syllable final consonant clusters in Arabic
'recognice'	German	lack of voicing contrast in final consonants in German

Orthographic regularities

Just as in L1 acquisition, a fair amount of the complexity of learning English spelling comes from the orthographic regularities that allow certain combinations and positions of letters. L2 users of English have to go beyond the alphabetic and logographic principles to the orthographic principle.

Figure 5.3 shows how L2 adult learners compare with L1 adults, using a test of mine derived from Treiman's Orthographic Constraints Test (Treiman 1993) mentioned above; the L1 results were discussed in Chapter 1. Both groups consisted of adult university students and so had similar educational levels. They had to decide 'which word looks like an English word' out of a pair of words on a computer screen, such as 'whon'/'nowh' (<wh> is only syllable-initial) and 'truve'/'truv' (word-final <v> without is <e> extremely rare in English). The L2 users' success-rate of 83.2% was not far off the native speakers' 88.0%. As well, the L2 users took 1.837 seconds to choose between the word pairs while the L1 users took 1.504 seconds: L2 users were slightly slower.

Both groups thus showed a high awareness of orthographic regularities, with the L2 users making slightly more mistakes and taking slightly longer. Interestingly, in a version of the same experiment that compared people with different L1s, the Chinese and Japanese speakers had the fastest response time, the Arabic speakers the slowest, with speakers of German and Romance languages coming in between. Hence orthographic regularities seem to be easiest for those whose L1 writing system is meaning-based, such as Chinese and Japanese, most difficult for those with a consonant-based alphabetic system such as Arabic.

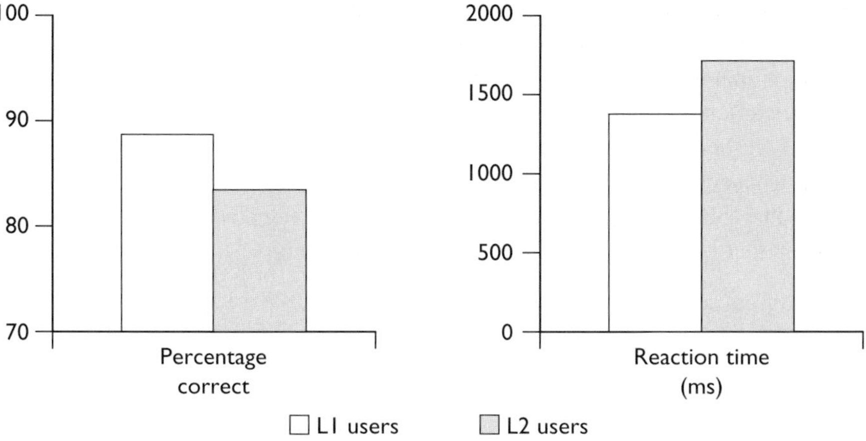

Fig. 5.3. Orthographic regularities in L2 users.

Lexical representation

Do L2 learners make any more use of lexical representation in spelling than L1 children? We saw above that L1 children did not find it a great help that the past tense morpheme 'ed' is consistently spelled in the same way regardless of pronunciation. Figure 5.4 compares 65 adult L2 students of English in Cambridge with the L1 children tested by Bryant *et al.* (1997) seen above, using a similar test of regular verbs, irregular verbs and non-verbs. L2 adults are much better at the regular 'ed' spelling, such as 'filled', than the L1 children but are also nearly as good at the irregular verbs, such as 'began', and the non-verbs, such as 'field'.

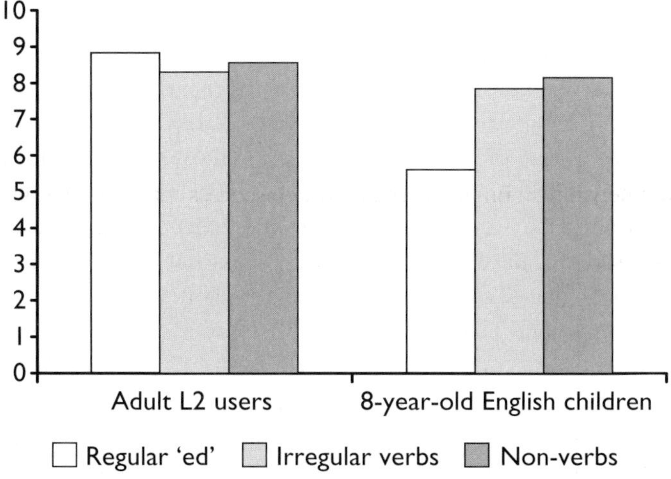

Fig. 5.4. Past-tense spelling in L2 users of English versus eight-year-old native children. (Source: Nunes *et al.* 1997)

The L2 pattern is then rather different from that for the L1 children. The lexical representation approach discussed in Chapter 3 claimed that English spelling is near-optimal for speakers of English, that is, those who already know English phonology. L2 adult learners who do *not* have the same English phonology as native speakers seem to have benefited more from the uniformity of morpheme spelling than native children whose phonology is probably far closer to that of native adults. One reason might be that this feature of English has been directly taught to them, another that it is something that adults can exploit more easily than children.

Phonological awareness

Do L2 users with a different L2 command of English phonology from native children also let their knowledge of writing influence their knowledge of speech? In an experiment with L2 students, Holm and Dodd (1996) contrasted English words that had the same number of written letters and of spoken phonemes, such as 'stamp' /stæmp/ (five letters, five phonemes) with words that had *more* letters than phonemes such as 'whistle' /wɪsl̩/ (seven letters, four phonemes). The aim was to see whether the English spelling system had influenced their phonological awareness so that they would perceive more phonemes than there actually were. Hong Kong students were the worst group at estimating the number of sounds for both types of words; mainland Chinese, however, were the second-best group at words with the same number of letters and phonemes, and best of all at those that had many letters to one sound. In mainland China, Chinese characters are taught via an intermediary phase based on a sound-based alphabet called 'pinyin'; up to 1997 Hong Kong schools taught the characters directly. That is to say, L2 learners who have developed phonological awareness in mainland China are less subject to overcounting than those who have been trained exclusively in a character-based script in Hong Kong. Phonological awareness of this kind is not a matter of learning any writing system but of learning a sound-based system.

I followed up the Holm and Dodd (1996) experiment with an amplified test of sound-counting on 74 adult L2 students with a wide range of first languages, testing only consonants; a sample of the test-words was used in Task 2 (*see* p. 133). The results differed both from those for L1 children and those found by Holm and Dodd (1996). Overall, L2 learners consistently said that there were *fewer* sounds than the proper amount rather than more, that is, they 'undercounted' by feeling that 'back' /bæk/ had two sounds, not three. *Over*counting occurred only on <gh> words and <tch/ge/dge> words, that is, they would say 'bought' /bɔːt/ had four sounds, not three, and 'edge' /edʒ/ had four, not two sounds. Why these results should be different is unclear.

L2 spelling and the National ESOL Curriculum

Lastly, how does spelling relate to English language teaching? Mainstream English course-books hardly teach the writing system at all. It does, however, figure in the *Adult ESOL Core Curriculum in England* (DfES 2001). The box below extracts the aspects of spelling described in the 'Entry Levels' for the core curriculum; these are followed by two other levels related to other UK qualifications but not linked to international levels such as the Common European Framework (Council of Europe 2001). As in the discussion of the L1 syllabus above, other aspects of the writing system such as punctuation have been omitted.

Adult ESOL core curriculum in England, 2001: spelling (extracted)
An adult will be expected to:

Entry Level 1	Entry Level 2	Entry Level 3
■ Spell correctly some personal key words and familiar words ■ Write the letters of the alphabet, using upper-case ■ Produce legible text	■ Spell correctly the majority of personal details and familiar common words ■ Produce legible text	■ Spell correctly common words and relevant key words for work and special interest ■ Proofread and correct writing for grammar and spelling

Entry Level 1 emphasizes the spelling of key words and letter names, which can be equated to the logographic phase for L1 children and the letter-name part of the sound-based phase. Entry Level 2 expands to the 'majority' of key words and producing 'legible text', presumably handwriting instruction. Entry Level 3 is yet more key words plus the skill of editing.

Compared with the L1 curriculum seen on p. 137, this curriculum lacks the major features of sound-based writing, namely the acquisition of the specific relationships between letters and sounds. Except for the letter-names, it might as well be a curriculum for a meaning-based writing system like Chinese. It shows no appreciation that the students come from a variety of different writing systems and so have a variety of possible problems. Nor does it mention the everyday problem EFL teachers in London face of students who are not literate in their first language, so that their first encounter with writing comes in their second language. Official guidelines in England in 2001 seem uninformed by the research into the L2 spelling of English of the past 20 years.

Yet it can be done differently. The European Framework (Council of Europe 2001) lists ways in which learners can 'develop their ability to handle the writing system of a language':

- by simple transfer from L1
- by exposure to authentic texts . . .
- by memorization of the alphabet concerned . . .
- by practising cursive writing . . .
- by memorizing word-forms . . .
- by the practice of dictation.

This is an admirable summary of an approach to teaching writing systems across languages, balancing different routes and different scripts in a principled fashion, uncluttered by the long history of the teaching of English spelling.

To sum up (see Table 5.3), children develop the English writing system in a fairly consistent way, even if they are surprisingly bound to features such as letter-names and the letters of their own names. They do not for some time rely on the orthographic principle or the lexical representation of spelling. L2 learners carry with them the baggage of their first language both in pronunciation and in writing system. Educational curricula have been developed in isolation from research into spelling development, perhaps with the exception of the Common European Framework.

Table 5.3 Second language acquisition of English spelling

- Many features of language are transferred from the writing system of the first language to that of the second
- L2 spelling mistakes reflect not just the L1 writing system but also the phonology of the L1 and pronunciation mistakes with English
- Lexical representation of morphemes is more available to adult L2 learners than to L1 children

DISCUSSION TOPICS

1 Prince Charles said 'All the letters sent from my office I have to correct myself, and that is because English is taught so bloody badly.' Do you agree? Is there anything in his remark that many teachers would take exception to?
2 Do you think that by and large English-speaking children are successes or failures at acquiring spelling? What do you attribute this to?
3 How important do you think it is to teach children the names of the letters of the alphabet and the order in which they come?
4 Do you think sounds are necessary to acquire letters or that letters are necessary to acquire sounds?
5 Why do some people fail to acquire English spelling?
6 Would you be pleased if you could spell a second language as well as a 15-year-old native speaker?
7 What do you think are the differences between acquiring a second spelling system and acquiring a first?
8 What would be on your list of things about English writing to teach (a) a child acquiring English as a first language, (b) an adult acquiring it as a second language?

ANSWERS TO TASKS

Task 2. Sound counting

	2 letters	3 letters	4 letters	5 letters
2 sounds	OF	who	edge	ought
3 sounds	OX	JET	page	judge
4 sounds		sex	COST	think
5 sounds			tuna	PLANT
6 sounds				music

Words with small capitals have the same number of letters and phonemes. Words *above* the small capital words in each column have more letters than sounds, words *below* have more sounds than letters (mostly <x> and <u>). (Note these word counts are specific to RP: dialects in some parts of Engand and the USA may, for example, have a correspondence between 'tuna' and /tuːnə/, that is, four sounds rather than five in RP /tjuːnə/).

Task 4. L2 learners' mistakes

Arabic: bicture, cuickly
Chinese: pratical, boyes
Dutch: wekk, thik
French: materiel, monney
German: higher archary (hierarchy), substitude
Greek: Grade Britain, Creek
Italian: wether, obbligation
Japanese: brack, difficulity
Urdu: countery, finall
Spanish: exclussive, inteligent

FURTHER READING

- Cook, V. and Bassetti, B. (eds) (in preparation). *Second Language Writing Systems and Biliteracy*. Clevedon: Multilingual Matters. Articles reporting diverse approaches to the second language acquisition of writing systems.
- Frith, U. (1985) Beneath the surface of developmental dyslexia. In K.E. Patterson, J.C. Marshall and M. Coltheart (eds), *Surface Dyslexia*. Mahwah, NJ: Lawrence Erlbaum, 301–30. The basic reference for the three principles.
- Nunes, T., Bryant P. and Bindham M. (1997) Spelling and grammar – the NECSED move. In C.A. Perfetti, L. Rieben and M. Fayol (eds), *Learning to Spell: Research, Theory, and Practice Across Languages*. Mahwah, NJ: Lawrence Erlbaum Associates, 151–70.

- Temple, C. *et al.* (1993) *The Beginnings of Writing* (third edition). Boston, MA: Allyn & Bacon. A fascinating and lively book.
- Treiman, R. (1993) *Beginning to Spell: A Study of First-Grade Children*. Oxford: Oxford University Press. The most comprehensive modern experiment-based treatment.

6 Historical changes in the English writing system

INTRODUCTION

This chapter describes the main historical changes in the English writing system from its early days in the Old English spoken before 1100 up to the present day, demonstrating not only how the writing system of English evolved and separated itself from other languages but also how some of its eccentric properties originated.

The history of English writing is interesting in its own right as showing how a writing system develops. It is also important to those studying English literature as the first step into a written literature of a previous time is through the written texts. Editors have often seen it as their job to adjust the earlier writing system towards modern systems in order to help the modern reader with punctuation, letter forms and the like rather than giving the texts in their authentic form.

Opinions on history and spelling reform

. . . a hopelessly inadequate alphabet devised centuries before the English language existed to record another and very different language. (George Bernard Shaw 1948)

To raise awareness of the alphabetic principle, its corruption during the long history of written English, and its more rational application in other languages. (Objective 2 of the Simplified Spelling Society 2001)

If the professors of English will complain to me that the students who come to the universities, after all those years of study, still cannot spell 'friend', I say to them that something's the matter with the way you spell friend. (Richard Feynman 1998)

English orthography is not a failed phonetic transcription system, invented out of madness or perversity. Instead, it is a more complex system that preserves bits of history (i.e. etymology), facilitates understanding, and also translates into sound. (Richard Venezky 1999: 4)

English is one of the few major languages that has been blessed *not* to have had any large-scale formally sanctioned spelling reforms during its history, this despite the numerous attempts on the part of various individuals for the past three hundred years. (Richard Sproat 2000: 192).

The history of English writing has also often led to a 'Golden Age' claim that English was at some previous point a pure model of a shallow sound-based alphabetic writing system that later fell from grace. Usually this decline is attributed to the invention of printing freezing the written language at the moment when the spoken language was about to undergo major changes in its vowel system and vocabulary. Modern accounts explain its decline in the spread of e-mails, text messages and spelling checkers, to be described in Chapter 7. The box above shows some typical opinions on the sins of the English writing system and their historical origins. The history of English then leads in the final part of the chapter to the belief that English spelling should be improved through deliberate change, usually called 'spelling reform'.

Usually the argument for spelling reform rests on a belief that the ideal writing system conforms to the 'alphabetic principle' that written letters correspond to phonemes, with its corollaries, the one-to-one principle that each letter links to a single sound and the linearity principle that letters occur in the same sequence as sounds, as discussed in Chapter 1. In other words the lexical route in reading and the orthographic regularities of English spelling are minimized or ignored. A typical view is that of an early pioneer of spelling change, John Hart, whose aim in 1569 was 'to vse as many letters in our writing, as we doe voyces or breathes in speaking, and no more; and neuer to abuse one for another, and to write as we speak: which we must needes doe if we will euer haue our writing perfite' (cited in Jones 1953). Looking at how English developed will show the extent to which Golden Age claims that English once had purely sound-based correspondences are justified.

English changed over the course of a thousand years in terms of grammar, phonology and vocabulary, as a quick comparison of Text 2, from the tenth century, and Text 4, from the seventeenth, will show. Since the discussion of English writing can never be divorced from the grammar, vocabulary and phonology of the language, this chapter sketches some of the more general language background, drawing on a wide range of sources mentioned in the references at the end. Unfortunately, apart from *A History of English Spelling* (Scragg 1974), most of these only make incidental comments on properties of writing in the midst of general discussion. Obviously the treatment here simplifies much of the complex writing systems of earlier English.

Focusing questions

- To what extent are any deficits of English spelling due to its history rather than to other aspects of the spelling system?
- Why do you think languages change over time?
- How much difficulty do you find in reading earlier forms of English, say Shakespeare or Chaucer? If you have not encountered them before, look at texts 2–4 below,

Key words

Old English (OE): was spoken before about 1100 AD.
Middle English (ME): was spoken between the Norman Conquest and about 1500.
Early Modern English: was spoken between about 1500 and 1700.
defunct letters: letters that are no longer used in Modern English include <þ> called 'thorn', <ð> nowadays called 'eth', <ƿ> 'wynn', <ȝ> 'yogh' and <æ> 'ash'.
Great Vowel Shift: this 'chain shift' affected all the spoken long vowels from Middle English to Early Modern English.
Anglo-Norman: was the type of French brought from Normandy by the French invaders, distinct from Parisian French.

6.1 BEFORE ENGLISH

Before looking at English itself, let us see how alphabetic sound-based writing systems originated. Text 1 below displays the first four letters of some early alphabets that influenced English. The concept of sound–letter correspondence is believed to have started in the Semitic languages of the eastern Mediterranean around 1700 BC, leading to scripts for Hebrew, Arabic and Phoenician. These used letters to correspond only to consonants and were written from right to left, as seen in Chapter 1. Hebrew and Arabic have remained consonant-based ever since. The Phoenician alphabet in Text 1A was written quickly with a reed brush. As can be seen, the letters have already been rotated 90° clockwise so that aleph 𐤀 no longer resembles the drawing of an ox's head on which it was based.

The Greeks took over the alphabet from the Phoenicians in the tenth or ninth century BC, eventually changing the writing direction from right to left to left to right and rotating the letters one more step, as seen in Text 1B. These changes may be partly a

Text 1. The letters <ABCD> in early alphabets

A. Phoenician	eighth to first centuries BC	𐤀𐤁𐤂𐤃
B. Early Greek	eighth to seventh centuries BC	ΑΒΓΔ
C. Trajan's column	114 AD	ABCD
D. Runes	fourth to seventh centuries AD	ᚠᛒᚲᛞ
E. Book of Kells	ca 800 AD	abcd
F. Carolingian	eighth to tenth centuries AD	abcd

consequence of using a split-reed pen, which is easier for a right-handed person to use from left-to-right without obscuring or smudging what they are doing (Jackson 1981). The crucial change, however, was adapting six Phoenician letters to correspond to vowel phonemes, thus creating the first fully alphabetic system where all the phonemes were represented, vowels and consonants alike. By about the beginning of the sixth century BC, this alphabet had reached Rome by complex cultural routes through the Etruscans, leading to the classic Roman alphabet carved, for instance, on the Trajan Column in 114AD, seen in Text 1C from which modern Roman fonts such as Times New Roman are ultimately derived, as discussed in Chapter 4. Its use of serifs shows the possibilities afforded by carving letters into stone with a chisel.

One strange survivor from the earliest times is the actual order of letters in the alphabet 'abcde . . .'. Children today still chant essentially the same order as the Phoenicians three and a half thousand years ago, apart from the few letters that have been lost or added. As a side effect, alphabetic order proved immensely useful as a way of organizing information, from dictionaries to phonebooks.

Due to the influence of Latin and the power of the Roman Empire, the Roman alphabet spread across Europe. The original letter-to-sound correspondences did not necessarily work in the diverse European languages. Hence new letters had to be added to the original Roman letters, leading eventually to <y> and <w> in English. Alternatively some letters effectively split in two, such as the fairly late division in mid-seventeenth century English of <i> from <j> and <u> from <v>.

In general the Roman alphabet consisted only of capital letters, as seen in Text 1C. The lower-case alphabet originated in the attempts of scribes to get a quick and flowing handwriting style using a quill pen. This innovation came to England via the influence of the Irish scribes of the seventh and eighth centuries AD, seen for example in the Book of Kells around 800 AD in Text 1E, in which the letters were still not joined up. Little is changed in the script used today for Irish and in the signs used on Irish pubs everywhere. Influence also came from the 'Carolingian minuscule', seen in Text 1F, in which the letters could be joined up continuously, which was invented around the end of the eighth century AD and became widespread across Europe. Both Irish and Carolingian scribes slanted the pen, thus giving a continuous variation of thickness to the line.

A further source of letters for a few English letters was the 33 letter runic alphabet, also known as the 'futharc' after its first six letters ᚠ <f> and Λ <u>, etc., which was used chiefly between the fourth and seventh centuries AD. Runic inscriptions occur in several parts of Northern Europe such as Denmark and Sweden; the letter forms are suitable for carving with a knife rather than writing with a pen. In England they have been found on crosses in Northumbria and on a knife retrieved from the Thames. The source of this alphabet is uncertain but it may be related to the mysterious Etruscan alphabet, believed to have acted as a bridge between the alphabets of Greece and Rome.

Punctuation marks started as an aid for reading Latin aloud, in the form of various dots and other marks. These were necessary because Latin was written without word spaces, making texts difficult to read aloud on sight. Around the eighth century AD, it became usual to put a space between words. According to Saenger (1997), this transformed reading from reading aloud to reading in silence. Without spaces, the reader had to test out loud what the text meant; with spaces, the reader could interpret the text without saying it aloud and they could read and write with greater privacy since their activity was not audible to other people; indeed Galileo saw the advantages of 'communicating one's most secret thoughts to any other person' (cited in Chomsky 2002: 45). Hence, once the lexical route became possible for reading European languages, authors became more daring individualists; and the speed of reading could be increased beyond the speed of articulation. As Harris (1986) put it, 'One is tempted to compare the introduction of the space as a word boundary to the invention of the zero in mathematics . . .'.

6.2 OLD ENGLISH

Old English (OE) refers to the varieties of English spoken from the fifth century AD till England was conquered by Normans in the late eleventh century. A specimen is given in Text 2. The display conventions are explained below.

Text 2. Old English: *The Wanderer*. Late tenth century

Version 1 Junius transcript; Version 2 'normalized' version; Version 3 rough translation.

A OFT hım anhaᵹa aꞃe ᵹebıꝺeð
Oft him ānhaga āre gebīdeð,
always the solitary man prosperity waits for

B meꞇuꝺeꞅ mılꞇꞅe þeah þe he moꝺceaꞃıᵹ
metudes miltse, þēah þe hē modcearig
the Lord's mercy although he sorrowful

C ᵹeonꝺ laᵹulaꝺe lonᵹe ꞅceolꝺe
geond lagulāde longe sceolde
throughout watery ways long has had to

D hꞃeꞃan mıꝺ honꝺum hꞃımcealꝺe ꞅæ
hrēran mid hondum hrīmcealde sǣ
stir with hands the ice-cold sea

E ƿaꝺan ƿꞃæꞇlaꞅꞇaꞅ ƿyꞃꝺ bıð ꝼul aꞃæꝺ·
wadan wræclāstas. Wyrd bið ful aræd!
travel paths of exile. Fate is quite inexorable.

Old English was originally brought to England by the invading tribes of Angles, Jutes and Saxons in the fifth century – hence older books sometimes call it Anglo-Saxon. Before discussing the OE writing system, some differences between Old English and Modern English need to be illustrated.

Starting with grammar, Old English had a complex system of cases for showing the grammatical functions that words played in the sentence, that is, grammatical subject, direct object, indirect object and so on. The box below gives the case inflections for three OE nouns, 'hond' ('hand'), 'stān' ('stone') and 'scip' ('ship'). The OE reader could immediately tell from the inflection that 'hondum' was in the dative or instrumental case in the plural (that is, 'with the hands'), that 'stānas' was nominative or accusative plural (subject or object of the sentence), and that 'scipes' was genitive singular ('the ship's (captain)'). Groups of nouns differed in the form of these case endings rather than all nouns having a single form.

Some examples of the case forms of Old English nouns

	'hond' ('hand')		*'stān' ('stone')*		*'scip' ('ship')*	
	singular	**plural**	**singular**	**plural**	**singular**	**plural**
nominative/accusative	hond	honda	stān	stānas	scip	scipu
genitive	honda	honda	stānes	stāna	scipes	scipu
dative/instrumental	honda	hondum	stāne	stānum	scipe	scipum

Much of the grammatical meaning of Old English was conveyed through such case endings, which applied to adjectives and to articles as well as to nouns. They play little role in the surface of Modern English, apart from the varying forms of pronouns 'he'/'him'/'his', the genitive ' 's' 'Peter's', and the plural 's' 'books', although syntacticians describe English nouns as having a deep Case that is rarely manifest on the surface of the sentence (Cook and Newson, 1996).

While OE verbs had forms for first, second and third persons in both singular and plural (indeed Old English also had a 'dual' category for two people), they lacked modern tenses formed with auxiliaries – 'he is coming', 'he has come', 'he will come' and so on. The form of the verbs also differed according to whether they were 'weak', 'strong' or 'irregular', bequeathing groups of irregular past tense forms that still exist today – 'break'/'brought', 'run'/'ran', 'sleep'/'slept' and others.

Much of the OE vocabulary still exists in Modern English in one form or another. OE vocabulary was more uniform in character than later stages of English, borrowing only a few words from Scandinavian, such as 'lagu' ('law'), and French, such as 'sòt' ('foolish'). Hence the spelling system had to cope with a narrower range of words than in later periods of English. Once the OE inflections are ignored and OE spelling modified, it is obvious that many of the nouns mentioned above still exist in Modern English: OE 'hondum' becomes modern 'hands', 'cyning' becomes 'king' and 'scipu' becomes 'ship'. The words did not necessarily have the same meaning a thousand years ago: in Text 2E above, line 1 ‘wadan’ meant ‘travel’, not ‘pass through water’ as now; ‘sellan’ meant ‘give’, not ‘sell’; ‘spedig’ meant ‘successful’, not ‘speedy’. The most deceptive element for a modern reader is perhaps OE words that have changed in meaning but not in form. Task 1 challenges the reader to work out the modern descendants of some OE words, anticipating some of the OE correspondence rules to be given below.

Task 1. Word identification

Identify the modern descendants of these OE words (given in normalized script).

āscian, blæc, cēap, dēofol, ecg, fēower, giefu, hlāford, hwēol, īeg, lēoht, mōnaþ, nǣdre, pund, sceal, tōþ, þicce, weg

Text 2 gives the opening of the OE lyric poem *The Wanderer*, dated between 950 and 1000 AD. OE texts only existed in a hand-written form. A completely faithful version is almost unreadable today without practice. Text 2 gives the text in three different versions. The first version is a transcription of *The Wanderer* into the Junius font (a downloadable font derived from an eighteenth-century print font for Old English, which is quite close to the appearance of the hand-written *Wanderer*). This gives an idea of the letter shapes and of the letters that no longer exist. The second version gives the ‘normalized’ Old English that appears in modern texts. This has been adapted to the needs of modern readers by changing the letters, punctuation and line-breaks, and adding a length mark < ¯ > to show long vowels, ‘hē’ (‘he’). The third version is a rough translation into Modern English, more or less word by word. The discussion will draw on both the Junius and the normalized versions where appropriate, using the Junius when forms of letters are at stake.

The Wanderer is written in a dialect of Old English called West Saxon, which seems to have constituted a standard written language. While there was variation between the OE dialects, for the most part the spelling was well established by this final stage of Old English.

Old English letter forms

- The actual forms of Old English letters sometimes differed from Modern English. Thus <d> is <ꝺ> in ‘honꝺum’ (Text 2, line 4, ‘hondum’, ‘hands’); <t> is <ꞇ> in ‘meꞇuꝺeꞅ’ (line 2, ‘metudes’, ‘lord’s’); <f> is <ꝼ> in <ꝼul> (‘full’); <s> is <ꞅ> in ‘ꞅæ’ (line 4, ‘sǣ’, ‘sea’); <i> is <ı> with no dot in ‘him’; and <r> is <ꞃ> in <ɑꞃe> (line 1, ‘āre’, ‘prosperity’) and so on. While these Junius letters represent a computer rendition of a print font, they seem fairly accurate versions of the original letter forms.
- Two distinctive letters that no longer exist in English are <þ>, called ‘thorn’, seen in ‘þeɑh þe’ (line 2), an ancestor of modern ‘though’, and <ð>, a crossed <d> nowadays called ‘eth’, seen in ‘ᵹebıꝺeð’ (line 1, ‘gebīdeð’), related to modern ‘bides’. Both these OE letters corresponded to the dental fricatives /θ/ and /ð/ in modern

'though' and 'think', but they did not consistently signal a difference between voiced /ð/ and voiceless /θ/, as these were not distinct phonemes. The form of <þ> comes from the runic letter ᚦ. The capital letter form of <ð> was <Ð>.

- The letter <ƿ>, called 'wynn', is seen in 'ƿaꝺan' (line 5, 'travel') and corresponded to /w/. It is usually written as <w> in normalized texts, 'wadan', and is derived from the runic character ᚹ.
- The letter <ᵹ>, called 'yogh', usually corresponded to /g/ before <æ a o u y> in 'gǣst' ('spirit') and to /j/ before <e i> 'ᵹeonꝺ' (line 3) (c.f. modern '(be)yond') and 'ꝺæᵹ' ('day'), and to the velar fricative /ɣ/ after back vowels, as in 'laᵹu' ('law') and 'ꝺꞃaᵹan' ('draw'). <ᵹ> is usually written as 'closed' <g> rather than open <ᵹ> in normalized text, that is, 'geond'.
- The letter <æ>, called 'ash', seen in 'ƿꞃæꞇlaꞅꞇaꞅ' (line 5, 'wræclāstas', 'paths of exile'), corresponded to /æ/ in 'fæder' ('father') and 'sǣ' ('sea') in short and long forms. Its capital letter form was <Æ>.
- Several letters of the modern alphabet either were not present in Old English, such as <q>, or were treated as variants of other letters, for example <j>/<i> and <v>/<u>. <cw> was used in words like 'cwēn' and 'cwað' where the modern spelling has <qu>, 'queen' and 'quoth'. <x> is sometimes found for <cꞅ> as in 'æx' ('axe').

Old English correspondence rules

The Old English writing system is commonly agreed to have been fairly shallow. Each vowel in the spelling of a word corresponded to a spoken vowel, apart perhaps from the first <e> in 'sceolde' ('should') (Text 2 above, line 3). Each vowel letter corresponded to both a 'short' vowel and a 'long' vowel, that is, two different phonemes. This is indicated by the length mark in normalized scripts, as in the <a>s in Junius 'anhaᵹa' (line 1, 'solitary man'), normalized as 'ānhaga', showing the first <ā> corresponds to long /ɑː/, the other <a>s to short /a/. Hence the <o> in Old English 'god' could correspond either to a short vowel /ɔ/, as in 'god' ('god'), or to a long vowel /oː/, as in 'gōd' (good). In addition to the usual five vowel letters, Old English <æ> had two short and long correspondences /æ/ /æː/ in 'bæc' ('back') and 'dǣd' ('deed'). <y> corresponded to two short and long central rounded vowels, /ʏ/ and /yː/ in 'yfel' ('evil') and 'lȳt' ('little') – that is to say <y> was not closely tied to <i>, as is the case in Modern English.

Old English consonant letters always corresponded to phonemes, as seen in the box below, that is, they formed a one-to-one system. Both <c> and <n> in 'cniht' ('youth', i.e. 'knight') corresponded to separate sounds, as did <h> and <l> in 'hlāf' ('loaf') or <p> and <r> in 'wrītan' ('write'). Hence doubled written consonants corresponded to two spoken consonants (or at any rate a consonant with doubled length) in say 'libban' ('live') or 'ridda' ('rider'). The main consonant digraphs are <sc> corresponding to /ʃ/ as in 'sceolde' ('should') (Text 2 above, line 3), 'scipu' ('ship') and 'sciellfisc' ('shellfish'), and <cg> corresponding to /dʒ/ in 'ecg' ('edge') and 'secgan' ('say').

Some Old English consonant correspondences
<h> ≡ /x/ 'riht' right
<h> ≡ /h/ 'hondum' ('hands')
<c> ≡ /k/ 'cald' ('cold')
<c> ≡ /tʃ/ 'cild' ('child')
<sc> ≡ /ʃ/ 'scipu' ('ship')
<ƿ> ≡ /w/ 'weg' ('way')

As Old English phonology differs from Modern English phonology in many ways, the actual OE correspondences between letters and sounds are often different:

- Voicing between the pairs of fricative consonants /v/ /f/, /s/ /z/ and /ð/ /θ/ was not distinctive as the voiced forms usually occurred only between vowels and in unstressed forms; in other words these pairs of consonants were not distinguished by voice and so did not constitute different phonemes. Hence 'fæt' corresponded to both modern 'fat' and 'vat'; <ð> and <þ> corresponded to both /ð/ 'þǣr' ('there') and /θ/ 'þing' ('thing'); <z> was missing as there was no need to distinguish voiced /z/ from voiceless /s/.
- <h> corresponded to the same /h/ phoneme as in Modern English before vowels, as for instance in 'hē' ('he') and 'hondum' ('hands'), but to a fricative with voiced /ç/ or voiceless /x/ variants after vowels, as in 'dohtor' ('daughter') and 'riht' ('right').
- <c> had similar restrictions to <ȝ>, usually corresponding to /k/ before <a o u y>, as in 'cald' ('cold') and 'cōc' ('cook'), and to /tʃ/ before front vowels, as in 'cȳse' ('cheese') and 'cild' ('child').
- Since the OE vowels probably differed from Modern English far more than the consonants, it is impossible to give all the details here. One striking difference is the six pairs of short and long vowels in Old English compared with the two pairs of Modern English phonemes that are distinguished primarily by length, /ɪ/ /iː/ and /ʊ/ /uː/. Another is the four OE diphthongs compared with the modern nine or so. Strang (1970) estimates Old English had 15–17 vowels and 15–19 consonants. Like Modern English, Old English had therefore to represent these 30–36 phonemes with the 24 or so distinct letters at its command.

Its solution, like Modern English, was to slacken the one-to-one principle of 'shallow' alphabetic languages by having one letter correspond to more than one phoneme, such as <h> or <æ>, or a digraph corresponding to one phoneme as in the correspondence of <sc> with /ʃ/. Old English also violated the linear order principle by making the correspondence of a letter depend on the letter that followed it; for example the correspondence of <c> was determined by the following vowel. Hence many of the deviations from strict sound – letter correspondences of Modern English are already present in Old English.

Punctuation

A comparison of the different versions of *The Wanderer* in Text 2 above reveals some of the OE typographic conventions and punctuation that were taken from the Irish scribes. The Junius transcript is written continuously without punctuation apart from the raised dot at the end of line 5. Old English was sparse in punctuation. In some texts a low dot indicated a short pause, a high dot a long pause (Strang 1970: 344): in other words, it was a correspondence punctuation system based on oral pausing, as described in Chapter 4.

As well as giving vowel length and modern closed <g>s, etc., the 'normalized' version shows the reader the structure of the poem by providing a comma, a full stop and an exclamation mark, and by dividing the poem up into lines and half-lines – the basic unit of Old English verse based upon a combination of stress and alliteration. The normalized version thus makes the text approachable rather than representing its original form. As Mitchell and Robinson (2001: 313) point out, the danger is that 'the use of modern punctuation can distort both the syntax and the meaning of OE texts'. The original *Wanderer* made little use of punctuation apart from word spaces. Yet the scribes who produced the text must have been aware of the extrinsic typographic properties of the page, which had produced such artistic feats as the Lindisfarne Gospels.

6.3 MIDDLE ENGLISH

Middle English (ME) refers to the English spoken between the Norman Conquest in 1066 and about 1500, that is, up to the time of Geoffrey Chaucer and *The Canterbury Tales*. During much of this period the ruling class in England used French for written literature, the courts and other public functions, but used Latin for scholarly and religious purposes. The rest of the population used English for their more humdrum lives. The dominance of writing in French in England meant little of this stage of written English was recorded. This multilingual situation exerted considerable influence on English, particularly from French, whether Anglo-Norman or the Parisian variety, in addition to the historical changes within English itself.

ME grammar differed from OE grammar in many ways, for instance reducing many of the case forms for nouns found in Old English to a final <e> – 'erthe' ('earth'), 'smale foweles' ('small birds') and 'yonge sonne' ('young son'). To balance this, Middle English relied increasingly on word order rather than case.

The diminished importance of case inflections had repercussions for the spelling system. Verbs were still divided into weak past tense 'lovede' ('loved'), strong 'bounde' ('bound') or irregular 'wiste' ('knew'). Some tenses formed with auxiliaries emerged, such as the perfect 'hath dronken' ('has drunk').

The vocabulary of English expanded during this period to take in many French or Latinate words such as – dates are the first occurrence in the *Oxford English Dictionary* (*OED* 1994) – 'assaut' ('assault', 1297), 'sege' ('seige', 1225) and 'treson' ('treason', 1225). Words also entered via the dialects spoken in the areas of

England occupied by speakers of Scandinavian languages. Sometimes the same word would enter English from two different sources, yielding for example modern 'skirt' from Scandinavian versus OE 'shirt' or indeed modern 'shorts', and 'dyke' (Scandinavian) versus 'ditch' (OE), or modern 'catch' (OE) versus 'chase' (Old French). The spelling system had to include words linked to the phonology of French or Scandinavian, unlike the comparatively uniform OE vocabulary.

As written Middle English was used at a local rather than national level, it had many dialects; 'ME is, *par excellence*, the dialectal phase of English' (Strang 1970: 224). The spelling system had to stretch to accommodate several dialects, unlike the comparative uniformity of Old English. In different areas the same word might be spelled 'betwen', 'bytuene' and 'bytwene', or 'nyght', 'niȝt', 'nyȝt', 'nycht' and 'nyht', or 'treuthe', 'trouthe', 'trowthe', 'trawþe' and 'truth'. Even the same individual might write, on different pages, 'strengðe'/'strenðe', 'aȝæin'/'aȝan' or 'after'/'æfter' (Scragg 1974). Although the London dialect in the works of Chaucer is most familiar to the modern reader, this is because it subsequently led to the modern standard, not because it was a standard in its own time (Smith 1999).

Text 3 gives the opening of *Sir Gawain and the Green Knight*, an Arthurian poem dated around 1390 written in the West Midland dialect and a descendant of the type of English verse seen in *The Wanderer*. As there is no computer font for Middle English equivalent to Junius for Old English, the text is given here in the normalized version used by modern scholars. In this case the normalization conventions seem closer to the original than those for Old English, for instance preserving the line-breaks, lacking vowel length marks and using the open <ȝ>, avoided in normalized Old English texts.

Text 3. Middle English: *Sir Gawain and the Green Knight*, circa 1390

1 Siþe þe sege & þe assaut watȝ sesed at Troye,
After the seige and the assault had ceased at Troy

2 Þe borg brittened & brent to brondeȝ & askeȝ,
The town destroyed and burnt to brands and ashes

3 Þe tulk þat þe trammes of tresoun þer wroȝt
The man who the schemes of treason there made

4 Watȝ tried for his tricherie, þe trewest on erthe.
Was tried for his treachery, the truest on earth.

Middle English letter forms

- The letter forms of Middle English in the normalized versions differ from those in the original handwritten manuscript. <s> was often written as a tall letter so that 'sesed' ('ceased') was 'ſeſeð'. The abbreviation for 'and' normalized as <&> was in fact <⁊>.

- The letter <þ> (thorn) was still used, as in 'þat' ('that') and 'þenk' ('think'). <þ> was often written as an open top letter so that <þe> was '**ye**'. The resemblance of <y>, the ME written form of <þ>, to a modern <y> led to the usage still found today of showing that something is quaintly old by spelling 'the' as 'ye' (usually with the word 'olde'), as in the pubs called 'Ye Olde Green Dragon' and 'Ye Olde Trip To Jerusalem'.
- The open letter <ȝ> (yogh) in 'wroȝt' ('wrought') was distinct from the closed <g> in 'vgly' ('ugly'), though this is not maintained consistently in the normalized texts.
- The letters <æ>, <ƿ> and <ð> were being superseded by <a> 'watter' ('water'), <w>/<u> 'trewest' ('trewest') and either <th> 'thenn' ('then') or <þ> 'þer' ('there').
- <u> was typically a variant of <v> 'leue' ('live'). The letter <j> was a word-initial variant of <i> 'joye' ('joy') versus 'ioye' rather than a letter in its own right. <y> was starting to be used for <i>, as in 'blysse' ('bliss'), 'tyme' ('time') and 'yrn' ('iron').
- The consonant pair <qu>, taken from French, was now the typical spelling for OE <cw> in words like 'quene' ('queen') or 'require' and <k> was substituted for OE <c> 'knyȝt' ('knight') and 'kyng' ('king').

Middle English correspondence rules

Like Old English, the ME writing system was shallow in that most letters corresponded to phonemes and no letters were silent, as seen in the box below. Unlike Old English, it had to accommodate a range of dialect pronunciations and many words from other languages. More use was made of consonant digraphs such as <ch> to correspond to one phoneme. The differences between the spelling of Middle English and Old English are partly due to changes of pronunciation, partly to changes of correspondences, partly to the prominence of Latin and French.

- The letter <þ> corresponded to what had developed into two 'th' phonemes, voiced /ð/ 'þat' ('that') and unvoiced /θ/ 'þenk' ('think'). However <th> was increasingly used for these correspondences, derived from Latin manuscripts, particularly with the start of printing.
- The open letter <ȝ> had multiple correspondences. Initial open <ȝ> corresponded to /j/ 'ȝere' ('year'), contrasting with closed <g> 'gere' ('gear'). After vowels <ȝ> corresponded to the fricative /x/ 'wroȝt' ('wrought') and 'ryȝt' ('right'), then changing to <gh> and finally having a zero correspondence when the velar /x/ sound was eventually lost in English). In Text 3 final <ȝ> corresponds to /s/ or /z/ 'watȝ' ('was') and 'askeȝ' ('ashes'), apparently due to an overlap between the letter forms <ȝ> and 'tailed' <z>, leading Scottish printers to use <z> to correspond to /j/ in names such as 'Menzies' and 'Dalziel' (now pronounced /mɪŋɪs/ and /diːel/ respectively in Edinburgh) (*OED* 1994). Closed <g> was used for the correspondence with /g/ 'borugh' ('town').

Some Middle English correspondences
<þ> ≡ /ð/ 'þat' ('that')
≡ /θ/ 'þenk' ('think')
<ȝ> ≡ /j/ 'ȝere' ('year')
≡ /g/ 'gear' ('gear')
≡ /x/ 'ryȝt' ('right')
≡ /s/ or /z/ 'watȥ' ('was')
<h> ≡ /h/ 'hungre' ('hunger')
≡ /ø/ 'oure' ('hour')
<y> ≡ /iː/ 'ryden' ('ride')
≡ /i/ in 'þyng' ('thing')
final <e> ≡ /ə/ 'scielde' ('shield')

- The correspondences of <c> and <k> became complex. On the one hand <k> gradually took over the correspondence with initial /k/ 'kyng' from <c> OE 'cyning'. On the other hand <c> corresponded to /s/ in 'lace' ('belt'), borrowed from French spelling.
- <h> corresponded to /h/ 'hungre' ('hunger') in words coming from Old English. As <h> in French had zero correspondence, that is to say, was silent, being effectively a leftover from Latin, French words that came into English mostly followed the original spelling with <h> but changed the pronunciation to match the spelling by adding an /h/, as in 'harmony' or 'humour'. ME spelling sometimes shows attempts to get rid of the unnecessary <h>, for example 'ost' ('host') and 'oure' ('hour'). A small number of words have kept the French /h/-less pronunciation, such as 'hour', 'honour' and 'honest'. A few have variants, 'herb' corresponds to /hɜːb/ in British English but to /ɜrb/ in American English; in my own speech I occasionally spot a silent <h> in 'historical' – 'an historical period'.
- <h> was also increasingly used as part of consonant digraphs. <th> was starting to replace <þ> in 'thenn' (*OED*: 1420). <sch> corresponded to /ʃ/ in 'schal' ('shall') (1200), replacing OE <sc> 'sceal'. <gh> was starting to replace <ȝ> in 'light' ('lyghte', 1398). <ch> replaced <c> for the correspondence to /tʃ/ as in 'cherche' ('church') from OE 'cyrice' ('chireche', 1200). <wh> replaced <hƿ> in 'what' from OE 'hwæt' ('whatt', 1200).
- Each of the six vowel letters had both a short and a long correspondence, for example <y> corresponded to /iː/ in 'ryden' ('ride') and to /i/ in 'þyng' ('thing'). In addition the London English spoken by Chaucer had eight diphthongs, such as 'day' and 'saugh' ('saw') (Strang 1970: 251). Vowel doubling sometimes indicated vowel length as in 'good' and 'feed'. Because of the dialect differences and individual quirks, the vowel correspondences varied considerably.
- final <e>. The different letters used in spelling the OE case inflections had now mostly changed to <e>, that is to say, OE 'nama' became 'name' in the thirteenth century according to the *OED*; the variant plural endings had now become 's' –

for example 'stānas' became 'stones' (*OED* 1400) – apart from a few modern survivors of the old plurals like 'goose' and 'oxen' <e> as a relic of the OE case system mostly corresponded to /ə/ as in 'scielde' ('shield'). It later became a 'silent' letter, though its use for showing preceding free vowels had yet to emerge systematically.

- <a> had now mostly replaced <æ> as in 'dai' ('day') from OE 'daeg' (1200) and 'þat' ('that') from OE 'þæt'.

In general, Middle English was more eclectic than Old English, largely due to its localized forms rather than a single standard form, allowing English writers a greater licence to spell in different ways, whether to reflect their own pronunciation or their own tastes. Though predominantly a shallow writing system, the one-to-one principle was broken, for instance in the multiple correspondences of <ȝ> and in the use of digraphs like <ch>. The linearity principle was also breached with the relationship of <c> and <k> with following vowels as in 'kyng'.

Task 2. The Canterbury Tales

Rewrite the opening lines of *The Canterbury Tales* (Chaucer 1387) from this normalized version into Modern English spelling.

Whan that aprill with his shoures soote
The droghte of march hath perced to the roote,
And bathed every veyne in swich licour
Of which vertu engendred is the flour;
Whan zephirus eek with his sweete breeth
Inspired hath in every holt and heeth
Tendre croppes, and the yonge sonne
Hath in the ram his halve cours yronne, . . .

Answer at the end of the chapter

Middle English punctuation

The four lines of *Sir Gawain* in Text 3 have no punctuation in the original manuscript, the commas and full stop of the normalized version being imposed by editors. The only punctuation marks in Middle English consisted of 'a low dot, an inverted semicolon and a virgule (/)' (Strang 1970: 159), used to indicate lengths of pause – short, medium and long. Like Old English, ME was correspondence-based rather than grammatically based and lacked marks such as the question mark and the exclamation mark that indicate grammatical punctuation. The normalized texts are therefore imposing a punctuation system on Middle English; the original ME writing system is being sacrificed to the convenience of a modern reader.

6.4 FROM EARLY MODERN ENGLISH TO MODERN ENGLISH

Early Modern English refers to English between about 1500 and 1700. The first printed books in English came just before the start of this period, coming from the first

English printers established by William Caxton in 1477. Most of the subsequent history of the English writing system has concerned the printed word rather than the hand-written word.

To a large extent, Early Modern English writing was standardized across the different regions of England, Scotland and Wales, though there were considerable changes in the spoken language over this period. It is often said that the pressure to standardize the spelling came from printers, whose descendants still play this role in modern times, as seen in Chapter 4. Brengelmann (1980) argues, however, that Elizabethan writers would have insisted that their views took precedence over those of any printing hack and that standardized spelling worked against printers by depriving them of flexible alternative spellings of words. For example, few of the actual spellings introduced by William Caxton have come down to Modern English. Brengelmann (1980) feels the work of scholars at changing spelling was a more important influence, to be discussed below.

The sample of Early Modern English in Text 4 is transliterated from Hamlet's soliloquy (Act II, Scene II) in the first folio edition of *Hamlet* printed in 1623, about the middle of the Early Modern English period, by which time most of the phonological changes from Middle English had taken place. The original edition can be inspected on-line at the Schoenberg Center for Electronic Text and Image (SCETI) (http://dewey.library.upenn.edu/sceti/). The extent to which this text differs from the familiar version reflects again the normalized forms of English in modern editions. No one can be certain of the extent to which the spelling and punctuation are derived from copies made for use in the theatre, the preferences of compositors, or Shakespeare himself (Partridge 1964).

Text 4. William Shakespeare, *Hamlet*.

First Folio edition, 1623, II.ii

Ham. I ſo,God buy'ye : Now I am alone.
Oh what a Rogue and Peſant ſlaue am I?
Is it not monſtrous that this Player heere,
But in a Fixion,in a dreame of Paſſion,
Could force his ſoule ſo to his whole conceit,
That from her working,all his viſage warm'd;
Teares in his eyes,diſtraction in's Aſpect
A broken voyce,and his whole Function ſuiting
With Formes,to his Conceit? And all for nothing?
For *Hecuba*?

The grammar of Early Modern English was largely similar to that of present-day English. Many distinctive features of Middle English had been lost. Word order had taken over from case forms, leading to a greater variety of word orders. Some of these are used more rarely today, for example inversion 'Had we but world enough and time', the opening line of Marvell's *To his coy mistress*. Prepositions were becoming more crucial to written English. The present simple tense 'I go' was used for events in progress where continuous forms with 'be' and '-ing' are more often used in Modern English 'I am going'. Romeo asks 'But soft, what light through yonder window breaks?', not 'But soft, what light is breaking through yonder window?' Case and number forms of nouns and pronouns are largely the same as Modern English, apart from the complex distinctions between singular 'thou' and plural 'ye'/'you'.

Vocabulary entered Early Modern English from a range of languages. While French and Latin were still important sources, English also took in 'brandy' from Dutch (*OED* first occurrence, 1622), 'zinc' from German (1661), 'sherry' from Spanish (1608), 'volcano' from Italian (1613), 'alcohol' from Arabic via Latin (1672), 'coffee' from Turkish (1598), 'tea' from Chinese via Dutch (1598) (also leading to the British variant 'cha'/'char'), 'chocolate' from Mexican Nahuatl (1604) and so on. In consequence, the spelling system of English had to accommodate words from many languages other than the French and Latin of Middle English. Conversely, many ME words had ceased to be part of the standard language: out of the ME words in Text 3 above from *Sir Gawain*, 'brittened' ('break up') is last recorded in 1535, 'tulk' ('man') in 1400 and 'wroȝt' ('made') is now only found in expressions such as 'wrought iron'.

Perhaps the most famous change in the history of the English language is the complex reshuffle of the phonological system of long vowels known as the Great Vowel Shift, which distinguishes Middle English from Early Modern English. It is called a 'chain shift' by Labov (1994) since the long vowels followed each other in a chain round the 'vowel space' in the mouth, moving upwards, and then becoming diphthongs when they couldn't move any further. Figure 6.1, taken from Cook (1997b), illustrates the movement of the back vowels. In terms of the vowel space of articulatory phonetics, the ME back vowel /ɔ:/ moved higher in words like 'goot' ('goat') /gɔ:t/ (rhyming with Modern English 'caught') to occupy the position of /o:/, and later changed into the diphthong /əʊ/ of modern /gəʊt/. The displaced /o:/ sound moved up to take the position of /u:/, turning ME 'root' /ro:t/ into modern /ru:t/. As ME /u:/ had nowhere to go, it became the diphthong /aʊ/, making ME 'dun' /du:n/ ('down') into modern /daʊn/.

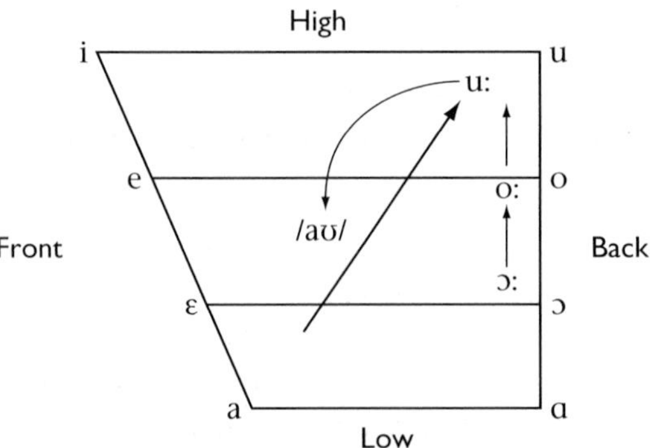

Fig. 6.1. The Great Vowel Shift shown on the vowel space (back vowels).

At the front of the mouth a similar chain shift occurred. ME /iː/ became a diphthong /aɪ/, so that 'wine' went from ME /wiːn/ to modern /waɪn/; ME /æ/ eventually became the diphthong /eɪ/ so that ME /naːmə/ ('name') evolved into modern /neɪm/, with similar stories for the other front vowels. The Great Vowel Shift thus profoundly shook up the English vowel system and led to many changes in the correspondences between vowel letters and vowel phonemes. Most of the Great Vowel Shift was effectively finished by Shakespeare's time in the standard language, with the exception of the upward move from ME /ɛ/ to Modern English /iː/, which was still at the /e/ position in Shakespeare's time when the word 'clean' had neither its modern correspondence /kliːn/ nor its ME correspondence /klɛn/ but a long /eː/ /kleːn/, not used in Modern English but similar to saying 'cleanliness' with lengthened /e/. The Great Vowel Shift did not, however, take place evenly across English dialects, some of which indeed still have unchanged correspondences such as /uː/ rather than standard /aʊ/ in words like 'town'.

The pronunciation of consonants changed little. ME /x/ was lost in words like 'right', making the digraph <gh> silent; /n/ was lost in some contexts, as in 'damn'; /l/ disappeared in 'half', /w/ in 'write' and /g/ in many words with <gn> such as 'sign'. These were now 'silent' letters as there were no longer corresponding phonemes in the spoken words in question. The voiced /ʒ/ phoneme was introduced into words such as 'measure'.

Early Modern English letter forms

In general the different technology of print led to changes in letter shapes (Jackson 1981). The punch-cutters who created the master letters from which moulds were made to cast the actual type were more like sculptors carving stone with a chisel than calligraphers copying manuscripts with a pen. Initially, Gutenberg had tried to mimic handwritten shapes, producing over 300 different letter forms for his celebrated Bible in 1455. The differences between quill pens and printing soon, however, led to distinctive print forms of the letters, for example reviving the carved classical Latin forms rather than the pen-strokes of handwriting, exemplified in some of the fonts seen in Chapter 4. Table 6.1 summarizes the history of English letter-forms.

The distinctive letters of Middle English such as <þ> and <ȝ> had given way in Early Modern English to <th> and <gh>. So the letters of printed Early Modern English differed little from those of Modern English, apart from the following:

- The form of <s> preserved the 'long' <ſ> of earlier periods in non-final word positions, as seen in Text 4 'ſoule' and 'diſtraction'. This letter survived in print until at least the late-eighteenth century, for example Richard Sheridan's *School for Scandal* (1780) has 'ſay', 'myſelf' and 'buſineſs'.
- Italics were used for certain special functions. In plays they occur for characters' names '*Ham.*' and '*Hecuba*' and stage directions '*Exeunt. Manet Hamlet.*' – the stage direction before Text 4 – as well as in Latin tags such as '*quondam*' or '*Vndique mors eſt.*'

Table 6.1 Comparing older letter forms with Modern English

	Shared letters	Extra letters	Variants of another letter	Rare letters	Unused letters
Old English (tenth century)	b c d f h l m n p r s t a e i o u y	ʒ ƿ þ ð æ	x (used for -cs occasionally æx)	k q z	g j v
Middle English (fourteenth century)	b c d f g h k l m n p q r s t w x z a e i o u y	ʒ þ (later th)	u (medial v) j (initial i)		
Early Modern English (1500–1700)	b c d f g h k l m n p q r s t w x z a e i o u y		u/v (till 1630) j/i (till 1640) 'long' ſ		
Modern English (1700–present-day)	b c d f g h j k l m n p q r s t v w x z a e i o u y				

- <v> and <u> had not yet separated into two letters in Text 4, <v> being preferred initially and <u> medially, as we see from 'ſlaue', and later in the same soliloquy 'vnpacke', 'Vnkle' and 'haue'. These letters separated in about 1630, according to the *OED* (1994).
- <i> and <j> were also not discrete letters: 'Iohn-a-dreames' and 'Iigge' occur in the same scene as Text 4. According to the *OED* (1994), they parted company in about 1640.
- <y> still functioned as a form of <i> in places where it is excluded today, for example 'voyce', and, later in the same soliloquy, 'Lye' and 'myraculous'. <ie> was used word-finally in places where <y> is now used. The title of *Hamlet* in the First Folio was 'The Tragedie of Hamlet', though the 1611 Quarto edition used 'Tragedy' in the running title at the top of each page.
- <z> now plays a full part, as in 'amaze' later in Hamlet's soliloquy.
- Capital letters were used in some books to indicate certain types of noun, 'Rogue', 'Peſant' and 'Player', and sometimes verbs and adjectives, though this usage is far from consistent. The Quarto *Hamlet* for instance had 'rogue', 'peſant' and 'player'. This usage persisted until at least the mid-eighteenth century.
- Capital <W> was sometimes in print literally a double <VV> as in 'VVell' and 'VVich' (Kyd 1592). This continued at least up to Otway's *The Orphan* (1680) 'VVomb', 'VVith' and 'VVhat', perhaps because of the use by printers of type from the Continent. Sometimes a form with two crossed <V>s is still found today, as in the logo for the publishers Wiley.

The box below summarizes the history of the disappearing letters of English and the letters that superseded them. This illustrates only some of the variant letter-forms, not for instance the multiple correspondences of <ȝ> in Middle English and their many descendants in Modern English.

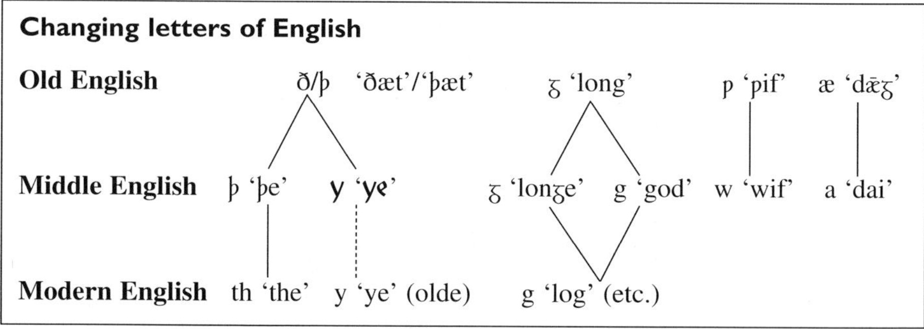

Early Modern English correspondence rules

On account of the Great Vowel Shift, by the end of the Early Modern English period most spoken correspondences for vowel letters had changed to something like their modern equivalent. The reason why English spelling fell out of step with speech was that the vowel system of the spoken language had moved on but by and large the vowels of the written language had not. Or as George Bernard Shaw (1948) put it, English has '. . . a hopelessly inadequate alphabet devised centuries before the English language existed to record another and very different language'. Present-day English in a sense has a Middle English letter-to-sound correspondence system and a Modern English phonological system. The relationship between the underlying lexical representation and the surface pronunciation, crucial to Chomsky's approach to spelling described in Chapter 3, can be interpreted as the links between an ME form of a word and its modern spoken form, though Middle English itself was far from having a standard set of consistent correspondences.

During the Early Modern English period scholars were becoming critical of English spelling and were suggesting how it could be improved. The box below gives the practice of Sir John Cheke (c. 1542), as worked out by Strype (1705) from his writings. Because of the perceived superiority of Latin as the language of learning, one pressure was to make English conform to Latin – 'the grosenes of oure owne Country language, whiche can by no means aspire to the hyghe lofty Latinists style' (Neville 1563).

The views on spelling reform of Sir John Cheke (c. 1542, as described by Strype 1705)

1 He would have none of the letter E put to the end of Words, as needless and unexpressive of any Sounds as in these Words *Excus, giv* . . . Vnless where it is sounded, and then to be writ with a double E, as in *Necessitee*.

2 Where the Letter A was sounded long, he would have it writ with a double AA in distinction from A short: as in *maad, Straat, Daar*.

3 Where the Letter I was sounded long, to be writ with double I, as in *Desiir, Liif*.

4 He wholy threw out the Letter Y out of the Alphabet, as useless, and supplied it ever with I, as *mi, sai, awai*.

. . .

7 Letters without sound he threw out; as in these Words, *Frutes, Wold, Dout, Againe for Against, hole, meen for mean*. And

8 changed the spelling in some Words to make them the better expressive of the sounds: as in *Gud, Britil, Praisabil, Sufferabill*

(Source: Jones R.F. (1953) *The Triumph of the English Language*)

So words that were thought to have Latin origins had their spellings changed to fit Latin or French patterns. ME 'langage' became 'language' from about 1300. 'Cors' early on acquired a <p> 'corps' which was pronounced by 1500; the final <e> was added in the nineteenth century, distinguishing 'corpse' from 'corps' in which the <p> is still silent. 'perfit' became 'perfect' by about 1590, gaining a spoken /k/ in due course. In these examples the added letter led to changes in the pronunciation of the words, even when this was not even justified by the correspondences in the source language. For example the <p> in French 'corps' is silent.

Some words, however, suffered only a change in spelling without a consequent change of pronunciation; the change from 'doute' to 'doubt' (1398) did not result in the <b> having any spoken correspondence; the change from 'Temes' to 'Thames' (1503) did not yield a pronunciation reflecting the <h>, and the change from ME 'sisours' to 'scissors' (1568) did not result in <sc> corresponding to /sk/, though I do have this variant in my own speech as a comic pronunciation /skɪzəz/. Added letters that have affected the spoken form included <d> in 'advance', <h> in 'habit' and <c> in 'verdict'. These changes were motivated by intuitions about the origins of words, sometimes right, often wrong. Thus 'iland' was remodelled as 'island' on the grounds of the French-derived 'isle' rather than its OE source 'ieȝ'; 'amiral' was changed to 'admiral' as it was thought to come from a Latin word with the prefix 'ad-' rather than from Arabic 'amir'. The overall principle was that English words should be made to conform to their Latin roots, a version of Venezky's principle seen in Chapter 3 'Etymology is honoured' except that is based on faithfulness to other languages not to English itself. Unlike 'silent' letters left stranded by historical changes in pronunciation, this type of wilful change created many silent letters with no function in present-day English correspondence rules, such as the <th> in 'asthma' or the <b> in 'subtle' discussed in Chapter 3, which prove a thorn in the side of approaches such as those of Albrow and Chomsky that assign particular values to silent letters.

A second contradictory principle common to most European countries at this time was the determination to see English as a language in its own right, independent of Latin. Some aspects of spelling were regularized to fit what were believed to be the patterns of English. So 'coude' became 'could' by analogy with 'would'; <w> was inserted in some words to get <wh> as in 'whore', 'whole' and 'whom', perhaps to provide a useful spelling contrast with 'hoar' and 'hole'. Many of the spelling reformers of this time were, however, concerned with making written English correspond better to the spoken English of its time, as seen in Cheke's practice in the box above. John Hart (1569) suggested dropping superfluous letters, such as <y>, <w>, <c> and silent <e> and all capital letters, since they have the same sound as their lower-case counterparts. Richard Mulcaster (1582) advocated the use of 'custom', that is, tempering the alphabetic principle for words that have well-established idiosyncratic spellings, and he saw the need for the spelling system to change constantly to keep up with the evolving spoken language.

Other more specific correspondence issues are:

- As Early Modern English was rhotic and /r/ could occur before consonants or silence, <r>s were not 'silent' in 'heere', 'Player', and 'warm'd' in the Shakespearean English illustrated earlier in Text 4, as they are in present-day British RP, but not in most US accents. The loss of post-vocalic /r/ also affected the pronunciation of the preceding vowel, leading eventually to diphthongs and long pure vowels /ɔː/ in 'more', /ɑː/ in 'part' and /ɜː/ in 'bird'.
- <l> was now silent in words such as 'half' and 'salmon'. Because of the tendency for spelling to influence speech, /l/ has crept back in to some words that lost it, such as 'salt'. To buy an Underground ticket to Holborn in London in the 1990s,

I needed to say /həʊlbən/ with an /l/ not the /həʊbən/ of my youth, though doubtless Estuary English will soon modify the /l/ to /w/. <l> was also introduced in words whose spelling was changed to appear like French, for example ME 'faute' ('fault'), again sometimes remaining silent as in 'almond'.

- The status of final <e> was complex. It partly survived as a relic of the OE case system 'dreame' and 'ſoule'; but it was also added to some words, perhaps to help silent <e> mark the preceding free vowel, as detailed in Chapter 3. The amount of variation in the use of <e> suggests that it must have been silent.
- <w>, <g> and <k> were now silent in clusters such as <wr> 'write', <gn> 'gnaw' and <kn> 'knew', as shown by such Shakespearean puns as 'ring' and 'wring' (Smith 1999).
- <gh> had entered English spelling as a descendant of <ȝ>, corresponding to the fricative /x/ in words such as 'sight' and 'thought'. As the /x/ sound had disappeared in Early Modern English, <gh> now had zero correspondence, apart from words in which the corresponding consonant had become /f/ such as 'laugh'. In a small group of words initial <g> corresponding to /g/ became <gh> as in 'ghost' and 'ghastly', mostly introduced in books printed by William Caxton and reflecting his earlier days in the Netherlands where this spelling was used, as in 'gherkin'; indeed his books also used 'gherle' for 'girl' and 'ghoot' for 'goat' (Scragg 1974).
- Though the Great Vowel Shift had affected virtually all the long vowels of spoken English by the end of this period, this was not accompanied by changes in the spelling. Many vowel correspondences had changed and have remained the same ever since.

Early Modern English punctuation

Punctuation was still largely correspondence-based rather than grammar-based in Early Modern English but used substantially the same set of marks as present-day English. Text 4 runs the gamut of commas, colons, semi-colons, full stops and question marks, even if the use of the question mark in exclamations seems eccentric 'Oh what a Rogue and Peſant ſlaue am I?' – the Quarto edition has an exclamation mark. The comma <,> had now replaced the virgule </>, appearing first in 1530 according to the *OED*.

One absentee is the quotation mark, which was used occasionally as a sign of quotation but placed at the beginning of the line, sometimes as a 'diple' <>>, revived in e-mails, as will be seen in Chapter 7. Its major use for indicating the beginning and ending of quotation within the text itself only came in during the eighteenth century. A word space following punctuation marks was not necessary 'in a Fixion,in a dreame', though there is a space both before and after the colon, following a French convention.

A comparison of the Folio and Quarto editions shows considerable variation:

Folio: *Ham*. I ſo,God buy,ye : Now I am alone.
Quarto: *Ham*. I ſo,God buy to you,now I am alone,

The marks corresponded to possible pauses or tone-group boundaries rather than to grammatical divisions.

The most striking new use of punctuation is perhaps the apostrophe <’> for contraction, seen in ‘warm’d’ (‘warmed’ often edited to ‘wan’d’ or ‘wann’d’), ‘in ’s’ (‘in his’, Quarto), that is, standing for letters that are left out; the rest of the soliloquy includes ‘what’s’, ‘damn’d’, ‘by’th’’ (‘by the’), ‘i’th’throat’ (‘in the throat’) and ‘upon’t’ (‘upon it’). The apostrophe for contraction attempted to make spelling correspond to speech, hence its use in plays that tried to convey ordinary speech from mid-sixteenth century on (Partridge 1964). It indicated what was felt to be one or more absent correspondences, whether omitting <e> ‘warm’d’, <hi> ‘in ’s’, <n> and <e> ‘i’th’’ or <i> ‘upon’t’. The apostrophe was not, however, used for the genitive as in present-day English ‘John’s’, as one can see in part of the ‘to be or not to be’ soliloquy in the First Folio:

> The Oppressors wrong, the poore mans Contumely,
> The pangs of dispriz’d Loue, the Lawes delay,

Changes from Early Modern English to the present-day

Chomsky’s approach, discussed in Chapter 3, suggested that it was advantageous to spell a morpheme in the same way despite variations in pronunciation. The example that has often been used in previous chapters is the uniform spelling of the past tense morpheme ‘ed’ as <ed> despite differences in pronunciation. The question arises of when this uniform spelling of the past tense morpheme manifested itself in the development of the English spelling system.

Figure 6.2 shows the regular ways in which the past tense ‘ed’ morpheme has been spelled in English over time. The evidence comes from original editions of plays, starting from 1592 *The Spanish Tragedie*, attributed to Thomas Kyd, and selecting a play about every 20 years on up to Sheridan’s *School for Scandal* in 1780, apart from 1742 where a lack of suitable plays means using the dialogue from an edited novel, Fielding’s *Joseph Andrews*. Essentially all the examples of regular past tense were included up to about 100, the lowest number being 51 for 1667. The past participle forms, which were more frequent, have been excluded as they may well show a different pattern. Although the data are not necessarily typical of the English of a particular period, they do suggest broadly how the spelling of the English past tense inflection developed.

- From 1613 to 1760 the <’d> spelling dominated, whether ‘charg’d’ (1613) or ‘preach’d’ (1760). The only exception is its low frequency in 1742, due to a rise in <t> as in ‘dropt’ and ‘drest’. <’d> corresponded both to /d/ ‘liu’d’ (1613), ‘forg’d’ (1633) and ‘fir’d’ (1760), and to /t/ ‘promiſ’d’ (1613), ‘hop’d’ (1633) and ‘eſscap’d’ (1760).
- The <ed> spelling started at 44% in 1592 as in ‘loued’, hovering around 20% up to 1723, and returned to 24% in 1760. In 1780 it became effectively the only form at 97%. In most cases <ed> corresponded to the usual /ɪd/ after /t/ or /d/, as in ‘parted’ (1633) or ‘deſscended’ (1742); in some cases it may have corresponded

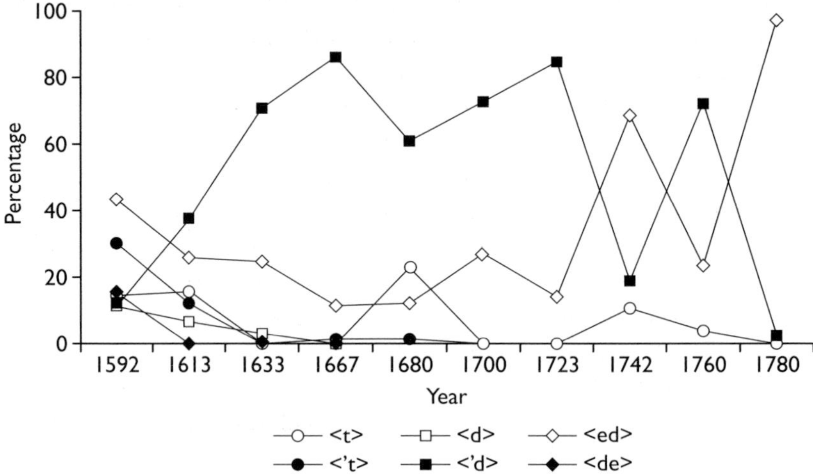

Fig. 6.2. Percentage of the <ed> past spellings at different periods. (Sources (all facsimiles except 1742): 1592 Thomas Kyd, *The Spanish Tradgedie*; 1613 Beaumont and Fletcher, *The Knight of the Burning Pestle*; 1633 Christopher Marlowe, *The Jew of Malta*; 1667 John Dryden, *The Indian Emperour*; 1680 Thomas Otway, *The Orphan*; 1700 William Congreve, *The Way of the World*; 1723 Ambrose Philips, *Humfrey Duke of Gloucester*; 1742 Henry Fielding, *Joseph Andrews* (edited by M. Battestin (1967). Oxford: Clarendon Press; 1760 Mr Kenrick, *Falstaff's Wedding*; 1780 Richard Sheridan, *School for Scandal*.)

to the full stressed form /ɪd/ after other consonants, as in 'strowed' (1592) or 'walked' (1633).

- Spellings with <t> and <'t> started with a combined 29% in 1613 but rapidly declined apart from a rise for <'t> in 1742. One difficulty, however, is knowing whether to include irregular verbs that still have <t>, such as 'left'. After an initial 13% in 1592, <d> vanishes rapidly, just as <de> is non-existent after 1592.

From this evidence it seems that the English spelling of the past tense inflection was not fully sound-based even at the beginning of this period. <'d> is used for past tenses regardless of whether it corresponds to /t/ 'look'd' (1633) or to /d/ 'hang'd' (1633). <ed> seems to correspond to a spoken /ɪd/ till say 1780. But <ed> did not take on the role of the invariant lexical spelling for 'ed' until 1780. Until this time there were at least two alternatives for the regular past tense 'ed'.

The consistent spelling of past tense 'ed' is then relatively recent in historical terms. The idea of representing the different correspondences of this morpheme by a single spelling did not emerge for several hundred years after printing. If such lexical spelling were a crucial factor in English spelling, it is surprising not only that children acquire it slowly over time, as seen in Chapter 5, but also that the English language managed without it for so long.

Deliberate improvements to English spelling

To conclude, is there now an answer to the question whether English spelling has deteriorated so much it should be reformed? The nearest English came to a single standard correspondence-based system was in late Old English around 1100, but even that was not fully shallow; each period since then has had difficulties in maintaining the shallowness of the writing system. The perceived problem is partly a matter of double standards: while people insist that words should have a single standardized form, with the partial exception of proper names, no one makes such claims for phonology or grammar: it would be just as advantageous to standardize dialect accents and words. English writing has a more established standard form than any other aspect of English – consider the mutual unintelligibility of English accents from different countries and dialects compared with the universality of the written language.

Since the sixteenth century, scholars have put forward alternatives to the current spelling of their day, going say from John Cheke to George Bernard Shaw. Sometimes this has meant changing the actual forms of the letters, as in the Shavian alphabet that won the prize bequeathed in Shaw's will for designing a new alphabet. More often it has meant rationalizing the letter-to-sound correspondences, for example the proposal called SR1 (Spelling Reform 1) to make all /e/s correspond to <e>, leading to 'meny', 'helth' and 'eny'. The box below presents the Cut Spelling system currently advocated by the Simplified Spelling Society, which 'modernizes' English spelling by eliminating unnecessary letters.

Cut Spelling

Rule 1: Cut letters irrelevant to the sound:

hed, dout, caut, wen, nife . . . etc.

Rule 2a: Cut unstressed vowels before L/M/N/R:

pedl, womn, vicr, caml, systm, victm, pistl, fathm, reasn, consl, albm, glamr

Rule 2b: Cut vowels in regular endings:

washd, washs, washng, washbl

Rule 3: Write most double consonants single:

eb, lok, wel, botl, hopd, hopng, acomodate.

Substitute letters:

- <f> for <gh>/<ph>: ruf, fotograf
- <j> for 'soft' <g>: jinjr, juj
- <y> for <igh> : sy, syt, syn

Use fewer capitals and apostrophes

- Only proper names with capitals: *France/french, Paris/parisian, Satrn/satrday.*
- Apostrophes for linking words: *she'd, it's, we'l, let's*, not for showing omission or possession: *oclok, hadnt, Freds house, our neibrs houses.*

(Based on the *Simplified Spelling Society Handbook* on-line at www.spellingsociety.org/pubs/leaflets/cutspelng.html)

The advocates of spelling reform believe above all in the alphabetical principle: 'An ideal spelling system matches letters to speech-sounds' (Simplified Spelling Society 2001). Cut Spelling would have to demonstrate that reduced forms such as 'womn' and 'washd' are as easy and rapid to use via the lexical route as their usual spoken counterparts; that losing the small number of lexical spellings is an advantage; that the current accessibility of written English to people all over the world almost regardless of dialect would not be sacrificed; that the compatibility of English with other languages, particularly on the web, is not compromised; and that the price of cutting off readers from previous periods of English is worth bearing, let alone any financial costs involved.

Historically speaking, attempts to change a writing system have been fairly unsuccessful apart from major switches in the whole system, such as the change from Arabic script to Roman script in Turkey in 1928, the introduction of simplified characters in China in 1956, and recent, still controversial, changes in the spelling of German. Perhaps the only changes to English that have stuck have been those adopted in the USA, to be discussed further in the next chapter.

To sum up, the English writing system has changed in complex ways over a thousand years, partly because of phonological changes, partly in response to new vocabulary introduced from other languages, partly to accommodate new technology such as the printing press and the computer. The actual letters took more or less their present-day forms in the Middle Ages, with some later divisions of letters such as <i> and <j>; modern punctuation marks were finally established during the eighteenth century. The letter-to-sound correspondences underwent a major upheaval with regard to vowels after the Great Vowel Shift. Aspects of lexical representation of morphemes such as the past tense 'ed' were adopted in the eighteenth century. Task 3 gets the reader to apply the descriptions in the chapter by dating a set of texts from different periods.

All in all, English has moved down the continuum of orthographic depth towards being a deep system. Whether this is a good thing or a bad depends on one's assumptions about the optimal balance between sound-based and meaning-based relationships in a language.

Task 3. Dates of texts

Put these passages in chronological order according to the spelling (some are normalized for their period).

A To them that demaund what fruites the Poets of our time bring forth, or wherein they are able to proue themselues necessary to the state. Thus I answere. First and for most, they haue cleansed our language from barbarisme and made the vulgar sort here in *London* (which is the fountaine whose riuers flowe round about *England*) to aspire to a richer puritie of speach, than is communicated with the Comminaltie of any Nation vnder heauen.

B THIS, my Lord, is my idea of an Englifh dictionary, a dictionary by which the pronunciation of our language may be fixed, and its attainment facilitated; by which its purity may be preferved, its ufe afcertained, and its duration lengthened.

C Ðā wæs ymb fēower hund wintra and nigon and fēowertig fram ūres Drihtnes menniscnysse þæt Martiānus cāsere rice onfēng and VII gēar haefde.

D The *Spanish* and the *Spaniard* both are Grave, the *Italian* and th'*Italians* Amorous, the *Dutch* as boisterous as the *Germans*, and the *French* as light as they themselves are. But the moderate Clime of *England* has indifferently temper'd us as to both: and what excess there is in either, must be attributed to the accession of something Foreign.

E In Ethiope all the ryueres and the watres ben trouble, and þei ben somdell salte, for the gret hete þat is þere. And the folk of þat contree ben lyghtly dronken, and han but litill appetyt to mete. . . . In þat contree ben folk þat han but o foot; and þei go so blyue it is meruaylle; and the foot is so large þat it schadoweth all the body aȝen the sonne, whanne þei wole lye and reste hem.

DISCUSSION TOPICS

1 To what extent is it right to alter the writing system of older texts to conform to the modern system, show length of vowels, etc., as done in most edited versions of older English texts?
2 How does a knowledge of the historical development of English aid the modern reader or writer of English?
3 To what extent is the writing system shaped by the technology of its age, whether the quill pen, the printing press or the personal computer?
4 Do you agree with Bill Bryson (1991: 199) that 'we have today in English a body of spellings that, for the most part, faithfully reflect the pronunciations of people living 400 years ago'? If so, is this a bad thing?
5 Have spelling reformers by and large had a good or a bad effect on the English writing system?
6 Does the lack of spelling uniformity for past tense 'ed' before say 1780 show that the different forms were not felt to be a single morpheme or a switch to a spelling more closely based on lexical representation?
7 What suggestions would you make for spelling reform based on the approaches to English spelling outlined in Chapter 3? Would these largely be the same as those advocated in Cut Spelling?
8 A well-known example of the iniquities of English spelling attributed to George Bernard Shaw (though apparently not found specifically in his writings) is that

'ghoti' is an alternative spelling for 'fish'. Using the approaches in Chapter 3, is this (a) a fair account of an alternative spelling of 'fish', (b) a proper criticism of English spelling?

ANSWERS TO TASKS

Task 1. Word identification (normalized script)

NB. The fact that the modern word is derived from an OE word does not mean it now has the same meaning.

āscian – ask blæc – black cēap – cheap dēofol – devil
ecg – edge fēower – four giefu – gift hlāford – lord hwēol – wheel
īeg – island lēoht – light mōnaþ – month nǣdre – adder pund – pound
sceal – shall tōþ – tooth þicce – thick ƿeg – way

Task 2. *The Canterbury Tales*

Word-by-word respelling with no other changes.

When that April with his showers sweet
The drought of March has pierced to the root,
And bathed every vein in such liquor
Of which virtue engendered is the flower;
When Zephirus eek with his sweet breath
Inspired has in every holt and heath
Tender crops, and the young sun
Has in the Ram his half course run, . . .

Task 3. Dates of texts

1 Extract C. *Bede's Ecclesiastical History* (731).
2 Extract E. *The Voiage and Travaile of Sir Iohn Maundeville* (c. 1400–1425).
3 Extract A. Thomas Nashe (1592), *Pierce Penilesse, His Supplication to the Divell.*
4 Extract D. Elisha Coles (1676), *An English Dictionary.*
5 Extract B. Samuel Johnson (1747), *Plan of a Dictionary.*

FURTHER READING

■ Jackson, D. (1981) *The Story of Writing*. London: Studio Vista. At one level a popular account, at another insights from a master calligrapher into the physical properties of writing technology.
■ Jones, R.F. (1953) *The Triumph of the English Language*. Stanford, CA: Stanford University Press. Memorable introduction to ideas about the English language current in 1476–1660.
■ Mitchell, B. and Robinson, F.C. (2001) *A Guide to Old English* (Sixth edition). Oxford: Blackwell. An approachable introduction.

- Parkes, M.B. (1992) *Pause and Effect: An Introduction to the History of Punctuation in the West*. Aldershot: Scolar Press.
- Saenger, P. (1997) *Space Between Words: The Origins of Silent Reading*. Stanford, CA: Stanford University Press. The main argument for the crucial role of word spaces.
- Scragg, D. (1974) *A History of English Spelling*. Manchester: Manchester University Press. The only book-length treatment.
- Strang, B. (1970) *A History of English*. London: Methuen. A mine of information despite its eccentric format of treating history backwards from the present.

Variation in the English writing system

7

INTRODUCTION

The English writing system has had to adapt to changing circumstances. Chapter 6 has already shown its flexibility in incorporating the changing vocabulary of English over the centuries. Its adaptation to different countries is the subject of Part 7.1 of this chapter through the contrasting British and American spelling styles. The English writing system is sufficiently well-established that it can be played with in names of products, visual puns, names of pop groups and many other ways, which is approached in Part 7.2. Written English has also taken hold of the internet, even if its grasp is gradually being loosened, and has been adapted to e-mails, chat-rooms and text messages, the subject of Part 7.3.

A crucial aspect of language is that it links to one's identity as a member of a group. In spoken language this is often achieved through accent. How you speak English proclaims who you are, whether from Toronto or Delhi, whether a man or a woman, whether a lawyer or a firefighter. As Firth (1951) put it, 'Surely it is part of the meaning of an American to sound like one'. Group loyalty manifests itself in several ways in the English writing system. At one level it becomes a matter of patriotism: your national identity is shown by whether you spell in a Canadian, a British or an American fashion. While people accept that speakers have different accents; they are far less tolerant about variations in spelling. A paper of mine was returned with the comment 'American spelling for an American journal': no one has ever required me to use an American accent for an American conference. As Jaffe (2000: 502) puts it, 'Orthography selects, displays and naturalises linguistic difference, which is in turn used to legitimise and naturalise cultural and political identity'.

At another level spelling can be a mark of regional or social group membership. The actual pronunciation of the group can be mimicked through unusual sound correspondences, as in dialect spelling such as 'Down Vizes way zom years agoo, When smuggal'n wur nuthen new . . .'. Or an arbitrary group standard can be adopted unrelated to pronunciation, for instance British 'colour' versus American 'color'. Particular conventions act as a way of excluding outsiders, say the chat-room convention of abbreviations such as 'LOL' ('laughing out loud'). Jargon makes insiders feel they belong and outsiders feel uncomfortable, whether the groups consist of teenagers, street gangs, football fans or syntacticians.

7.1 DIFFERENCES OF REGION: 'BRITISH' AND 'AMERICAN' SPELLING STYLES

Focusing questions

- Can you identify from spelling alone whether something is written by a person from England, the USA or Australia? How? (Test yourself on Task 1 if not sure.)
- Do you use British 'honour' or American 'honor'? Are you consistent with other words?
- Do you think it matters whether you use British or American spelling? Why?

Key words

eye-dialect: deviant spelling conventionally intended to show non-standard speech, while actually corresponding to a standard spoken form.

The English language is used by vast numbers of people all over the world, both native speakers and second language users. English has adapted itself to different countries and different uses. Considerable academic attention has been paid to the characteristics of the English used in the various parts of the world, such as Australia, England, Singapore, India and many others, whether in terms of accent, grammar or vocabulary.

Controversies have raged over whether some varieties of English should have more status than the others, particularly in a teaching context: should a Japanese be taught Australian, American or British English for example? Does English 'belong' in some sense to the native speakers in England, New Zealand and a small number of other countries? Many now regard English as independent of native speakers (Cook 1999): L2 users need English as an international language to communicate with each other rather than with native speakers, say a Danish businessman negotiating with a German on the phone about a contract in English, or two Arabic-speaking businessmen exchanging e-mails in English (Cook 2002).

The sheer variety of spoken English is not, however, found in written English. If one looks at a range of English language newspapers on-line, say the *Tehran Times*, the *Daily Nation* (Kenya), the *Japan Times*, the *New York Times*, *The Star* (Malaysia) and the *Herald Sun* (Australia), it is impossible to tell where they come from in terms of the English writing system alone. Unlike the spoken language, there is no written 'accent' that betrays the person's origin, beyond the American/British styles of spelling. Written English has not so much adapted to local circumstances as remained constant regardless of the variations in writers and readers. In a way it resembles the success of the Chinese writing system at unifying speakers of many dialects through a single writing system. Written English too can be read by people who might find it difficult to understand one another in speech.

Yet this does not mean that there is complete uniformity within the English writing system. The most obvious variation that most people are aware of is that between British and American spelling. Task 1 tests some of the familiar shibboleths. Let us go over some of the salient differences between these two styles of spelling. Usage is often not firmly demarcated to particular language communities. Nor are the rules applied consistently within one language area. They also vary from person to person, or publisher to publisher. Furthermore, the differences are mainly based on the pronouncements of manuals of style and spelling rather than on the description of large corpora of written English. Both in Britain and in the USA, such manuals differ among themselves as to the preferred spelling for particular words. Sources for the following are mainly the British Carney (1994) and the American Venezky (1999).

Task 1. American and British variants

Which are British variants, which American?

	American	British		American	British
1 kerb	☐	☐	7 ameba	☐	☐
2 enrollment	☐	☐	8 kidnapper	☐	☐
3 traveller	☐	☐	9 judgement	☐	☐
4 favor	☐	☐	10 litre	☐	☐
5 defense	☐	☐	11 analyze	☐	☐
6 tyre	☐	☐	12 catalog	☐	☐

Answers at end of chapter

British <-our> versus American <-or>

One give-away to the source of a text is the difference between 'colour' and 'color', 'honour' and 'honor', and 'favourite' and 'favorite'. American spelling prefers the <-or> ending, British the <-our>. A similar rule applies to <oul> in some words; British style tends to keep the <u>, American to drop it, as in 'mould' versus 'mold' and 'smoulder' versus 'smolder'. This is not to say that some American words do not preserve <-our> such as 'glamour' and 'saviour', and some British words do have <-or>, for instance derived forms such as 'honorary', 'coloration' and 'laborious', and nouns like 'stupor', 'terror' and 'squalor', even though 'terrour' is found in the *OED* as late as 1712 and 'squalour' in 1635.

British <-re> versus American <-er>

Another familiar contrast is between 'centre' and 'center', 'theatre' and 'theater', and 'litre' and 'liter', in which British style prefers <-re>, American <-er>. One small advantage of the British <-re>, according to Carney (1994), is that it allows a distinction between 'agent' nouns like 'meter' (instrument for measuring things) and other nouns like 'metre' (unit of length). Some words nevertheless have the <-re> spelling in American English such as 'acre', 'genre' and 'ogre'. Venezky (1999) points out that the American <-er> is not extended to derived forms such as 'central' ('centeral') and 'theatrical' ('theaterical'). However, it is apparently now fashionable for various institutions in the USA to style themselves 'centres' rather than 'centers'.

Consonant doubling

Many words with single <l> in British style have double <l> in American, for example, 'appal' versus 'appall', 'enrol' versus 'enroll' and 'fulfil' versus 'fulfill'. On the other hand, many words have double <l> before an ending in British English that have single <l> in American, such as 'jeweller' versus 'jeweler', 'traveller' versus 'traveler' and 'woollen' versus 'woolen'. Similar variation is found with some other consonants, <g> in British 'waggon' versus American 'wagon' and <pp> in British 'kidnapping' versus American 'kidnaping'.

Regional spellings of English

the differences between American and, say British English spelling are quite modest (Cummings 1988: 26)

Although American customs in spelling have never differed widely from British, such differences as have existed have nevertheless been treated as though they were matters of some moment, as though the Americans had really done something startling to spelling (Krapp 1960: 328)

All that can be safely asserted of the contemporary conventions of standard Canadian English spelling, when there is a British/American choice, is that the norm is not yet to choose either indifferently for the same word in the same text (Pratt 1993: 59)

The Australian Government Style Manual 'arbitrates on many of the currently variable points of English spelling, generally adhering to what is often thought of as British rather than American practice' (Peters and Delbridge 1989: 129)

You'll find a cat today must be a hepster. Don't mind if you don't find the word in Webster. He's as square as a bear' (lyric to 'Are You Livin', Old Man?', Evans, Higginbotham, Silver, 1945)

<-ise> versus <-ize>

American spelling tends to use <-ize> in verbs and verb-derived forms where British uses both <-ize> and <-ise>. American 'apologize' is usually 'apologise' in British spelling, 'recognize' 'recognise' and 'criticize' 'criticise'. While the <-ize> form is clearly American in many cases, there are nevertheless American spellings with <-ise> as in 'advertise', 'televise' and 'improvise'; in reverse, British spelling has <-ize> in 'capsize' and 'seize'. In addition American spelling has some <-yze> forms where British has <-yse> as in American 'analyze' versus British 'analyse', 'paralyze' versus 'paralyse' and 'breathalyze' versus 'breathalyse'. According to McArthur

(1992: 43), among British publishers <-ize> 'is preferred by Cassell, Collins, Longman, Oxford, <-ise> by the Readers Digest (UK); Chambers has <-ise> for its native-speaker dictionaries, <-ize> for its EFL learners' dictionary'.

<-ce> versus <-se>

American style has <-se> in a number of words that have <-ce> in British style, as in American 'defense' versus British 'defence', 'offense' versus 'offence' and 'pretense' versus 'pretence'. In some cases British English signals nouns versus verbs by the <-ce>/<-se> contrast, for example nouns 'advice', 'practice', 'licence' and 'prophecy' versus verbs 'advise', 'practise', 'license' and 'prophesy', though often British speakers are uncertain of this distinction.

<ae> versus <e>

Some Latin or Greek-derived words that originally had <æ> or <œ> disassembled the letters into <ae> and <oe> in British but reduced them to <e> in American so that British 'paediatric', 'faeces' and 'haemorrhage' are American 'pediatric', 'feces' and 'hemorrhage'. British English vacillates over other words such as 'encyclopaedia'/ 'encyclopedia', 'mediaeval'/'medieval' and 'paeony'/'peony' where American typically has the <e> spelling. Other words have <ae> or <oe> in both British and American spelling, for instance 'canoe', 'reggae' and 'paella'.

Individual words

Some words vary arbitrarily between the two styles of spelling. One group of words alternates <-ogue> and <-og>: American 'dialog', 'prolog' and 'catalog' versus British 'dialogue', 'prologue' and 'catalogue'. A brief list of other differences between British and American spelling is given in the box below.

Some differences between 'British' and 'American' spelling (tendencies rather than absolute)

American	British	American	British	American	British
jail	gaol/jail	mustache	moustache	airplane	aeroplane
check	cheque	sulfur	sulphur	karat	carat
curb	kerb	program	programme/	cozy	cosy
plow	plough		program	aluminum	aluminium
skeptic	sceptic	wagon	wagon/waggon	ax	axe
draft	draught	tire	tyre	pajamas	pyjamas
gray	grey/gray	z (/zi:/)	z (/zed/)	namable	nameable
judgement	judgment/judgement	carcase	carcass/carcase		

Often, as British spelling allows both forms and American English allows only one, the alternative British spellings may distinguish different words, for instance 'to tire'/'a rubber tyre', 'to check something'/'to cash a cheque', 'a computer program'/'a theatre programme', 'to live on the second storey'/'to tell a story' and so on. Making letter-to-sound correspondences consistent destroys some of these possible ways of showing meaning.

Different as British and American pronunciation may be, most of these variations of spelling have little to do with pronunciation, let alone with the letter-to-sound correspondence rules in any wide sense, but concern orthographic regularities affecting a limited range of letter combinations and idiosyncratic words. None of them affect the major systems and rules described in Chapter 3, perhaps with the exception of some consonant doubling.

One place where pronunciation might be relevant is the rules for the letter <r>. Standard American English is a rhotic dialect in that /r/ is present in all positions and British English RP is non-rhotic in that /r/ is absent before consonants and silence, as seen for instance in Chapter 3. One neat demonstration is that characters who hesitate in British novels say 'er', whereas those in American novels say 'uh', though the sound is doubtless the same. The American correspondence of <er> would have to be /ər/, not the usual hesitation noise /ə/, whereas <uh> can correspond to /ə/ in a more straightforward way.

The main differences between British and American spelling come down to the reforms of one nineteenth-century man, Noah Webster. At various times he suggested cutting extra vowels, 'doctrin' and gazell', cutting extra consonants 'chesnut' and 'crum', and reducing digraphs to a single letter 'fether' and 'nusance'. His influential dictionary, published in 1828, established several of the distinctively American forms, in most cases chosen from alternatives within the spelling system of the period. His chief overall argument was that these promoted consistency: 'The irregularities in the English orthography have always been a subject of deep regret' (Webster 1828). Hence he advocated in the preface to the 1828 dictionary:

- <or> rather than <our> 'honor', 'labor' (difference 1 above)
- <er> rather than <re> 'scepter', 'center' (2 above)
- <se> rather than <ce> 'defense', 'offense' (5 above).

His dictionary also incorporated many other individual words with American spelling such as 'appall', 'enroll', 'apologize', 'feces', 'hemorrhage' and 'curb'.

Other proposals for changing the spelling system were made later in the USA. In 1898, the National Education Association scheduled 12 words for change, namely: 'tho altho thru thruout thoro thoroly thorofare program prolog catalog pedagog decalog'. Some are now the accepted American form, for example the <g> for <-gue> spellings and the single <m> in 'program'. The rest are seen in notices if not in academic prose, say the spellings without <gh> such as 'thoro'.

So the British and American writing styles differ in quite minor respects. Some of the differences in punctuation were described in Chapter 4, such as variation between single and double quotation marks and use of capitals after colons. American style spelling is not so much a systematic reworking of English as a minor tinkering with spelling reform. The differences between them is more like a designer label sewn on to the clothes than the clothes themselves – 'British' and 'American' styles – having nothing to do with systematic differences in sound-to-letter correspondence. Had American English been reworked to correspond better to American pronunciation or had the whole system been reformed on a logical basis then something more general and less arbitrary might have emerged.

Other varieties of world English mostly place themselves somewhere in between these two alternative styles, as seen in the box below, which gives the forms found in four countries and also gives two of the historical sources, the dictionaries by Johnson and Webster. Both Australian and Canadian spelling systems are seen as distinct systems of their own, usually claiming to be more towards the British end of the spectrum. Despite this, one analysis of Australian newspapers shows that two and a half times as many readers are exposed to 'color' as to 'colour' (Peters and Delbridge 1989); indeed, the political party is the 'Labor Party', though New Zealand has a 'Labour Party'. In Canada 'colour' was officially sanctioned by an Order-in-Council in 1890 and was preferred by 75% of freelance editors in a poll. Usage varies between Canadian provinces, Ontario having the highest number of <-our> spellings such as 'honour' and 'favour', Alberta the lowest proportion (Pratt 1993). Canadians tend to prefer British <-re> in 'centre' and 'theatre', but American <-ize> in 'dramatize' and have some one-off American spellings such as 'aluminum' and 'tire'.

Variation for key words in different countries

In many cases these are tendencies rather than absolute rules in a country

British *OED* (1994)	Canadian	Australian	US New Collegiate (1979)	Webster (1828)	Johnson (1755)
colour	colour	colour	color	color	colour
labour	labour	labour (but Labor Party)	labor	labor	labour
centre	center		center	center	centre
woollen	woollen		woolen	woolen	woollen
enrol/enroll	enroll		enroll	enroll	enroll
apologise/ apologize	apologize	apologise	apologize	apologize	apologize
defence	defence		defense	defense	defence
encyclopedia/ encyclopædia	encyclopedia	encyclopaedia	encyclopedia	encyclopedia	encyclopedia
catalogue	catalogue		catalog	catalogue	catalogue

Sources: dictionaries as named, otherwise articles and web sources

To some extent these differences are felt to be a matter of national identity: the American spelling <-or> according to Webster (1828) 'commenced or received its most decided support and authority at the revolution' and he cites *George Washington's Letters* (1795) in support. Such regional differences do not extend outside this small area of spelling. It is odd that the only variations in the global English spelling system should be the work of a single dictionary maker in 1828. Webster made perhaps the only successful attempt at spelling reform of English. But it only affected a small area of spelling in an erratic way, showing perhaps how difficult it would be to implement the far more rational and extensive reforms mentioned in Chapter 6.

Table 7.1 British and American styles of spelling

Differences between British and American styles of spelling:

- are small in number
- have little to do with dialect differences in pronunciation
- are not consistently followed in either the UK or the USA
- mostly affect selected words
- are to do with <-our> versus <-or>, <-re> versus <-er>, consonant doubling, <-ce> versus <-se>, <-ise> versus <-ize>, <ae>/<oe/ versus <e>/<o>
- can mostly be traced to spelling reform by Noah Webster or the National Education Association

Representation of non-standard dialect

Regional differences in the writing system extend to the use of spelling to indicate dialect. A simple way is to use the existing letter-to-sound correspondences to indicate a non-standard accent. Task 2 calls for identification of the types of speech from three sources. Variations of pronunciation are shown by different vowels 'git' ('get'), 'agoo' ('ago'), 'hud' ('had') or consonants 'dat' ('that'), 'zom' ('some') or by apostrophes 'jes'', 'smuggal'n' or omission 'wi'' ('with'), in each case assuming that the reader can reconstruct dialect accent from the standard correspondences for <i>, <oo> and so on. As seen in Chapter 5, children learning to read English carry out a similar task of reconciling the spelling system with their own accent, which may differ considerably from the standard dialect.

Task 2. Dialect spelling in novels and poems

Which part of the world do you think the speech represented in the following literary sentences are supposed to come from?

1 'Where you *git* all dis lyin' an' drinkin' an' gamblin' an' runnin' roun'? You *knows* I ain't raised you like dat! An' don't think dis jes' me talkin'! Tilda ain't no fool, she jes' ain't let you know she seein' right through you, too!'

2 Down Vizes way zom years, agoo,
When smuggal'n wur nuthen new,
An people wurden nar bit shy
Of who they did ther sperrits buy.

3 The problem wi Begbie wis . . . well, thirs that many problems wi Begbie. One ay the things thit concerned us maist wis the fact that ye couldnae really relax in his company, especially if he'd hud a bevvy.

Answers are at the end of the chapter

A second way of showing dialect is to use spelling that indeed represents the sounds but is not the expected spelling. The sounds corresponding to the <in'> ending of 'lyin'', that is /ɪn/ rather than /ɪŋ/, are found everywhere in the English-spelling world, chiefly associated with male speakers. Similarly, /ən/ is a weak spoken form of 'and' so that representing it as <an'> in effect shows an ordinary spoken variant rather than a dialectal form. Spellings like <in'> and <an'> have become a label for a non-standard accent although they in fact correspond to ordinary spoken forms of English. Michael Moorcock in *The Condition of Muzak* conveys London speech *inter alia* by using 'wot' ('what'), 'woz' ('was'), 'corled' ('called'), 'shore' ('sure'), ' 'e' ('he') and 'yer' ('your'), all of which would be usual in the speech of many English speakers, not just that of Cockneys. This convention has been called 'eye dialect', that is to say the use of written forms that are labelled as non-standard through their deviant spelling but do not represent the actual pronunciation.

It is a moot question whether the representation of dialect speech in these ways actually conveys an appropriate image for the character and their group. Standard spelling marks the status and education of the speaker; hence non-standard spelling shows lack of status (Jaffe 2000). Spellings like those in Task 3 below imply at some level not just that the people speak a dialect, but that they are illiterate or at best quaint.

7.2 NOVEL SPELLINGS OF POP GROUP AND BUSINESS NAMES

Focusing Questions

- What pop groups can you think of with non-standard spellings for their names? What brand names?
- Why do groups choose such names?

Key words

letter-name and number-name spellings: use letters and numbers to correspond to syllables, particularly monosyllabic function words, for instance '4 U' and 'Toys R Us'.

Once a writing system has come into existence, the rules can be deliberately flouted, whether for serious or frivolous purposes. Underlying much use of English in technology-based communication are the traditional ways of playing with English, some of which are described in this section. Areas to look for such novel spellings are invented proper-names in television programmes, 'Klingons', or Dickens novels, 'Mr

Cheeryble', concocted business names, 'Rite Bite Restaurant' and made-up names for pop groups, 'Gorillaz'.

Thirty percent of the business names in the corpus analysed in Praninskas (1968) indeed used novel spelling. Jaquith (1976: 301) points out that novel spellings are seldom used for high-class restaurants or goods: ' "Fast food franchise" focuses on the criteria which overwhelmingly are characteristic of AF [advertising forms] products/services (1) high volume, (2) low price, (3) quick turnover, (4) quick expendability'. Fast food chains in England include 'Spud-U-Like' and 'Dunkin' Donuts'; fish and chip shops 'Sea Gee's', 'Frydays' and 'A Salt 'N' Battered'.

The box below provides a sample from Praninskas (1968), supplemented with some modern British examples, using essentially the same categories discussed for spelling 'errors' in Chapter 5, namely omission (styled 'elimination') 'Glasbake', substitution 'Fly Kop' and simplification of consonant clusters 'Everbrite'. An addition is 'syllabic representation' in which letters correspond to whole syllables rather than to individual phonemes. This too has been encountered in Chapter 5, which described children's early letter-name spellings such as 'nit' ('night') and 'blo' ('blow').

Graphemic manipulations in trade names

1 *Elimination of symbols*: Glasbake, Pic-a-puf, Kut 'n Serv, Hi Tec Autos, Sound Attak
2 *Substitution of symbols*: Fly Kop, Numzit, Jerm-o-nox, KwikFit, Beazer Homes
3 *Simplification*: Everbrite, Lash-Kote, Walkrite Shoes, Hi-Spec Opticians, Rentokil
4 *Syllabic representations*: Gard-n-Gro, Part-T-Pak, Q8 Petroleum, The Four Cs, 2 Bad Mice Publishers

(Source: Praninskas (1968), supplemented with some modern names)

Novel spellings

It is a poor mind that cannot think of more than one way to spell a word (Andrew Jackson)

Principle 1 . . . is that 'Variation is tolerated'. This is an egregious understatement, in that variation is actually invited in English orthography (Venezky 1999: 16)

All in all, there is no mistaking the kall of 'k' over our kountry, our kurious kontemporary kraving for it, and its konspicuous use in the klever koinages of kommerce (Pound 1923)

'new' and non-standard orthographies change the relationship between reader and text. They interrupt (if only for a fraction of a second) the seamless experience of meaning through text (Jaffe 2000: 510)

our culture and its bearers are sufficiently flexible to tolerate, even encourage, something like two writing systems for one language (Jaquith 1976: 306)

A novel spelling has to draw on aspects of the existing spelling system. Chapter 3 described the main spelling correspondences and orthographic regularities of English, which are thoroughly exploited in the creation of novel spellings. If, however, inventions went too far beyond the current system, they would no longer be comprehensible to the users.

This section draws on two main sources of novel spellings: the names of pop groups as spelled in listing magazines and the names of businesses as given in *Yellow Pages*, both primarily taken from UK sources. Task 3 displays some names of contemporary pop groups and tests whether they fit the categories of Praninskas' analysis.

Task 3. Novel spellings in pop group names

Test Praninskas (1968) in the box on p. 187 against this sample of pop group names.

> Reprazent, Pollen 8, Eminem, U2, Guns 'n' Roses, No Way Sis, Mu-Ziq, Black II Basics, 'N Sync, OP8, Serial Thrillaz, Sugababes, The Noize, The Pharcyde, Motörhead, B-witched, Propa-Ghandi, 4-Hero, The Bruvvers, Fun Lovin' Criminals, Ko-egzist, Mellon Collee, Slaughta, The Diaboliks, Headrillaz, Ezey Ryder, Soula Power

Novelty through alternative correspondences

One way of creating a novel spelling is to utilize a letter that corresponds to the correct sound but is unusual for a particular position in the word, thus creating the appearance of novelty without any change in the overall system. For instance, while both <k> and <c> correspond to /k/ at the beginning of words, <c> also corresponds to /s/ depending on the following vowel, whether <e>, <i> or <y> for /s/ 'cell', 'acid' and 'cycle', or <a>, <o> or <u> for /k/, 'cave', 'come' and 'cube', as seen in Chapter 3. So, in defiance of the usual positional rules, a business may call itself 'Kans Kar Wash' or a pop group 'Ganja Kru'. The usual word-final correspondence for /k/ is <ck> rather than <k>, so novel words can end in <k> as in 'Bostik' or 'Statik Sound System'. Indeed, 'pak' is almost the standard spelling for 'pack' in brand names and business names – 'Cardpak', 'Voltpak' and 'Hotpak' – just as 'lok' is the common spelling of 'lock' – 'Loktite', 'Bordalok' and 'Paralok'. Initial <qu> corresponds to /kw/ in words like 'quiz' and 'queen', so another easy novelty is to use <k> as in 'Kall Kwik Printing'.

The use of <k> in invented spellings was commented on as far back as the 1920s. Pound (1926) noted alliteration of <k> in such product names as 'Kwality Kut Klothes' and in the 'Ku Klux Klan'. The simple device of using <k> when the orthographic regularities predict <c>, <ck> or <q> is enough to give a distinctive feel to the word without interfering with the reader's comprehension. What else could <k> correspond to other than /k/ in 'Kreed', 'Tragik Roundabout' or 'The Diaboliks'? When <c> corresponds to /s/, the novel alternation is indeed between <s> and <c> as in

'A-Cyde' and 'Sellophane Sun'. The basis for this alternation of <k>, <c> and <s> goes back to Old English spelling, as detailed in Chapter 6.

A similar way of creating novel spellings is found with <z> and <s>, mostly involving <z> for <s> in plural inflections, for example 'Metalheadz', 'Jazzie B and the Boyz' and 'Footprintz Records', undoing one of the morphemic elements in English spelling. Medial <z> rather than <s> also corresponds to /z/ in a range of trade names such as 'Aztek Signs', 'Sizzer' and 'Lazertype' and even in 'was' in the pop group 'Dadi Waz A Badi'. <z> was a problematic letter historically, as indicated in the insult spoken by Kent in *King Lear* (II: ii), 'Thou whoreson zed! Thou unnecessary letter!', and has been scheduled for elimination by various spelling reformers.

Other ways of exploiting the less likely correspondences of a phoneme in a particular position to create a novel word include:

- *correspondences for /f/.* The letter <f> corresponds to the phoneme /f/ in names 99% of the time, according to Carney (1994). However, /f/ corresponds to <ph> in Latinate system words such as 'physics' and 'seraph'. Hence a novel word can be created by extending this <ph> correspondence to other occurrences of /f/, for example 'Phish' and 'Puppy Phat no 1', or by treating <ph> words as if they had <f> as in 'Foto Plus', 'Atmosfear' and 'Freefone Taxis'. /f/ also corresponds to <gh> in a handful of words such as 'laugh' and 'tough'. A novel spelling needs nothing more than the normal <f> correspondence in these words as in 'Eat-E-Nuff' or 'Daddy Ruffnek'.
- *<j>/<dg> alternation.* The usual initial correspondence of /dʒ/ is <j> as in 'just' while its final correspondence is <dg> as in 'ridge'. Hence a quick novelty is provided by substituting <j> for <g>, 'Peter Djonz', 'Danjerous' and 'Mirrir Imaj'.
- *<i>/<y> alternation.* The word-final correspondence for /ɪ/ is usually <y>; so novel spellings can use <ee> as in 'Dazee' and 'Wishee-Washee' or <i> 'Joi' and 'Melodi Muzik'. The less common medial <y> can also be exploited, as in 'Mynk', 'Krystal Snack Bar' and 'Tymes Electric Ltd'. Both alternates can be used together as in 'Wylie Coyote'.

Novelty through omission or addition of silent letters

Notices, advertisements and the like feature conventionalized spellings with omission of silent letters, such as:

- <-ite> for <-ight>, whether 'Mr Byrite', 'Staybrite' or 'Hi-Liting Ltd'.
- <lo> for <low> and <hi> for <high>, as in 'Lo-Fidelity Allstars', 'Lo-Cost Foodstores', 'Toyota Hi Lux' and 'Columbian Hi-Rise'.
- <nu> for <new>, such as 'Nu-Troop' and 'Nuvax Electronics', though this also involves substitution.
- <c> or <k> for <ch>. In business names to do with electronics the digraph <ch> reduces to <c>, 'Moretec Electronics', or to <k> in 'Eltek Ltd', thus allowing a range of possibilities such as 'Hi Tec Autos', 'Hytek Windows' or even <x> 'Hytex Communications'.

- <h>. Some omissions of <h> are found 'Ryme nor Reason', and some added <h>s 'Bhang II Rites'.

Jacobson (1966) gives examples of many other omissions such as double consonants reduced to single letters 'Milkeeper' or repeated digraphs reduced to one 'Wristrap'.

Novelty through letter-names and numbers

Although abbreviations such as 'UN' are pronounced as a string of letter-names /juːen/, some shade over into words with normal correspondences, for example 'UNESCO' /juːneskəʊ/. Sometimes the former are called 'initialisms', the latter 'acronyms'. Novel spellings are often created out of letter-names. One method is to spell out the letter-names as letters with their usual correspondences, say 'Esso' ('SO'), 'Eminem' ('M&M'), 'Bejay News' and 'Emangee Clothing', though sometimes these might be words from other languages. More commonly, however, the letter-name corresponds to a syllable such as <n> to /en/ 'N-Trance', <c> to 'sea' 'The Four Cs', <x> to /eks/ 'Xpert Stationers', or <f> for /ef/ 'Just FX', particularly when the letter correspondence happens to coincide with a function word: <r> for 'are' in 'CDs-R-Us', <u> for 'you' 'U Sexy Thing', <b> for 'be' 'B-secure Locksmiths' and <y> for 'why' 'Y B Sober'.

These possibilities extend to novelties based on number-names, such as 'DV8' and 'Pearls B4 Swine', particularly when they overlap with function words: <2> for 'to' 'Back 2 Back', <4> for 'for' 'Out 4 Just Iz' and '4 U Employment Agency'. Even roman numerals can be used: <II> for 'to' 'Boyz II Men', 'Bad II the Bone' and <IV> for 'for' 'Four IV Design Consultants'.

In some ways this approach treats English as a syllabic writing system in which a letter corresponds to a syllable rather than a phoneme and exploits the letter or number names as syllables. Other syllable-based novel spellings divide the word into its syllables with hyphens, 'Fun-Da-Mental', 'Hip-Nosis' and 'Ease-E-Load'.

Novelty through fake antiquity

One minor way of creating novel spellings for business names, particularly pubs and shops, is through a small number of conventionally archaic spellings. The use of 'ye' for 'the' in 'Ye Olde Red Lion' was explained in Chapter 6. 'Ye' is often combined with an extra final <e> as in 'olde' 'Ye Olde Curiosity Shop' and 'shoppe' 'Ye Olde Leather Shoppe', or with <ck> instead of <c> 'publick' 'Ye Olde Publick Fair' and 'musick' 'Ye Penguin Archive of Musick'. The last occurrence of 'publick' in the *OED* was 1727, of 'musicke' 1700, so these are at least possible historical spellings, though 'publique' and 'musique' have as much of a historical case to be made for them; Caxton in fact used 'musycque'.

Representations of non-standard pronunciations

A novel spelling can also be an attempt to represent non-standard pronunciation. The use of <a> for <-er> with actor meaning is one such device, 'Killa Instinct', often with the plural <z> 'Headrillaz' and 'The Gravediggaz'. While <a> corresponds quite normally to /ə/ 'banana', the <a> and <az> forms now seem to suggest Jamaican or American accents. Business names use <a> either for comparative <-er> as in 'Supa Shop' and 'Betaware' or for adjectives in <-ar> 'Solaglas Windscreens', but with no implication of non-standard pronunciation. Pop groups rarely attempt to show a non-standard British accent, except perhaps for the 1960s group 'Joe Brown and the Bruvvers', or the modern group 'The Bruvvas', reflecting the Cockney, later Estuary English, substitution of /v/ for /ð/ mentioned in Chapter 5.

Another link is to gender. A well-known sociolinguistic difference in several varieties of English is that between /ɪŋ/ and /ɪn/ for verb endings such as 'walking' and 'flying'. There is some tendency for the standard RP /ɪŋ/ to be used in 'ing' endings more by women than by men, and greater tendencies for it to be used more by the middle-class than the working class and more in formal than informal contexts. The non-standard /ɪn/ can be represented in spelling by replacing the <g> with an apostrophe to show contraction – 'walkin'' and 'flyin''. In phonological terms there is no 'dropping' of /g/, or indeed any contraction at all, but only an alternation between the phonemes /n/ and /ŋ/. The names of pop groups frequently use the <in'> convention as in 'Fun Lovin' Criminals' and 'Screemin' Ab-Dabs'. It is even commoner in the names of pop songs 'Marchin' Already' and 'Fallin' From Planes' or jazz standards 'Movin'' and 'Walkin''. The <in'> spelling presumably aligns the word with an image of informal masculine working-class solidarity conveyed by the /ɪn/ pronunciation. It extends to other uses of <-ing> like 'Hello Darlin''. Interestingly the only business names with <in'> are in the music industry, 'Stormin' Records' and 'Talkin' Loud'.

Many novel spellings hint at informality or non-standard speech through eye-dialect. <and> is reduced in various ways, whether <'n'> 'Heads 'N' Extras', <N> 'Thugs-N-Harmony' or <n> 'Rock n roll animal'. The weak unstressed form of 'and' as /n/ or /ən/ is normal in speech, not just the sign of a non-standard speaker. The same is true of 'wimmin' for 'women' /wɪmɪn/ 'Jon Pleased Wimmin', 'wot' for 'what' /wɒt/ 'Wotsits', neither of which could really be said much differently, and the reduced forms of 'going to' /gənə/ 'Never Gonna Let You Go', and 'want to' /wɒnə/ 'The Wannadies'. These novel spellings convey novelty and informality purely through the spelling, rather than corresponding to any new pronunciations. The pop group Slade was indeed famous for the spelling of their song titles, such as 'Cum On Feel The Noize' and 'Mama Weer All Crazee Now'.

None of these novel spellings radically change English, not even as much as the American/Webster changes seen in Part 7.1; they play with the margins of the English spelling system. They go far enough to sound alternative and daring without taking any risk that people might not understand them.

The same is true of the novel names created with punctuation and typography. The apostrophe can be exploited to give an unusual appearance to a word, as in 'Hear'Say'; an umlaut can be introduced, 'Motörhead' or 'Häagen-Dazs'; or an <@> can be used, 'The B@D Sound System' (presumably here corresponding to /æ/ not to

/æt/). Capital and lower case letters can be played with as in 'The hKippers', 'k.d. lang' or 'GongYOUreMIXED'. Business names commonly eliminate the word-space but retain the capital letter, 'NatWest' and 'PizzaExpress', particularly in the names of computer products – 'FrontPage', 'RealOne Player' and 'HotBurn', to take three examples on my PC start-up menu. Other typographic effects are occasionally found, such as letters in reverse order 'Skoobs Books' or letter doubling 'Duuo Motors'. A further step towards sheer design is to turn the letter forms themselves into a logo as with the distinctive appearance of Coca-Cola or McDonald's signs.

Some novel spellings would be applauded by spelling reformers, as detailed in Jacobson (1966). Eliminating unnecessary letters is often suggested for English, 'Hedspace' and 'Kollektiv'. More transparent links between letters and sounds are approved, in line with 'The Noize' and 'Skandalous'. The omission of <gh> has often been recommended, nicely represented in <-ite> business names such as 'Flo-Rite', 'Flitecall' and 'Nite Star Restaurant', as well as in some pop group omissions 'Life thru a lens', though spelling reformers such as Wijk (1966) have not generally approved of 'nite'.

The box below gives the brief categorization of novel spellings made by Venezky (1999), using his American examples. Novel spelling needs to give the impression of deliberate breaking of the rules rather than illiterate ignorance. Very few correspond to the typical mistakes made by adults, even if the letter-name conventions resemble children's early steps. There are nevertheless a few exceptions, perhaps accidental, 'The Pheonix Band', 'Polloneze' and 'Pyscho Daisies', or deliberate, 'Theakston's Old Peculier' beer.

Categories of novel spellings (Venezky 1999: 42)

1 *Completely legal*: The Beatles, Tylenol
2 *Marginal*: Mixit, Read 'Em
3 *Clear violations*: Sudz, Exxon
4 *Unorthodox symbols and letter names*: Thöz Nuts, 2night

Table 7.2 Novel spellings

Novel spellings create a different appearance, usually without changing the substance, by:

- using alternative correspondences such as initial <k> ≡ /k/ before <a>/<o>/<u>: Kall Kwik Printing, Klipp Joint
- omitting silent letters such as <gh> and <w>, Speedrite Transport, Doorflo
- using letter-names and number-names to correspond to syllables and to function words: 4 U Employment Agency, Pizza-U-Like
- using antique-looking spelling: Thee Newe Worlde Inne, Ye Olde Antique Purse Shoppe
- using traditional eye-dialect spellings: Wot-A-Gem Jewellery

7.3 ADAPTING ENGLISH TO MODERN MEANS OF COMMUNICATION

Focusing questions

- What would you say were the orthographic characteristics of e-mails? Of text messages?
- What are the reasons for these?

Key words

computer-mediated communication (CMC): is communication via the computer through the internet and other means.
asynchronous communication: in which messages are exchanged linearly one after the other.
synchronous communication: in which messages are created and exchanged in real-time.

The first section described how some minor aspects of English spelling were altered by fiat in the USA. The second section saw how spelling can be altered playfully to produce novel spellings and words. This section looks at how English writing has adapted itself to the age of the computer.

The overall label for language used via the computer is computer-mediated communication (CMC), involving entering messages into a computer from a keyboard, transmitting them to the recipient by some electronic means and reading them on a monitor screen. One type of CMC is e-mail, sent through the internet to individuals or to large numbers of addressees. From a handful of users with access to large computers in the 1980s, e-mail grew into almost the standard written form of correspondence for untold millions during the 1990s. A second type of CMC is computer chat-rooms in which several people take part in exchanges on-line, again now used by vast numbers of people from primary school age upwards.

A third type is text messages sent through mobile phones, alias cell-phones, popular because of their cheapness, convenience and privacy, seen in Task 4. Although text messaging does not directly involve a computer, messages are nevertheless inputted through a form of keyboard, transmitted and then displayed on a mini-screen. For technical reasons the SMS (Short Message System) is not available on phone systems in some parts of the world. Other CMC varieties which we will not touch on here are web pages, interactive games such as MOOs and the web diaries known as blogs, all of which partly overlap with other CMC registers in spelling and typography.

Task 4. Decipher these authentic text messages

A R U in 4 T?
B We gt punto rnt dey nice

C Wow! Do U need anything? We r at st johns
D Make sure U stop 4 something 2 eat
E The p'lice said oif people want 2 sit down n blok picca-circus l8er they will let them
F IS IT POS 2 HAVE A COPY OF SOC. SER FORM BY THURS 4 CHRIS E?
G Sory to bover u:-/ tell Knae we fink they're brilliant if u c him. Werf a lsten

E-mails and spoken language

The issue that has most exercised researchers is whether e-mails are more like spoken or written language. Text 1 contains sample e-mails taken more or less at random from my own hard disk. Let us test some of the issues about the relationship between speech and writing raised in Chapter 2 against this sample.

Text 1. Sample e-mails

A MA diss second marking . . . I have 4 hanging around . . . so will pass one to each of you spreading blessings evenly . . . Hope that is OK . . . and of course reciprocate!
B Sorry was in physically on FRiday pm but di nto check e-mail!
C This MONDAY, 21st OCTOBER, 8PM. PUBLIC MEETING, COLCHESTER QUAKER FRIENDS MEETING HOUSE (behind Mercury Theatre), Church Street. With expert speakers on the current situation.
D chris says he will make the nut roast but he needs the recipe from last year as it was sooo gooood,he says he will also make roast potatoes.jo [nee brown] has gone blonde-i wonder if she has more fun? happeee christmas
E p..s do you know how to save and/or print this file in Word. EVerytime I try to save it or print my chapter, I get nothing.

Spoken language is spontaneous first draft, written language is final draft

The e-mails in Text 1A resemble first drafts, for example the erratic use of capitals and lower-case 'p..s' and 'EVerytime' in Text 1E and the lack of capitals in Text 1D, the typing mistakes 'di nto' (Text 1B), the scarcity of punctuation (Text 1D), and the apparent looseness of links with <. . .> in Text 1A.

Spoken language has a shared context between speaker and listener, writing does not

In most e-mails the context is not spelled out but taken for granted. Though prefaced with 'p..s', Text 1E in fact constitutes the entire message, which makes reasonable sense in the context of a joint book in progress but conveys little taken out of its shared environment. Only Text 1C behaves like an ordinary written announcement with its specificity of time and place: 'MONDAY, 21st OCTOBER, 8PM.'

Speech attributes specific roles to the listener, writing indefinite roles

Text 1C is a general announcement to an anonymous audience of anybody interested, though confined to a particular e-mail list, and resembles many written notices, for instance in the use of capital letters as seen in Chapter 4. The other texts are geared to a specific reader with a particular relationship to the writer, whether professional as in texts 1A, 1B and 1E, or family as in Text 1D. Hence the bias seems to be towards the specific roles of spoken language.

Speech is processed 'on-line', writing is stored 'off-line'

Many e-mails are undoubtedly typed straight out rather than edited before being sent, as the sample e-mails well show. In the early days of e-mail, the technology made it difficult or impossible to edit what one was typing; my own attempts at correcting e-mails simply added meaningless control characters to the texts. People tend to reply instantly to e-mails and thus they can easily send messages that they regret on second thoughts. E-mail is believed by its users to be as ephemeral as a phone-call, despite the embarrassing 'private' e-mails that get transmitted to a wider audience from time to time. Users treat e-mail as if it employed the fleeting memory processes of speech rather than the permanent storage of writing. Yet e-mails have an indefinite life within computers and continue to exist somewhere in fairly permanent electronic form.

Speech uses intonation, writing uses punctuation

E-mail makes use of a variety of graphic devices, whether repeated vowels for emphasis 'sooo gooood' (Text 1D) or capital letters 'QUAKER MEETING HOUSE' (Text 1C). It also pioneered the use of punctuation marks as graphic devices in the 'smileys', alias emoticons, usually representing human faces sideways :-), which rapidly degenerated, at least according to the manuals, into such arcane symbols as :-& 'tongue-tied'.

Many of the properties of e-mails are closer to spoken than written language, with the unique exception of emoticons. A crude distinction between speech and writing is not, however, very revealing. Collot and Belmore (1996) applied Biber's dimensional analysis of registers, described in Chapter 2, to e-mails (Figure 7.1). They compared e-mails taken from bulletin boards with Biber's corpus. In terms of grammar, e-mails have fewer past tenses, passives and third-person pronouns than the general corpus, while they have more first-person 'I', verb + 'that' and sentence relatives.

A main dimension of variation in Biber's scheme is between involved and informational production. The plus and minus scores for the relevant categories locate e-mails on this dimension. Collot and Belmore (1996) believed that there would be a difference between e-mails constructed off-line and those that were composed on-line because of the different relationships of the writer to the text. Although some messages could be identified as off-line from the computer tags inserted by some programs, the remainder were not distinctly identifiable as on-line since they might have been prepared off-line in programs that did not identify themselves. Hence the distinction had to be between 'off-line' and 'other'.

Collot and Belmore (1996) fitted the overall scores for the two types of e-mail into Biber's continuum of involved and informational production, as seen in Figure 7.1. Putting together the different scores for categories such as contraction 'MA diss' (more involved), first-person pronouns 'I have 4 hanging around' (less involved), nouns (less involved), prepositions 'in on Friday' (less involved) and the other categories, there was very little difference between off-line messages and the 'others'. If the 'others' were indeed on-line, there is apparently no difference in behaviour when composing an e-mail spontaneously and more deliberately.

Figure 7.1 shows that e-mails come close to the involved production end; this can be compared to Figure 2.2 on page 48 in Chapter 2, the original Biber continuum. They score less for involved features than the spoken registers, of telephone conversation but score more than involved features in other spoken registers such as broad-

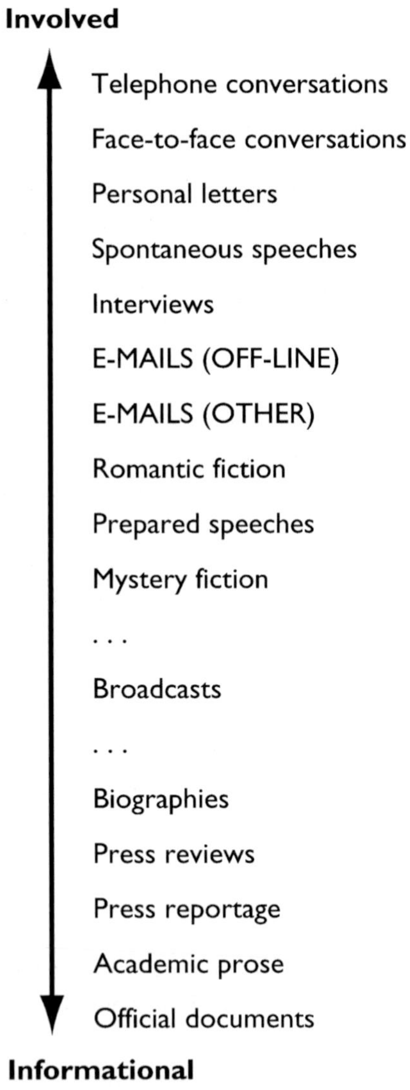

Involved

Telephone conversations
Face-to-face conversations
Personal letters
Spontaneous speeches
Interviews
E-MAILS (OFF-LINE)
E-MAILS (OTHER)
Romantic fiction
Prepared speeches
Mystery fiction
. . .
Broadcasts
. . .
Biographies
Press reviews
Press reportage
Academic prose
Official documents

Informational

Fig. 7.1. The place of e-mails on Biber's dimension of involved versus informational production (truncated). (Source: Collot and Belmore 1996.)

casts. They were less involved than the written register of personal letters. In terms of Biber's other dimensions:

- on the non-narrative/narrative dimension marked, for example, by amount of public verbs like 'say', e-mails are similar to letters and phone conversations rather than romantic or general fiction
- on the situation-dependent/explicit dimension marked by numbers of relative clauses, e-mails are in the middle of the scale along with humour, press reports and science fiction rather than near the two extreme registers of situation-dependent broadcasts and explicit official documents.

E-mails are therefore analysable in the same terms as other registers of language and in many ways cluster with spoken language registers.

Using a different style of analysis on e-mails to discussion groups, academic written texts and spoken lectures, Gruber (2000) showed that, on grammatical measures such as the number of words per clause, e-mails resembled letters or academic papers. On other measures such as lexical density, involvement (use of 'I') and hedges ('normally', 'usually') they were like spoken lectures, contradicting an earlier result that the lexical density of e-mails in conferencing was closer to written than spoken language (Yates 1996). Baron (2000) summarized the nature of e-mail in terms of four dimensions, similar to those already mentioned:

- *Social dynamics*: e-mail behaves like writing because the physical separation of the participants 'fosters personal disclosure'.
- *Format*: e-mail is permanent, like writing, but unedited, like speech.
- *Grammar*: e-mails use the first-person pronouns, present tenses and contractions of speech, but some of the denseness of writing, say subordinate clauses.
- *Style*: e-mails are informal, and often emotional, like speech.

The overall lesson is that the difference between speech and writing is not either/or but a merging of factors on several distinct dimensions, as we have already seen with other registers in Chapter 2.

The punctuation of CMC has been extended by the practical needs of e-mails and the web, not just through the invention of emoticons. Web addresses need separators to show different components. One is the full stop <.>, known as 'dot', reviving a traditional use of full stops as separators.

vivian.c@ntlworld.com

Another is </>. now known as 'forward slash'. This was the medieval equivalent of the comma, known as 'virgule', mentioned in Chapter 6:

http://titles.cambridge.org/journals/

E-mail programs have a convenient reply function which can include the original message in the new text, but distinguished from it by <>> at the left-hand side:

Thanks very much – I appreciate it! R

> Well yes that's what said! Will try to tackle but may not be fully informed as I had hoped not to be.

Before the use of quotation marks to show quotations within the text, the medieval convention was to use 'diples' <>> in the left-hand margin (Parkes, 1992), as mentioned in Chapter 6 – an amazing revival! A computer punctuation convention, more often found on web pages than e-mails, is to underline web addresses and sometimes to signal them in blue:

http://www.bbc.co.uk/england/essex/

Another computer adaptation to CMC is the use of <@> for location 'at':

docai@essex.ac.uk

Previously <@> was only familiar from certain traditional forms of bills 'five books @ £6.99 each'. It does, of course, correspond to different spoken forms in different languages. E-mails do not, however, seem to make great use of letter-name spellings, unlike pop group names.

Like other in-group fads such as CB Radio, e-mails have been accompanied by a rash of advice in manuals and on websites as to what should or should not be done, known as 'Netiquette'. Books such as *The Elements of E-mail Style* (Angell and Heslop 1994) proffer advice that would not have been out of place in Lord Chesterfield's *Letters to his Son* (1775) such as 'Make sure the subject and verb agree in number'. The ostensibly forward-looking *Wired Style Handbook* gives advice in its on-line version (http://hotwired.lycos.com/hardwired/wiredstyle/) such as 'If a noun is merely the generic name for a thing (network), spell it all lowercase'. As soon as a new in-group jargon emerges, self-appointed gatekeepers try to control it, sometimes giving the same prescriptive advice that has been used for hundreds of years.

One distinctive Netiquette rule concerns capital letters, probably reflecting the computer's preference for capitals in its early days. The manuals' advice is usually to avoid them: 'Typing your message all in upper-case letters is known in the world of e-mail as **shouting**' (Angell and Heslop 1994: 11). Hence Text 3C above 'MONDAY, 21st OCTOBER, 8PM. PUBLIC MEETING' is bad e-mail style.

Since its early in-group days, e-mail has settled down as a medium for every sort of communication. While the properties described above apply broadly to the whole register, the uses of e-mail are now as extensive as those of any other register such as letters. Informality may, however, continue to be preserved in e-mails by the growing practice of putting formal texts like memos or lists in attachments, keeping the e-mail essentially as a cover note.

Chat-rooms

E-mails are usually exchanged consecutively like letters, thus ruling out the interruptions that are a normal part of spoken language interaction. Chat-room discussions by contrast take place simultaneously; all the participants can intervene at any time. Hence a distinction has been drawn between *asynchronous* communication, in which messages are exchanged linearly one after the other, with any amount of time in between them, as in e-mails, lists and bulletin boards, and *synchronous* communication, in which messages are created and exchanged simultaneously in real-time.

Chat-rooms have become massively popular through systems such as ICQ, particularly with children, and have multiple uses and users, creating a wide range of registers rather than a single form of communication. The box below summarizes some properties of chat-room English described by Cherny (1999). In many ways these are more striking than the features of e-mails. Some reflect the problem of conducting a conversational interchange when the participants cannot see or hear each other. Without seeing the writer, you need to be told 'Mike cools' or 'Anthony ohboys'. The lack of gestures and the problem of identifying the speaker and addressee are compensated for by a program that expands key words into phrases: a command 'whuggle John' becomes 'Peter whuggles John' by supplying the missing subject and verb forms ('whuggle' means 'web-hug', that is, a verbal substitute for a physical gesture).

Properties of chat-room English

Verb-formation:

'emoted' verb as short form: 'Mike cools', 'Anthony ohboys'

contractions: 'anne gonna go see', 'Lenny bops you onna head', 'Jon runs atta Ted'

Deletion:

prepositions: 'Jon laughs lynn', 'Karen giggles Rick'

'is': 'Penfold bad mood', 'Rick getting there'

Reduplication: 'Ray nodsnodsnods', 'laughslaughs'

Abbreviations: 'LOL' ('laughing out loud'), 'filfre' ('feelfree'), 'bbl' ('be back later')

Anti-social commands (word typed in is converted by program): 'whuggle Y' > 'X whuggles Y' (a virtual hug); 'cathedral Y' > 'X comes down on Y like a ton of cathedrals'

Punctuation: speech bubbles: '. o 0' ('whew')'

Extra letters: 'slooooowwww', 'hmmmm', 'arrgh', 'ummmm', 'noooo00ooo'

(Source: Cherny, L. (1999) *Conversation and Community: Chat in a Virtual World*)

Although chat-room language also uses some forms found in e-mails, such as contractions 'Lenny bops you onna head' and extra letters 'noooo00ooo', it also uses letter abbreviations for phrases on a large scale, for example 'LOL' (laughing out loud) and 'bbl' (be back later). A selection is given in Text 2, taken from various on-line guides and checked by a teenage user, in this case probably the most accurate sources. There are many precedents from earlier registers of written English, such as the message written on an envelope 'SWALK' ('sealed with a loving kiss'), the radio disk jockey's farewell 'TTFN' ('ta-ta for now') or indeed long-standing written abbreviations like 'ASAP' and 'PLS'. This initialism (use of initial letters of phrases) should be distinguished from the novel spelling letter-names for syllables, though this too occurs in the chat-room, say 'filfre' ('feelfree'), 'B4' and 'GR8'.

Text 2. Chatroom abbreviations

A/S/L – Age/Sex/Location	AFK – Away From Keyboard
ASAP – As Soon As Possible	B4 – before
BFN – Bye For Now	BRB – Be Right Back
CU – See You	F2F – Face To Face
GF – Girl Friend	GR8 – great
IAE – In Any Event	LOE – Lack Of Education
LOL – Laughing Out Loud (Lots Of Love)	LY – Love You
PLS – please	SY2SB – Send You to Sin Bin
Tanx – thank you	

Chat-room language also exploits computer programming by changing brief commands into full forms, say by transforming the input 'cathedral Peter' automatically into 'John comes down on Peter like a ton of cathedrals'. Some chat systems offer a range of commands such as 'bored' that are converted into the appropriate smiley face. Chat-room language also has grammatical oddities such as repeating syllables for emphasis 'Ray nodsnodsnods'. While such reduplication is used meaningfully in some languages, for example Bahasa Malay, it is limited in English to forms such as 'very very very interesting'. Omission of prepositions is common, 'Jon laughs lynn', and of auxiliaries, 'Rick getting there'. In some ways this resembles the truncated form of telegrams paid for by the word and the early stages of English spoken by children and L2 learners.

One of the key characteristics of chat-room English must, however, be the way that participants interweave several threads of conversation simultaneously, illustrated in the extract of chat-room discourse in Text 3. Users A and B are having a discussion of a friend's surgical operation; User B is having a conversation with D about the curious behaviour of Jim: C and E seem to be making remarks into a vacuum. These exchanges break many conventions of normal spoken conversation, but this does not apparently affect the comprehension or the enjoyment of the participants.

Text 3. Chat-room sample

Users' names have been removed and replaced by letters in square brackets.

A: what did he have surgery for, [B]?

C: you handsome thing

D: would you believe it or not [B] last night fishman Jim's name was lit up on my friends list?

B: he had 3 vertebra fused [A]
C: my wine person left here now, where am i gonna get more??
E: nanna??????
D: but when i pmmed him,, no-one answered my pm
D: yes [F]?
A: ewww, my brother had that, it's no picnic
B: probably one of his brothers names

Partly this fluidity of exchange is necessitated by the technical features of communication via the internet. Participants may have to work on their answers on the keyboard while other things are occurring on the screen; delays in transmission distort the usual sequence by separating say question and answer by other material. As always, such features may be more a proud badge of belonging than any real change to English writing.

Text messages

Like e-mails, text messaging mushroomed from small beginnings to a point where the Mobile Data Association claimed 1.68 billion messages were sent in the UK during July 2003. While immensely popular with children, it has become an accepted part of most people's lives within a few years. Many of the conventions of text messages come out of the CMC roots of e-mails and chat-rooms.

One difference in the actual medium is that messages have to be limited to 160 characters, though some systems are starting to be more generous. Although much is made of this need for brevity by its devotees, in fact the average chat-room contribution is only a few words and many e-mails are equally brief. The mobile's keyboard is rudimentary in that a key has to be pressed several times to get most letters, increasing the amount of time spent typing. Hence many users employ predictive spelling that supplies frequent words from the opening letters.

Text 4. Sample text messages

A Wot time r u goin 2 b home? Hv 4got10 keys, ring asap.
B Home, nd 2 spk 2 pls rng l8r
C Gon 2 twn with m8s, wil b l8 home, prob c u 2moro
D Cant w8 til bak 2gethr cu 2moro yors 4evr
E Mik wrkin l8 cant go 2 Sbry rd eadt! Pls sve prog 4 both of us
F Wot am I goin 2 do no1 had n e brsl sprouts 4 t. Car fxd w8in 4 u in car port gd as nu.
G Bit l8 4t ud b in bed ages ago, nite

(Note: eadt = *East Anglian Daily Times*; Sbry = Sudbury, rd = read, brsl = Brussels)

Text 4 gives a selection of text messages received by a frequent text user. The striking features are:

- *Letter-name and number-name syllabic spelling*: as in Text 4A 'r' ('are'), 'u' ('you'), '2' ('to'), 'b' ('be'), '10' ('ten') and Text 4F 'n e' ('any'), 't' ('tea').
- *abbreviations*: are ubiquitous either where letters stands for words: 'asap' 'as soon as possible' (4A), 'eadt' (*East Anglian Daily Times*) (4E) or time-honoured abbreviations such as 'pls' 'please' (4E) or clipped spellings 'prob' 'probably' (4C) and 'prog' 'programme' (4E).
- *traditional novel and eye-dialect spellings*: are frequent: 'wot' (4A), 'nite' (4G) and 'nu' (4F).
- *punctuation*: is mostly minimal, no apostrophe in 'cant' (4D and 4E), no punctuation marks at all in Text 4F, apart from sentence-final full stops.
- *letter omission*: compared with the other CMC registers, the unique feature of text messages is the omission of letters. Sometimes this is the conventional reduction of final <ng> to <n> 'goin' (4F) and 'wrkin' (4E), but without the apostrophe, <ck> to <k> 'bak' (4D) and double letters to single 'til' (4D), sometimes the omission of final 'silent' vowels 'hv' (4A), 'gon' (4C). Mostly, however, it is the omission of vowels that usually have spoken correspondences, whether single vowels such as <o> 'twn' (4C), 'wrkin' (4E), 'rng' (4B), or all the vowels in the word 'fxd' (4F), 'gd' (4F), and even some consonants 'Sbry' ('Sudbury') (4E), almost changing English to a Arabic-like consonantal script. This usage overlaps with the abbreviations seen in newspaper small ads, whether for cars, 'f.s.h.', 'v.g.c.', 'met blue', or for lonely hearts, 'GSOH' ('good sense of humour'), 'LTR' (long term relationship'), 'WLTM' ('would like to meet'). However, the omissions in text messages amount to far more than the use of standardized abbreviated forms: any major element of any word can be left out, such as 'brsl' ('Brussels'), 'prob' ('probably') and 'fxd' ('fixed').

Public attention to text messages has voiced the usual concerns about whether a fad will get into dictionaries: Judy Pearsall, Publishing Manager for Oxford English Dictionaries, says, 'It is a phenomenon we have been tracking with ever greater focus here in Oxford, and we felt the time was right to treat it as an integral form of English' (www.askoxford.com/betterwriting/emoticons/). A host of popular books have displayed the more extreme oddities to the world, such as *WAN2TLK Little Book of Text Messages* (O'Mara 2001) and *The Joy of Text* (2001). This has led to the usual laments about the decline of spelling: 'according to British academic Dr Ken Lodge . . . mobile phone SMS "text messages", . . . are ruining the English language.' (*The World of English* www.woe.edu.pl/2001/4_01/sms.html); ' "So much of American society has become sloppy or laissez faire about the mechanics of writing," Baron said' (www.govtech.net/news/news.phtml?docid=2003.02.13–40642).

Which of these peculiarities could be attributed to the actual properties of the medium? Text messages are kept short to stay within the 160 character limit. Yet most chat-room contributions and e-mails are about the same length, without having such intense use of syllabic and consonantal spelling. The use of letter-names and numbers is seen by users as increasing the speed with which they can input message. On my mobile phone, however, typing <2> takes seven key-presses, typing <to> takes only four. Typing <4go10> takes 37 key-presses (4 for <4>, 13 for <1>, 12 for <0>), whereas typing <forgotten> takes only ten. In terms of actual keyboard effort the use of numbers is unrewarding on my phone, chiefly because they appear at the end of a list of alternatives: typing <1> means scrolling through <. ,'?!@-:;"/\>. A proficient teenager with another model of mobile took 2 presses to type <2>, 17 to type <4go10> and 19 to type <forgotten>, hardly a massive saving. It is possible to take out some of the drudgery through predictive spelling, but it is hardly possible to combine this with reduced spelling. As with CMC proper, the idiosyncracies of text messages are more like a jargon to show membership of a group than the product of the technology itself.

The other difference from CMC is the extreme specificity of the messages to a person, a time and a place. Text messages provide even less background than e-mails and chat-room contributions. The messages in Text 4 are so restricted in terms of addressee and topic that they do not make much sense without more detail. Yet this does not resemble speech; omitting vowels would render spoken English fairly incomprehensible since vowels are the indispensable nucleus of the syllable, unlike say the predictable vowels in languages that do use consonantal writing such as Hebrew and Arabic.

Table 7.3 Computer-mediated communication

E-mails:
- are closer to spoken than written language in many respects
- are closer to involved production than informational production on Biber's scale of involved versus informational production
- use some punctuation marks as emoticons :-/, others to separate elements and show quotation >

Chat-room messages:
- have many similar characteristics to e-mails
- use letter names and number names for syllables and function words: B4, GR8
- use abbreviations: LOL, PLS
- have some grammatical innovations: laughslaughs, nodsnodsnods
- have interweaving conversations

Text messages:
- use letter-name and number-name syllabic spelling: 4got10, c u 2moro
- use many abbreviations: brsl, asap
- exploit traditional novel spellings: nite, nu

This chapter has shown that English writing has succeeded in adapting to a range of circumstances without so far losing its asset of being understood anywhere that English is spoken. The spelling system has been exploited by its users, partly for serious purposes of branding products, partly for new forms of communication via the internet, partly as an amusing recreation and sign of group membership. With the exception of American style spelling, few of these adaptations have arisen as a logical response to the real difficulties of using English.

DISCUSSION TOPICS

1 How major are the differences between British and American styles of spelling?
2 To what extent is conformity to a single style of spelling important or could spellings differ as much as accents?
3 Why are novel spellings mostly found in brand names for cheaper or older products?
4 What names would you predict for future pop groups and what names do you think they would avoid?
5 Have the processes of novel spelling always been with us as part of English or are they modern innovations?
6 Are the adaptations found in computer-mediated writing due to the technology or because of fashion?
7 Will mobile phones with video abolish the need for text messaging?
8 How meaningful is the debate over whether e-mails are closer to speech or writing?

ANSWERS TO TASKS

Task 1. American and British variants

Which variants are British, which American?

	American	British		American	British
1 kerb	☐	✔	7 ameba	✔	☐
2 enrollment	✔	☐	8 kidnapper	☐	✔
3 traveller	☐	✔	9 judgement	✔	✔
4 favor	✔	☐	10 litre	☐	✔
5 defense	✔	☐	11 analyze	✔	☐
6 tyre	☐	✔	12 catalog	✔	☐

Task 2. Dialect spelling in novels and poems

1. Haley, A.P. (1976) *Roots: The Saga of an American Family*. (Southern USA Black)
2. Slow, E. (1894) *Wiltshire Rhymes and Tales in the Wiltshire Dialect*.
3. Welsh, I. (1993) *Trainspotting*. (Edinburgh)

FURTHER READING

- Crystal, D. (2001) *Language and the Internet*. Cambridge: Cambridge University Press. Extremely informative.
- Pemberton, L. and Shurville, S. (eds) (2000) *Words on the Web*. Exeter: Intellect. An up-to-date collection of articles.
- Herring, S. (ed.) (1996) *Computer-Mediated Communication*. Amsterdam: John Benjamins. Collection of the first articles on this area.
- Baron, N.S. (2000) *Alphabet to E-mail*. London: Routledge. Useful section on e-mail. All sources about CMC obviously go rapidly out of date.

References

Akamatsu, N. (1998) L1 and L2 reading: the orthographic effects of Japanese on reading in English. *Language, Culture and Curriculum* 11, 9–27.

Albrow, K.H. (1972) *The English Writing System: Notes towards a Description.* London: Longman.

Angell, D. and Heslop, B. (1994) *The Elements of E-mail Style.* Boston, MA: Addison-Wesley.

Aronoff, M. (1992) Segmentalism in linguistics: the alphabetic basis of phonological theory. In P. Downing, S.D. Lima, and M. Noonan (eds), *The Linguistics of Literacy.* Amsterdam: Benjamins, 71–82.

Bailey, B. (2000) Human interaction speeds, human factors. *Internal e-Newsletter.* (www.humanfactors.com/downloads/aug00.asp).

Baines, P. and Haslam, A. (2002) *Type and Typography.* London: Laurence King.

Baron, N.S. (2000) *Alphabet to E-mail.* London: Routledge.

Bayraktar, M., Say, B. and Akman, V. (1998) An analysis of English punctuation: the special case of the comma. *International Journal of Corpus Linguistics* 3, 33–57.

Bebout, L. (1985) An error analysis of misspellings made by learners of English as a first and as a second language. *Journal of Psycholinguistic Research* 14, 569–93.

Bernard, M., *et al.* (2001) A comparison of popular online fonts: which is best and when? *Usability News* 3, 1.

Bennett, J.A. and Berry, J. (1991) Cree literacy in the syllabic script. In D.R. Olson and N. Torrance (eds), *Literacy & Orality.* Cambridge: Cambridge University Press, 90–104.

Besner, D. and Chapnik Smith, M. (1992) Basic processes in reading: is the orthographic depth hypothesis sinking? In R. Frost and L. Katz (eds), *Orthography, Phonology, Morphology and Meaning.* Amsterdam: Elsevier Science Publishers, 45–66.

Biber, D. (1988) *Variation across Speech and Writing.* Cambridge: Cambridge University Press.

Biber, D. (1995) *Dimensions of Register Variation.* Cambridge: Cambridge University Press.

Biber, D., Conrad, S. and Reppen, R. (1999) *Corpus Linguistics: Investigating Language Structure and Use.* Cambridge: Cambridge University Press.

Bloomfield, L. (1933) *Language.* New York, NY: Holt.

Brengelmann, F.H. (1980) Orthoeptists, printers and the rationalisation of English spelling. *Journal of English and Germanic Philology* 79, 332–54.

Bringhurst, R. (1992) *The Elements of Typographic Style*. Vancouver: Hartley & Marks.

British National Corpus (*BNC*) (1995) Oxford University Computing Services. (www.hcu.ox.ac.uk/BNC/).

Bromley, T. (2002) *Dialect Spelling: A Study of the Effects of a Child's Dialect on their Spelling*. MA dissertation, University of Essex.

Brooks, G., Gorman, T. and Kendall, L. (1993) *Spelling It Out: the Spelling Abilities of 11- and 15-year-olds*. Slough: NFER.

Brown, G. (1977) *Listening to Spoken English*. London: Longman.

Brown, T. and Haynes, M. (1985) Literacy background and reading development in a second language. In T.H. Carr (ed.), *The Development of Reading Skill*. San Francisco, CA: Jossey-Bass, 19–34.

Bruce, D.J. (1964) The analysis of word sounds by young children. *British Journal of Educational Psychology* 34, 158–70.

Bryant, P.E., Nunes, T. and Bindman, M. (1997) Children's understanding of the connection between grammar and spelling. In B. Blachman (ed.), *Linguistic Underpinnings of Reading*. Hillsdale, NJ: Erlbaum, 219–40.

Bryson, B. (1991) *Mother Tongue: the English Language*. Harmondsworth: Penguin.

Burchfield, R.W. (1996) *The New Fowlers Modern English Usage* (3rd edition), edited by R.W. Burchfield. Oxford: Clarendon Press.

Cameron, D. (1995) *Verbal Hygiene*. London: Routledge.

Carey, G. (1960) *Mind the Stop*. Cambridge: Cambridge University Press.

Carney, E. (1994) *A Survey of English Spelling*. London: Routledge.

Castles, A. and Coltheart, M. (1993) Varieties of developmental dyslexia. *Cognition* 47, 149–80.

Catach, N. (1993) *L'ortographe. Que-sais-je*? Paris: PUF.

Chafe W. (1988) Punctuation and the prosody of written language. *Written Communication* 5, 396–426.

Cherny, L. (1999) *Conversation and Community: Chat in a Virtual World*. Stanford, CA: CSLI.

Chesterfield, Lord P.C. (1775) *Letters to his Son*. Reprinted, London: Folio Society, 1973.

Chikamatsu, N. (1996) The effects of L1 orthography on L2 word recognition. *Studies in Second Language Acquisition* 18, 403–32.

Chomsky, C. (1970) Reading, writing and phonology. *Harvard Educational Review* 40, 287–309.

Chomsky, N. (1972) Phonology and reading. In H. Levin (ed.), *Basic Processes in Reading*. London: Harper & Row, 3–18.

Chomsky, N. (2002) *On Nature and Language*. Cambridge: Cambridge University Press.

Chomsky, N. and Halle, M. (1968) *The Sound Pattern of English*. London: Harper & Row.

COBUILD English Dictionary (1995) London: HarperCollins.

Collins, F.H. (1973) *Authors' and Printers' Dictionary* 11th edition. Oxford: Oxford University Press.

Collot, M. and Belmore, N. (1996) Electronic language: a new variety of English. In S. C. Herring (ed.), *Computer-mediated Communication: Linguistic, Social and Cross-cultural Perspectives*. Philadelphia, PA: John Benjamins, 13–28.

Council of Europe (2001) *Common European Framework of Reference for Languages*. (www.coe.int/T/E/Cultural_Co-operation/education/Languages/Language_Policy/Common_Framework_of_Reference/)

Cook, V.J. (1997a) L2 users and English spelling. *Journal of Multilingual and Multicultural Development* 18, 474–88.

Cook, V.J. (1997b) *Inside Language*. London: Edward Arnold.

Cook, V.J. (1999) Going beyond the native speaker in language teaching. *TESOL Quarterly* 33, 185–209.

Cook, V.J. (2002) Background to the L2 user. In V.J. Cook (ed.), *Portraits of the L2 User*. Clevedon: Multilingual Matters, 1–28.

Cook, V.J. (ed.) (2003) *Effects of the Second Language on the First*. Clevedon: Multilingual Matters.

Cook, V. and Bassetti, B. (eds) (in preparation) *Second Language Writing Systems and Biliteracy*. Clevedon: Multilingual Matters.

Cook, V.J. and Newson, M. (1996) *Chomsky's Universal Grammar* (second edition). Oxford: Blackwell.

Coulmas, F. (1996) *The Blackwell Encyclopedia of Writing Systems*. Oxford: Blackwell.

Crystal, D. (2001) *Language and the Internet*. Cambridge: Cambridge University Press.

Cummings, D.W. (1988) *American English Spelling: an Informal Description*. Baltimore, MD: John Hopkins University Press.

Danielewicz, J. and Chafe, W. (1985) How 'normal' speaking leads to 'erroneous' punctuating. In S. Freedman (ed.), *The Acquisition of Written Language*. Norwood, NJ: Ablex, 213–25.

de Saussure, F. (1916) *Cours de Linguistique Générale*. C. Bally, A. Sechehaye and A. Reidlinger (eds). Paris: Payot. Trans. W. Baskin (1959) *Course in General Linguistics*. London: Peter Owen.

DeFrancis, J. (1984) *The Chinese Language: Fact and Fantasy*. University of Hawaii Press.

DeFrancis, J. (1996) How efficient is the Chinese writing system? *Visible Language* 30, 6–44.

Derwing, B.L. (1992) Orthographic aspects of linguistic competence. In P. Downing, S.D. Lima and M. Noonan (eds), *The Linguistics of Literacy*. Amsterdam: Benjamins, 193–210.

DfES (2001) *Adult ESOL Core Curriculum in England*. London: DfES. (www.dfes.gov.uk/curriculum_literacy/).

Diringer, D. (1953) *The Book Before Printing*. New York, NY: Dover.

Dixon, C. (2001) Systematizing the platypus: a perspective on type design classification. In E. Kindel, *Typeform Dialogues*. London: Hyphen Press.

Donaldson, M. (1978) *Children's Minds*. London: Fontana.

Ethnologue: Languages of the World: Fourteenth Edition. (1996) On-line document: http://www.sil.org/ethnologue/.

Faber, A. (1992) Phonemic segmentation as epiphenomenon: evidence from the history of alphabetic writing. In P. Downing, S.D. Lima, and M. Noonan (eds), *The Linguistics of Literacy*. Amsterdam: Benjamins, 111–34.

Feynman, R.P. (1998) *The Meaning of It All: Thoughts of a Citizen Scientist*. New York: Helix Books.

Firth, J.R. (1951) Modes of meaning. In J.R. Firth, *Essays and Studies*. London: English Association, 118–49.

Fowler, H.W. (1926) *A Dictionary of Modern English Usage*. Oxford: Clarendon Press.

Fries, C.C. (1952) *The Structure of English*. London: Longman.

Frith, U. (1985) Beneath the surface of developmental dyslexia. In K.E. Patterson, J.C. Marshall and M. Coltheart (eds), *Surface Dyslexia*. Hove: Lawrence Erlbaum, 301–30.

Funnell, E. (1983) Phonological processes in reading: new evidence from acquired dyslexia. *British Journal of Psychology* 74, 159–80.

Gill, E. (1931) *An Essay on Typography*. London: Lund Humphries.

Glen, D. (2001) *Printing Type Designs*. Fife: Akros.

Golden Apostrophe Awards, The (2003). http://www.sharoncolon.com/.

Goody, J. (2000) *The Power of the Written Tradition*. Washington, DC: Smithsonian Institute.

Goswami, U. (1999) Integrating orthographic and phonological knowledge as reading develops: onsets, rimes, and analogies in children's reading. In P. McMullum and R. Klein (eds), *Converging Methods for Understanding Reading and Dyslexia*. Hillsdale, NJ: Erlbaum, 57–75.

Goswami, U. and Bryant, P. (1990) *Phonological Skills and Learning to Read*. Hillsdale, NJ: Erlbaum.

Greengrocer's Apostrophe, The (2003). http://homepage.ntlworld.com/vivian.c/ApostGrocers.htm.

Gruber, H. (2000) Scholarly email discussion list postings: a single new genre of academic communication? In L. Pemberton and S. Shurville (eds), *Words on the Web*. Exeter: Intellect, 36–43.

Hall, N. and Robinson, N. (eds) (1996) *Learning about Punctuation*. Clevedon: Multilingual Matters.

Halliday, M.A.K. (1975) *Learning How to Mean*. London: Edward Arnold.

Halliday, M.A.K. (1985) *Spoken and Written Language*. Oxford: Oxford University Press.

Hanson, V.L., Goodell, E.W. and Perfetti, C.A. (1991) Tongue twister effects in the silent reading of hearing and deaf college students. *Journal of Memory and Language* 30, 319–30.

Harris, R. (1986) *The Origin of Writing*. London: Duckworth.

Hart, J. (1569) *An Orthographie, conteyning the due order and reason, howe to write or paint thimage of mannes voice, most like to the life or nature*.

Hartley, J. and Burnhill, P. (1971) Experiments with unjustified text. *Visible Language* V, 265–78.

Hart's Rules for Compositors and Readers at the University Press, Oxford (1983) 39th edition. Oxford: Oxford University Press.

Haynes, M. and Carr, T.H. (1990) Writing system background and second language reading: a component skills analysis of English reading by native-speaking readers of Chinese. In T.H. Carr and B.A. Levy (eds), *Reading and its Development: Component Skills Approaches*. San Diego, CA: Academic Press, 375–421.

Herring, S. (ed.) (1996) *Computer-Mediated Communication*. Amsterdam: John Benjamins.

Holm, A. and Dodd, B. (1996) The effect of first written language on the acquisition of English literacy. *Cognition* 59, 119–47.

Huang, H.S. and Hanley, J.R. (1994) Phonological awareness and visual skills in learning to read Chinese and English. *Cognition* 54, 73–98.

Hughes, R. (1996) *Comprehending Oral and Written Language*. London: Routledge.

Hurford, J. (1994) *Grammar, a Student's Guide*. Cambridge: Cambridge University Press.

Ibrahim, M. (1978). Patterns in spelling errors. *English Language Teaching Journal* 32, 207–12.

Jackson, D. (1981) *The Story of Writing*. London: Studio Vista.

Jacobson, S. (1966) *Unorthodox Spelling in American Trademarks*. Uppsala: Almqvist & Wiksell.

Jaffe, A. (2000) Non-standard orthography and non-standard speech. *Journal of Sociolinguistics* 4, 497–514.

Jaquith, J.R. (1976) Digraphia in advertising. *Visible Language* X, 295–308.

Jarvie, G. (1992) *Chambers Good Punctuation Guide*. Edinburgh: Chambers.

Johnston, E. (1905) *Writing & Illuminating & Lettering*. London: Pitman.

Jones, R.F. (1953) *The Triumph of the English Language*. Stanford, CA: Stanford University Press.

Joy of Text, The (2001). London: Corgi.

Katz, L. and Frost, R. (1992) Reading in different orthographies: the orthographic depth hypothesis. In R. Frost and L. Katz (eds), *Orthography, Phonology, Morphology and Meaning*. Amsterdam: Elsevier, 67–84.

Katzner, K. (1986) *The Languages of the World*. London: Routledge.

King, G. (2000) *Collins Wordpower: Punctuation*. London: Collins.

Koda, K. (1987) Cognitive strategy transfer in second language reading. In J. Devine, P. Carrell and D. Eskey (eds), *Research in Reading in English as a Second Language*. Washington DC: TESOL, 127–44.

Krapp, G.P. (1960) *The English Language in America*. New York, NY: Continuum.

Kreiner, D. (1992) Reaction time measures of spelling: testing a two-strategy model of skilled spelling. *Journal of Experimental Psychology: Learning, Memory and Cognition* 18, 765–75.

Kress, G. (2000) *Early Spelling*. London: Routledge.

Labov, W. (1994) *Principles of Linguistic Change: Internal Factors*. Oxford: Blackwell.

Leech, G., Rayson, P. and Wilson A. (2001) *Word Frequencies in Written and Spoken English*. Harlow: Longman.

Levinson, S.C. (1996) Relativity in spatial conception and description. In J.J. Gumperz and S.C. Levinson (eds), *Rethinking Linguistic Relativity*. Cambridge: Cambridge University Press, 177–202.

Longman Dictionary of Contemporary English (1978) Harlow: Longman.

Lowth, R. (1775) *A Short Introduction to English Grammar*. Delmar, NY: Scholars' Facsimiles & Reprints, 1979.

Luria, A.R. (1976) *Cognitive Development: Its Cultural And Social Foundations*. Cambridge, MA: Harvard University Press.

Lyons, J. (1968) *Introduction to Theoretical Linguistics*. Cambridge: Cambridge University Press.

Macdonald-Ross, M. and Waller, R. (1975) *Open University Texts: Criticisms and Alternatives*. Milton Keynes: Open University.

Maddiesen, I. (1984) *Patterns of Speech*. Cambridge: Cambridge University Press.

Malinowski, B. (1923) The problem of meaning in primitive languages. In C.K. Ogden and I.A. Richards, *The Meaning of Meaning*. London: Routledge and Kegan Paul.

McArthur, T. (ed.) (1992) *The Oxford Companion to the English Language*. Oxford: Oxford University Press.

McCaskill, M.K. (1998) *Grammar, Punctuation, and Capitalization: A Handbook for Technical Writers and Editors*. Hampton, VA: NASA SP–7084. (www.cs.wcu.edu/res/nasa_sp7084/)

McIntosh, R. (1990) *Hyphenation*. Halifax: Hyphen House.

Merriam–Webster's Guide to Punctuation and Style (2002) Springfield, MA: Merriam-Webster.

Meyer, C.F. (1987) *A Linguistic Study of American Punctuation*. New York, NY: Peter Lang.

Mitchell, B. and Robinson, F.C. (2001) *A Guide to Old English* (sixth edition). Oxford: Blackwell.

Morison, S. (1968) *Letter Forms: Typographic and Scriptorial*. Vancouver: Hartley & Marks.

Mulcaster, R. (1582) *The First Part of the Elementarie*. Edited by E.T. Campagnac. Oxford: Clarendon Press, 1925.

Nation, I.S.P. (2001) *Learning Vocabulary in Another Language*. Cambridge: Cambridge University Press.

National Curriculum for England: English (1999) London: Qualifications and Curriculum Authority.

Neville, A. (1563) *Oedipus* (translation, with preface).

Noon, J. (1995) *Pollen*. London: Pan.

Nunberg, G. (1990) *Linguistics of Punctuation*. Stanford, CA: CSLI.

Nunes, T., Bryant, P. and Bindham M. (1997) Spelling and Grammar – The NECSED move. In C.A. Perfetti, L. Rieben and M. Fayol (eds), *Learning to Spell: Research, Theory, and Practice Across Languages*. Mahwah, NJ: Lawrence Erlbaum Associates, 151–70.

Olson, D.R. (1996) Toward a psychology of literacy: on the relations between speech and writing. *Cognition* 60, 83–104.

Olson, R.K., Kleigl, R., Davidson, B.J. and Foltz, G. (1985) Individual and developmental differences in reading ability. In G.E. Mackinnon and T.G. Waller (eds), *Reading Research: Advances in Theory and Practice Vol. 4*. New York, NY: Academic Press, 1–64.

Ong, W.J. (1982) *Orality and Literacy: the Technologizing of the Word*. London: Methuen.

Oxford English Dictionary (*OED*) (1994) CD-ROM version 1.13. Oxford: Oxford University Press.

Parkes, M.B. (1992) *Pause and Effect: An Introduction to the History of Punctuation in the West*. Aldershot: Scolar Press.

Partridge, A. (1964) *Orthography in Shakespeare and Elizabethan Drama*. London: Edward Arnold.

Partridge, E. (1953) *You Have A Point There*. London: Routledge & Kegan Paul.

Patterson, K.E. and Morton, J. (1985) From orthography to phonology: an attempt at an old interpretation. In K.E. Patterson, J.C. Marshall and M. Coltheart (eds), *Surface Dyslexia*. London: Erlbaum, 335–59.

Pemberton, L. and Shurville, S. (eds) (2000) *Words on the Web*. Exeter: Intellect.

Perera, K. (1984) *Children's Writing and Reading: Analysing Classroom Language*. Oxford: Blackwell.

Perfetti, C.A. (1999) Comprehending written language; a blueprint of the reader. In C. Brown and P. Hagoort (eds), *The Neurocognition of Language*. Oxford: Oxford University Press, 167–210.

Perfetti, C.A., Zhang, S. and Berent, I. (1992) Reading in English and Chinese: evidence for a universal phonological principle. In R. Frost and L. Katz (eds), *Orthography, Phonology, and Meaning*. Amsterdam: North Holland, 227–48.

Peters, M. (1985) *Spelling, Caught or Taught: a New Look*. London: Routledge.

Peters, P. and Delbridge, A. (1989) Standardisation in Australian English. In P. Collins and D. Blair (eds), *Australian English*. Queensland: University of Queensland Press, 127–37.

Petersen, K.M., Reis, A., Askelöf, S., Castro-Caldas, A. and Ingvar, M. (2000) Language processing modulated by literacy: a network analysis of verbal repetition in literate and illiterate subjects. *Journal of Cognitive Neuroscience* 12, 364–82.

Pinker, S. (1994) *The Language Instinct: the New Science of Language and Mind*. London: Allen Lane.

Port Royal Grammar (1660) Trans. into English 1753. Reprinted 1975. The Hague: Mouton.

Pound, L (1923) Spelling-manipulation and present-day advertising. *Dialect Notes* 5, 226–32.

Pound, L. (1926) The Kraze for K. *American Speech* 1, 43–44.

Praninskas, J. (1968) *Trade-Name Creation: Processes and Patterns*. The Hague: Mouton.

Pratt, T.K. (1993) The hobgoblin of Canadian English spelling. In C. Clarke (ed.), *Focus on Canada*. Amsterdam: John Benjamins, 45–64.

Punctuation Project (1999) www.partnership.mmu.ac.uk/punctuation/.

Punctuation Design Standards. www.microsoft.com/typography/developers/fdsspec/punc.htm.

Quirk, R., Greenbaum, S., Leech, G. and Svartvik, J. (1972) *A Grammar of Contemporary English*. London: Longman.

Robinson, P. (1980) The philosophy of punctuation. *New Republic* April 26, 1980. (www.press.uchicago.edu/Misc/Chicago/721833.html).

Rozin, P., Poritsky, S. and Sotsky, R. (1971) American children with reading problems can easily learn to read English represented by Chinese characters. *Science* 171, 1264–7.

Saenger, P. (1997) *Space Between Words: The Origins of Silent Reading*. Stanford, CA: Stanford University Press.

Sampson, G. (1985) *Writing Systems: A Linguistic Introduction*. London: Hutchinson.

Sassoon, R. (1995) *The Acquisition of a Second Writing System*. Exeter: Intellect.

Sassoon, R. (1999) *Handwriting of the Twentieth Century*. London: Routledge.

Scragg, D. (1974) *A History of English Spelling*. Manchester: Manchester University Press.

Scribner, S. and Cole, M. (1981) *The Psychology of Literacy*. Cambridge, MA: Harvard University Press.

Seidenberg, M.S. (1992) Beyond orthographic depth in reading: equitable division of labour. In R. Frost and L. Katz (eds), *Orthography, Phonology, Morphology and Meaning*. Amsterdam: Elsevier, 85–118.

Seidenberg, M.S. and McClelland, J.L. (1989) A distributed, developmental model of word recognition and naming. *Psychological Review* 96, 523–68.

Simplified Spelling Society (2001) *Simplified Spelling Society Handbook*. (On-line at www.spellingsociety.org/pubs/leaflets/cutspelng.html).

Shemesh, R. and Waller, S. (2000) *Teaching English Spelling*. Cambridge: Cambridge University Press.

Smith, J. (1999) *Essentials of Early English*. London: Routledge.

Sproat, R. (2000) *A Computational Theory of Writing Systems*. Cambridge: Cambridge University Press.

Strang, B. (1970) *A History of English*. London: Methuen.

Strype, J. (1705) *The Life of the Learned Sir John Cheke*.

Tannen, D. (ed.) (1982) *Spoken and Written Language: Exploring Orality and Literacy*. New Jersey: Ablex.

Temple, C., Nathan, R., Temple, F. and Burris, N. (1993) *The Beginnings of Writing* (third edition). Boston, MA: Allyn & Bacon.

Tinker, M. (1963) *The Legibility of Print*. Iowa, LA: Iowa State University Press.

Todd, L. (1995) *The Cassell Guide to Punctuation*. London: Cassell.

Tomasello, M. (2000) *The Cultural Origins of Human Cognition*. Cambridge, MA: Harvard University Press.

Trask, L. (1997) *The Penguin Guide to Punctuation*. London: Penguin.

Treiman, R. (1993) *Beginning to Spell: A Study of First-Grade Children*. Oxford: Oxford University Press.

Treiman, R., Kessler, B. and Bourassa, D. (2001) Children's own names influence their spelling. *Applied Psycholinguistics* 22, 555–70.

Treiman, R., Zukowski, A. and Richmond-Welty, E.D. (1995) What happened to the 'n' of 'sink'? Children's spelling of final consonant clusters. *Cognition* 55, 1–38.

Tschichold, J. (1928) *The New Typography*. University of California Press edition, 1998.

Tschichold, J. (1991) *The Form of the Book*. Point Roberts, Washington DC: Hartley & Marks.

Twyman, M. (1982) The graphic presentation of language. *Information Design* 2, 2–22.

United Nations. *Universal Declaration of Human Rights*. (www.unhchr.ch/udhr/navigate/alpha.htm).

VanDyck, W. (1996) *Punctuation Repair Kit*. London: Hodder Childrens Books.

Venezky, R.L. (1970) *The Structure of English Orthography*. The Hague: Mouton.

Venezky, R.L. (1999) *The American Way of Spelling*. New York, NY: Guilford Press.

Vygotsky, L.S. (1962) *Thought and Language*. Trans. E. Hanfmann and G. Vakan. Boston, MA: MIT Press.

WAN2TLK Little Book of Text Messages (2001). London: Michael O'Mara Books.

Webster, N. (1828) *An American Dictionary of the English Language*. New York, NY: Johnson Reprint Corp., 1970.

Wells, J.C. (1982) *Accents of English 2: The British Isles*. Cambridge: Cambridge University Press.

Wijk, A. (1966) *Rules of Pronunciation for the English Language*. London: Oxford University Press.

Wing, A.M. and Baddeley, A.D. (1980) Spelling errors in handwriting: a corpus and a distributional analysis. In U. Frith (ed.), *Cognitive Processes in Spelling*. London: Academic Press, 251–85.

Yates, S.J. (1996) Oral and written linguistic aspects of computer conferencing. In S. Herring (ed.), *Computer-Mediated Communication*. Amsterdam: John Benjamins, 29–46.

Yule, V. (1978) Is there evidence for Chomsky's interpretation of English spelling? *Spelling Processes Bulletin* 18, 10–12.

Yule, V. (1991) *Orthographic Factors in Reading: Spelling and Society*. PhD dissertation. Australia: Monash University.

IPA transcription of English phonemes

The phonetic alphabet used in this book for British English Received Pronunciation (RP) is equivalent to the IPA found in Wells (1982) *Accents of English*, Cambridge University Press. The keywords used here show some of the variability in letter-to-sound correspondence.

1 /ɪ/ pill
2 /e/ head
3 /æ/ hand
4 /ɒ/ rot
5 /ʌ/ bun
6 /ʊ/ good
7 /ə/ about
8 /ɑː/ spa
9 /ɜː/ bird
10 /iː/ sheep
11 /eɪ/ day
12 /ɔː/ bought
13 /əʊ/ wrote
14 /uː/ food
15 /aɪ/ fight
16 /ɔɪ/ boy
17 /aʊ/ out
18 /ɪə/ ear
19 /ɛə/ bear
20 /ʊə/ tour (not in all RP speakers)
21 /p/ pub
22 /b/ bin
23 /t/ Thames
24 /d/ date
25 /k/ call
26 /g/ ghost
27 /f/ laugh
28 /v/ vast
29 /s/ sun
30 /z/ rose
31 /ð/ this
32 /θ/ theme
33 /ʃ/ rush
34 /ʒ/ genre
35 /m/ moon
36 /n/ know
37 /ŋ/ tongue
38 /tʃ/ watch
39 /dʒ/ jet
40 /w/ white
41 /h/ hot
42 /j/ yes
43 /l/ light
44 /r/ red

Index

P

Q

R